CU00793649

Analysing English Grammar

A practical step-by-step introduction to the analysis of English grammar, this book leaves the reader confident to tackle the challenges analysing grammar may pose. The first textbook to take an integrated approach to function and structure in grammatical analysis, it allows students to build experience, skill and confidence in working with grammar. The innovative, hybrid approach combines an introduction to systemic functional theory with a solid grounding in grammatical structure. The book approaches grammar in an incremental way, enabling students to develop grammatical skill in stages. It is of particular value to those starting to work with functional grammar but it is also relevant for experienced readers who are interested in developing a more systematic approach to grammatical analysis.

LISE FONTAINE is a lecturer in the Centre for Language and Communication Research at Cardiff University.

Analysing English Grammar

A systemic functional introduction

LISE FONTAINE
Cardiff University

CAMBRIDGE
UNIVERSITY PRESS

CAMBRIDGE UNIVERSITY PRESS
Cambridge, New York, Melbourne, Madrid, Cape Town,
Singapore, São Paulo, Delhi, Mexico City

Cambridge University Press
The Edinburgh Building, Cambridge CB2 8RU, UK

Published in the United States of America by Cambridge University Press, New York

www.cambridge.org
Information on this title: www.cambridge.org/9780521151931

First published 2013

A catalogue record for this publication is available from the British Library

Library of Congress Cataloging-in-Publication data

Fontaine, Lise, author.
  Analysing English grammar : a systemic-functional introduction / Lise Fontaine, Cardiff University.
    pages   cm
  ISBN 978-0-521-19066-4 – ISBN 978-0-521-15193-1 (Paperback)
1. English language–Grammar.   I. Title.
  PE1112.F616 2012
  425–dc23

                                                                        2012015818

ISBN 978-0-521-19066-4 Hardback
ISBN 978-0-521-15193-1 Paperback

Contents

Contents

Preface

In many ways this book is the sum of my life so far as a lecturer in functional grammar at Cardiff University. It has come from working closely with my students and trying to help them map the expressions of language functions onto grammatical structures and vice versa. Many students are apprehensive about the study of grammar but there is merit in working through it. One student described it once as climbing a mountain; very challenging but very satisfying when you finally get it. This is the real motivation behind this book. I wanted to offer something that would unlock some of the mysteries. I hope that this book will let people see grammar as a thing of interest and something that we shouldn't be afraid of. I also hope that it will raise curiosity and lead readers to pursue an even more detailed understanding.

I am grateful to many people who have helped me write this book. My students have contributed indirectly. I would like to thank Cardiff students, past and present, who have taken Describing Language or Functions of Grammar with me. They have been incredibly supportive and encouraging. Although it seems like a lifetime ago, I was also a linguistics student once, at York University in Toronto, Canada. I am grateful to have had such inspiring and dedicated professors and I'd like to thank Ian Smith, Ruth King, Susan Ehrlich and Sheilah Embleton especially.

I owe thanks to Michael Halliday, the founder of systemic functional linguistics, for such inspirational writings and for the depth of thinking that shows through his work. I would also like to thank Robin Fawcett in particular for welcoming me to Cardiff and being so generous with his time and his work. I am grateful to all my colleagues in the Centre for Language and Communication Research at Cardiff University for their support and encouragement. I have also been greatly influenced by Geoff Thompson as well as Meriel Bloor and Tom Bloor, who have written very successful introductory textbooks to systemic functional linguistics. Both of these books were life-saving to me when I was new to this theory and I still refer to them regularly. I hope that this book will merit sitting on a shelf alongside theirs.

Work of this nature requires more than intellectual inspiration and moral support. I have been very lucky to have a supportive family who allowed me the time to write and complete this book. I am especially indebted to my mother, Gael Fontaine, for her many hours of proofreading. I would also like to thank Clyde Ancarno for her constant support and comments on draft versions. Two former students deserve special thanks for commenting on drafts: Michael Willett and David Schönthal.

Last but certainly not least, I would like to thank the anonymous reviewers for their comments, which have led to a greatly improved final version of this book.

Chapter 1: Introduction to functional grammatical analysis

1.1 INTRODUCTION

People are interested in language and in understanding how we think language works for lots of different reasons. Becoming more knowledgeable about language often means having to learn something about grammatical analysis whether it is to teach children language skills, to work with those who have some kind of language difficulty or impairment, to teach a foreign language, or to master a command of a given language for a particular agenda such as speech writing or media communication. Understanding how language works means understanding how grammar works.

Grammar may seem like a very mysterious thing to many people. To use language, and even to use it well, we don't really need to have an explicit understanding of it. However, if we want to work with language we need a way to talk about it and we need a way to identify the bits and pieces that it involves so that we can work with it more masterfully and more professionally.

There are many analogies for the kind of relationship we need to have with language when it becomes an object of study, but essentially we find the same distinction as with other walks of life where the lay person and professional differ in how they work with and talk about their area. I can walk and run but I'm not a professional athlete by any stretch of the imagination. I don't need to know which muscles work when I need to use them. If something happened to my body – my knee, for example – I would see a professional and say something like 'my knee hurts'. The relevant professional will know about the individual muscles and they will also understand what happened and how to fix the problem. Athletes and physiotherapists know what they need to do to maximize performance, and when they discuss these things together they use shared terminology to make communication work better. Similarly I can drive a car and I may be able to do basic repairs like change a tyre or replace a light bulb, but for most other problems I have to take my car to a professional mechanic. He or she knows all about how my car works, including the names of the various components of the engine and many other things that I am simply not aware of. If I wanted to be able to work with my car professionally (analyse and interpret it), I would need to learn about the components and how they interact, and in order to be able to talk about it with someone else I would also need the right terminology.

This is also true for becoming more professional about grammar. In order to be able to talk about it, we need some terminology so that we can be clear and precise. We also need to know how to recognize the relevant components and we need to learn about how they interact in language. This is why, with each chapter in this book, new terminology will be introduced along with the skills for recognizing the main grammatical components of the English language.

1.1.1 The motivation for this book

Most people I speak to either do not like grammar or they think they are not very good at it. They often say it is too difficult. This is an odd perspective because without knowing how our grammar works we would not be able to communicate – even if this knowledge remains largely unconscious and implicit. Negative attitudes towards grammar, like those towards mathematics, are unfortunately products of our education system and often depend on the attitudes of the teachers. These attitudes are damaging because we can be left with a sense that some are better at it than others, or, worse, that we just are not good at it. I usually ask my students whether they were ever taught grammar by a teacher who really loved it. Unfortunately the answer is rarely 'yes'. This book is not about fixing that problem because it is not going to try to challenge the education system with respect to how English grammar is taught. However, what it will do is offer one way of approaching language from an analytical perspective and it will be presented by someone who really loves working with language. If you end up enjoying grammar even just a bit more than before then this book will have been a great success.

Having taught functional grammar for many years, I know there is a need for a book that concentrates on how to actually do the analysis, a systematic step-by-step procedure for analysing grammar. In presenting the practical 'how-to' aspects of analysis, this book draws from various existing descriptions of the theory of systemic functional grammar. Primarily, it relies on my own experience of teaching grammar. I offer one way to analyse grammar and there are of course other ways. I am convinced though that being consistent and systematic makes the job much easier.

Although the approach developed here falls within the framework of systemic functional linguistics generally, it isn't trying to promote one single particular theoretical stance within systemic functional theory. Consequently, the book does not try to explain the theory in detail and the presentation draws on a variety of sources. Clearly the underlying theoretical framework has implications for the analysis but theoretical discussions are left aside wherever possible and, where appropriate, pointers are given for further reading on the topic.

1.1.2 Goals of the chapter

This chapter is very much an introductory overview of analysing grammar in a functional framework. It will explain why a functional approach is important but it will also emphasize that structure has to take a more prominent position in functional analysis than is the case in many existing books. The goal of this chapter is to lay the foundation for the functional–structural approach to analysis that is presented in the rest of the book. The remaining chapters cover individual topics in detail, so this chapter gives a bird's-eye view of the functional view of language and what this kind of analysis looks like. It is a bit like looking at a photograph of a particular dish before starting to follow the instructions in the recipe. This way you get a glimpse of where we are headed before we dive into the details.

This chapter will also introduce some of the terminology used in this book. Each chapter will introduce more terms as we need them. Some terms will be capitalized just like personal names and place names. In principle, functional elements of the clause (such as Subject or Actor) will take a capital letter, which is standard practice in systemic functional linguistics. This is to remind us that these terms refer to a specific use of the term rather than the general meaning of the word in everyday use. It would be distracting to write every term with an initial capital letter, but hopefully this practice will help to reduce the potential for confusion between general words and specific terms for clausal elements.

1.1.3 How the chapter is organized

In the next section we will cover the basic principles of analysing grammar within a functional framework and explain why a functional–structural view of language is the most appropriate one for the analyst. Following this is a general overview of systemic functional linguistics. At the end of the chapter there are two sections for further practice and reading. First there are some short exercises for you to try, which will give you some practice working with language analysis. Then there is a section which gives you some indicators for further reading if you are interested in learning more about some of the ideas presented in this chapter.

1.2 ANALYSING GRAMMAR WITHIN A FUNCTIONAL FRAMEWORK

All speakers of a language do something with it; they use language. They may play with it, shape it, but ultimately they use it for particular purposes. It serves a function. The ways in which people use language is always driven by the context within which people are using language and the speaker's individual goals or objectives (conscious or subconscious). In this sense, we could say that language is primarily functional; in other words, for any language context (casual conversation, letter to the editor, political speech, etc.) language is being used to do a job for the speaker; it is being used by the speaker. On a day-to-day basis, it is the function of language that is most important to people using it. This is not to say that the form or structure of language is not important – it is. In many cases it is impossible to separate function and structure. Anyone who has tried to communicate with someone in an unfamiliar language or with a two–year-old will know that being grammatically correct is almost irrelevant. Meaning is what counts, and getting the right meaning is what is most important. By looking only at grammatical structure, we miss out on the important perspective we can gain by considering functional meaning. However, without a firm understanding of the grammar of language, or how language is structured, it is nearly impossible to analyse the functions of language effectively.

1.2.1 A functional–structural view of language

The problem we are faced with when we are analysing language is that we have to be able to segment it into sections first before we can complete the analysis. Otherwise it's a bit like playing pin the tail on the donkey, where we hope that we've matched the right bits of language to the functional analysis. This is why a functional–structural approach is needed.

In order to try to prove this point, let's consider a rather famous joke told by Groucho Marx. The example will probably work best if you haven't already heard the joke.

> This morning I shot an elephant in my pyjamas ...
> How he got into my pyjamas, I'll never know!

What makes this example interesting is that it provides evidence of our ability to recognize functional and structural relations. Why does this joke work? It is based on the fact that the sentence is ambiguous; in other words it has more than one meaning or interpretation. However, the ambiguity is hidden because no one would recognize it initially. In the first part of the joke, the only understanding we have is that one morning while Groucho was still wearing his pyjamas, he shot an elephant. This sense corresponds to our real-world expectations because if there is a connection to be made amongst a man, pyjamas and an elephant, the association will be between the man and the pyjamas. So we understand immediately that the phrase *in my pyjamas* is telling us about how he (the speaker) shot an elephant. However, in the second part of the joke, we are forced to restructure our interpretation of the language used in order to form new relations and get a different meaning; we have to reinterpret what he said. By forcing a connection between the elephant and the pyjamas, we now understand that the elephant was wearing Groucho Marx's pyjamas when he shot it. The function of *in my pyjamas* is now to describe the elephant. There was an inherent ambiguity in the first sentence that went unnoticed and this is where the humour comes in. It might make us laugh or maybe groan, but one thing the joke does very well is force us to reconsider how we grouped or structured the words in order to make meaningful relations. This is what is meant by grammar – how words and structures come together to make meaningful relations.

We need to be able to look at language analytically if we want to be able to understand how it is working. This means being able to identify the components and their groupings or relations and how they are functioning. Learning to analyse grammar in a functional framework requires a good understanding of the relationship between function and structure. This relationship is one we deal with on a regular basis. For example, we can consider this relationship by looking at what is probably our most common tool: the knife and fork.

Most of us will use these every day. There is an obvious relation between the shape or structure of each piece and the function it has. Without too much technical understanding, we appreciate that the structural representation (i.e. the form or shape) of these tools is well suited for their purpose and that this will have evolved over time. It is also possible to modify or adapt the form to fit the needs of the user: for example, a child's fork has different relative dimensions and someone with arthritis may prefer to use an adapted shape. However, the general relation is that we use the fork to stab or hold food to raise it to our mouths and we use the knife to cut food. We could use the fork to cut and the knife to eat but generally this isn't how we use these tools. So we can say that the main function of the knife is to cut food and that we need the tool to have form or a structure in order to do this.

Language is very similar. The function of language is what it is doing for the speaker (or rather what the speaker is doing with language) and in order to achieve this function, language is shaped into a structural form.

- Function is what language is doing (for the speaker).
- Structure is the form or shape of language and, specifically, how language is organized (by the speaker and determined by the language).

It is impossible to have one without the other. To ask which came first or which is more important is like asking whether the chicken or the egg came first. We need to accept that they work together. However, we stated above that, in terms of communication, we give priority (usually) to function or meaning.

The combination of function and structure gives us meaning. This is what lets us understand language and what lets us express what we want to say. Hopefully, the 'elephant in my pyjamas' example has proved this point. If we change the structural relation, we get a different meaning. The relationship between function and structure will be discussed in more detail in the next section.

1.3 AN OVERVIEW OF SYSTEMIC FUNCTIONAL LINGUISTICS

Systemic functional linguistics (SFL), as its name implies, focuses on the functions of language. The system part of the name has to do with the way in which these functions are organized. The theory of SFL was developed originally by Michael Halliday in the late 1950s and early 1960s. There are some very good introductory descriptions of the theory and you will find references to these in the further reading section at the end of this chapter.

For Halliday, language is one type of semiotic system, which simply means that language is a system (or that it is organized systemically) and it represents a resource for speakers so they can create meaning. The view in SFL is that the ways in which we can create meaning through language are organized through patterns of use. The idea here is that language is organized as a system of options. This system organization is what enables speakers to create meaning, by selecting relevant options. The structure of language has a less prominent role in SFL since it is seen as 'the outward form taken by systemic choices, not as the defining characteristic of language' (Halliday and Matthiessen, 2004: 23). In other words, the primary driving force in language use is function but we need structure in order to express function. It is a complex relation which we will come back to throughout the book.

1.3.1 Functions of grammar

Function has an important place in SFL and is very much connected with the social uses of language. After all, language is primarily used for social communication. Halliday explains that 'the internal organization of language is not arbitrary but embodies a positive reflection of the functions that language has evolved to serve in the life of social man' (1976: 26). Therefore, at the foundation of SFL is the view of language as a social function.

The functions of language include both the use that language serves (i.e. how and why people use language) and linguistic functions (i.e. the grammatical and semantic roles assigned to parts of language). What is fundamental for Halliday is that language serves a social purpose. Therefore, his position is that a theory of linguistics must incorporate the functions of language in use.

1.3.1.1 Choice and meaning

In systemic functional linguistics, language is viewed as a system and since it is a system which relates meaning to form, it is a system of signs. We are all familiar with sign systems since we encounter them all the time. A traffic light can be seen as an example of a very simple sign system. We all recognize three signs: [red light], [amber light] and [green light]. Each one means something different. The relationship between each meaning and sign (simplified for the purposes of this discussion) is shown in Figure 1.1. Basically this represents the whole system, which in this case involves only three semantic options: stop, caution and go.

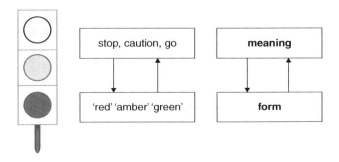

Figure 1.1 Simple sign system (adapted from Fawcett, 2008 and Eggins, 2004)

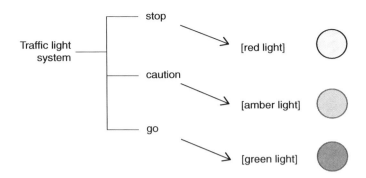

Figure 1.2 Simple sign system in system notation

We can represent this relationship using system notation. This is generally how such systems are represented in SFL. An example of this is shown in Figure 1.2, where we find the meanings (stop, caution and go) along with their 'realization' or structural form: in other words, [red light], [amber light] and [green light]. The notation of the lines indicates that for this system of traffic control there are three options and you must select one of them. This is what we call an OR relation (i.e. select 'stop' OR 'caution' OR 'go'). More complex systems may involve AND relations or combinations of both, as would be the case if, for example, we were trying to model the system of traffic flow for a given city.

What this simple example also shows is the relation between function and structural form or what we will now call realization. We need to relate this explanation to our study of language. Function is what forms the basis of the organization of meaning in language but structure (linguistic expression) is needed to realize or convey the meaning. If there was no red light showing, how would we know to stop?

We can now think of language in two ways:

1. Language as system, a resource for communicating meanings to our fellow human beings. As a system it includes the full potential of the language.
2. Language as text, the realized output of the language system. As text (e.g. spoken, written), it is an instance of language in use.

Language, when viewed as a system, is not a simple system as with the traffic light example, where each meaning maps onto one form. With language the relationship between meanings and forms is complex and there is not a one-to-one relationship, as Figure 1.3 attempts to show. This book will not be exploring this complexity or attempting to demonstrate it. We just need to accept that it is a complex relation. This isn't a problem for what we are trying to achieve here because to do good analysis and to develop a good understanding of how language works we don't really need to know everything there is to know about the theoretical representation of the language system.

In SFL the relationship between meaning and form is one of realization. The various potential meanings in the language are represented as connected (or networked) systems. A system is simply a representation of a set of options. For example, when we want to refer to a person, we can do so in a variety of ways. One option is to refer to them by name if this seems appropriate, another option is to describe the person, and another option is to use a personal pronoun. As an example, imagine we are at a party and there is a man standing in the kitchen talking to the host and, in this scenario, I want to say

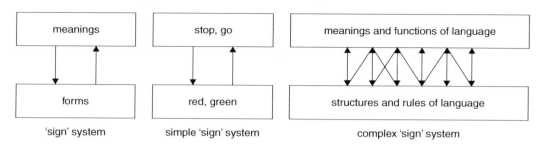

Figure 1.3 Relation of meanings and forms in a semiotic ('sign') system

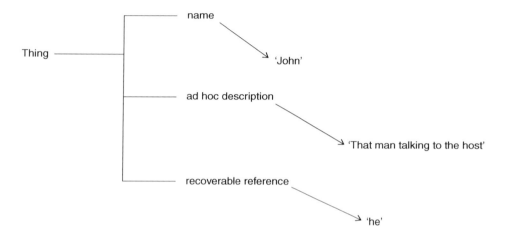

Figure 1.4 An example of a system for Thing

something to you about that particular person. To illustrate the three options mentioned above, I might say one of the following: *John works for the FBI*; *That man talking to the host works for the FBI*; or *He works for the FBI*. How we refer to entities will be covered in detail in Chapter 3 but for the moment we can see that there are at least three options in English for how we can refer to someone: (1) using their name; (2) using a description (an ad hoc description); (3) using a personal pronoun (a recoverable reference). This set of options can be represented systemically as in Figure 1.4, where the system here indicates the three options illustrated in the examples above: *John, that man talking to the host* and *he*. The system is labelled 'Thing' (short for 'referent thing') because it covers the options for referring to a referent when the referent is a thing (people, objects, ideas, places, concepts, etc.).

There are three other considerations for the system representation of language in SFL. The first is that each system has what is called an entry condition. In other words, there is a condition that must be met for each system. In the system shown in Figure 1.4, the system can only be accessed when the language being produced concerns an entity of some kind (in this case a person). In SFL there is a system for every set of options being modelled in the language. Systems are networked, which means that they are all connected to some extent. The second consideration is that each system has what are called realization rules or statements, which make the connection between the option concerned and the way in which that option is realized in the language. For example it is not enough to simply describe what options are available to the speaker; there has to be some description of what this triggers in the language system. In the sample system shown in Figure 1.4, the selection of name will determine that a person's name (for example, 'John') will be selected and used at that point. Finally the third consideration involves frequencies. This relates to the fact that certain options will be more or less frequent than others. In the sample system below, the option of recoverable reference is far more frequent than the other two. Recoverable reference involves the use of personal pronouns but these are only used if the speaker feels confident the addressee will be able to recover who is being referred to. For example, once the speaker has referred to a person by name (e.g. *John works for the FBI*, as above), they are highly unlikely to repeat the name to refer to this same person. Instead, the speaker is far more likely to use a pronoun (e.g. *He lives in New York*). In fact, a repeated name in most contexts will tend to cause confusion. However, in an example such as sentence (1) below, it is not at all clear who is being referred to for the second use of the personal pronoun, *he*. It is most likely that it is John who had the sinus infection and it is also most likely that it is the doctor who did the tests, but we can't be sure who did the saying because it could be John or the doctor. However, what this example does show is that referring to a Thing is most commonly done by use of a recoverable reference such as the personal pronoun *he*. If we replace all pronouns by the relevant name, we quickly see that it sounds completely unnatural, as shown in example (2). Similarly, if we only used (ad hoc) descriptions, the text would sound equally odd, as in (3), but in this case it not only sounds odd, it causes confusion and could suggest that there was another person involved.

(1) John went to see the doctor and he did some tests and he also said he had a sinus infection. I'm glad he finally went

(2) John went to see the doctor and the doctor did some tests and John also said John had a sinus infection. I'm glad John finally went

(3) A man I know went to see the doctor and the doctor did some tests and the man also said the man had a sinus infection. I'm glad the man finally went

The system notation is meant to explain language production from the perspective of the speaker. 'Speaker' is used in this book to include all instances of someone producing language (i.e. someone speaking or writing). As in the example above, it is the speaker who has to determine how to refer to the person they want to say something about. What we are interested in is analysing language and this is always language as text, the output of the language system (e.g. language that has been spoken or written). As analysts we are trying to pick apart and analyse language that has already been produced. In this book we won't be focusing on the system networks at all except for illustrative purposes when appropriate, because discussing the system networks is really beyond what we can achieve in this book. We will try to develop a very basic understanding of what is meant by the system organization of the functions of language and how this relates to grammatical structure. In the further reading section at the end of this chapter, there are references to books which do explore the system networks in some detail. However, no books explore them fully for the same reason – they are simply too large to represent.

1.3.1.2 Function and context

So far we've talked about language output as text but text itself has not been defined and we won't try to define it here. We'll just consider, in vague terms, that text is the actual language expressed, for example by writing or speaking, and that it is expressed through chunks or units from the grammar of the language. The main unit of grammar that we are going to be focusing on in this book is the clause. The clause is a unit that is similar to the orthographic sentence. More will be said about this in Chapter 2 but for now we can just think of a clause as being more or less the same as a simple sentence.

The clause is a multifunctional unit of language. The grammatical functions are represented in the clause, and this means that each clause expresses more than one type of meaning. Halliday adopted a three-way view of linguistic functions, offering insight into what he considers to be the three main functional components of language.

The first type of meaning sees the clause as a representation of some phenomenon in the real world, and this is referred to as experiential meaning since it covers the speaker's experience of the world. The experiential component serves to 'express our experience of the world that is around us and inside us' (Halliday, 1976: 27). This view is concerned with how speakers represent their experience. The notion of representing experience was further developed under the heading of the Ideational meaning, which includes experiential meaning as well as general logical relations. However, when discussing the various meanings of the clause, the logical is often left out. It won't be dealt with in this book. There are references in the further reading section at the end of this chapter which offer detailed descriptions of the logical metafunction.

The second type views the clause as social interaction and reflects both social and personal meaning. It is referred to as interpersonal meaning. The interpersonal component expresses 'the speaker's participation in, or intrusion into, the speech event' (1976: 27).

Finally, the third type of meaning relates the clause to the text and this is called textual meaning. However, the textual component, in Halliday's view, is somewhat different from the other two as this function is 'an integral component of the language system' and he considers it to be 'intrinsic to language' since it has the function of creating text (p. 27).

To illustrate how these three meanings interact in the clause, I will use an example from my own experience. Last year on my birthday I was given a Jamie Oliver recipe book. Although this is probably not really news to write home about, I usually do email my family and friends about birthday-related events. Depending on who I was talking to and what my goal in communicating was, I might have said one of the following sentences.

(4) Kev gave me the new Jamie Oliver recipe book for my birthday

(5) I was given the new Jamie book for my birthday

(6) For my birthday, Kev gave me the new Jamie book

(7) Who gave me the Jamie book for my birthday?

(8) Kev gave me the Jamie book for my birthday, didn't he?

(9) The recipe book was given to me for my birthday

We can infer a different context and set of assumptions for each of the six sentences above. In all cases, the situation being described is one of someone giving me something for my birthday so we might be tempted to say that all of these sentences are saying the same thing, or that they mean the same thing, whereas in fact they all differ from each other with respect to the three types of meaning we just mentioned. In terms of experiential meaning (what is being represented), these examples are very similar. The first example is probably the fullest representation of what happened since it represents who gave the book, who received the book and why the book was given. Examples (5) and (9) differ most from the others in this sense because they do not represent the person who gave the book and the others do (even if in example (7), we don't know who that person is). Examples (7) and (8) differ from the others when we consider how the language is being used to interact with the person being addressed. These sentences require a response, whereas the other sentences are simply giving information. Finally, we can recognize differences in textual meaning by looking at how the sentences begin and how they are each organized. Examples (4), (7) and (8) each begin by focusing on the person who gave the book but in (6), for example, the focus is on *my birthday*. We could go through each example in detail but what should be clear is that each example represents the same situation differently and each reflects a different social context.

By the end of this book, the analysis of these clauses will seem quite straightforward and the similarities and differences could be discussed in detail.

1.3.2 The multifunctional nature of the clause

The central unit of analysis in SFL is the clause. As discussed above, there are three main functional components to the grammar and these are integral to understanding the types of meaning identified in the clause. The components are referred to as metafunctions within SFL.

With the experiential component (or metafunction), the clause is seen as representation: the speaker's representation of a particular situation involving particular processes and participants. The interpersonal component sees the clause as exchange: the speaker's action and interaction with the addressee. Finally, with the textual component, the clause is seen as message: the speaker's means of organizing the message and creating text. Each type of meaning expressed in the clause has associated to it specific systems which express the meaning potential of the grammar. The clause, as an instance of language, therefore holds traces of these meanings, which are recoverable through analysis.

This is a good place to recall that there is a difference between the view of the metafunctions in language production and in language analysis. In producing language the speaker makes selections from the systems for the metafunctions in an integrated and simultaneous way; the meanings are brought together in one unit – the clause. The analyst tries to separate the metafunctions artificially in order to get a better understanding of the meanings represented in the clause. A useful image for this is that of the prism, which refracts white light into its component colours. In Figure 1.5,

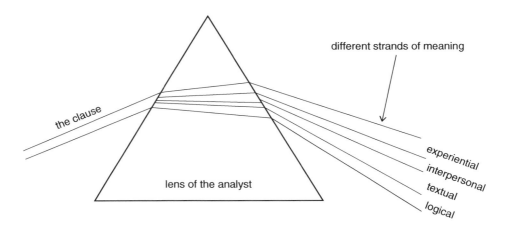

Figure 1.5 Analyst's view of the clause

Clause	Kev	gave		me	the new Jamie Oliver recipe book	for my birthday
Experiential meaning	Actor	Process: material (active)		Beneficiary	Goal	Circumstance: Cause
Interpersonal meaning	Subject	Finite	Predicator	Complement	Complement	Adjunct
	Mood					
Textual meaning	Theme	Rheme				

Figure 1.6 Three-strand analysis of the clause in example (4)

this imagery is used to show how the analyst views the clause in its component parts, even if, in real terms, the various strands are not really able to be separated from one another.

The three-strand analysis is illustrated in Figure 1.6, using example (4) from above (*Kev gave me the new Jamie Oliver recipe book for my birthday*). There is considerable terminology in Figure 1.6 and in this paragraph which will be unfamiliar to you. These will all be introduced in the relevant chapters. This example is simply to give you a glimpse of the multifunctional view of the clause that we will be developing in this book. In a sense the description in this example is an illustration of our goal in analysing the clause; this is what we want to achieve. As stated above, the experiential metafunction covers the range of processes and their participants. A very common process type is the material process, and the analysis shown in Figure 1.6 is an example of this. Each process type has specific participants associated to it. The most obvious of these for the material process is Actor, which represents the referent thing (person, place, object, concept, etc.) performing the process. One of the main functions of the clause within the strand of interpersonal meaning is that of Subject, which together with the Finite verbal element serves to determine the Mood structure of the clause. This is also illustrated in the example in Figure 1.6. Finally, the main element of relevance within the clause in terms of the textual metafunction is Theme, which functions as a means of 'grounding what [the speaker] is going to say' (Halliday and Matthiessen, 2004: 58). This is typically the very first part of the clause. Figure 1.6 shows how these three strands (or types) of meaning can be identified in a single clause.

If we compare this clause to example (5) given above (*I was given the new Jamie book for my birthday*) as presented in Figure 1.7, we get a sense of how these two clauses are similar and how they are different. The Theme element of the clause is different in each case yet it is the first element in both cases. We can also see that what is missing or different in Figure 1.7 is that the Actor (*Kev*), the person who did the giving, is not represented. As we progress through each chapter, we will develop our understanding of the individual strands of meaning, but perhaps more importantly we will develop our skill at being able to identify the functional components of the clause.

Clause	*I*	*was given*		*the new Jamie book*	*for my birthday*
Experiential meaning	Beneficiary	Process: material (active)		Goal	Circumstance: Cause
Interpersonal meaning	Subject	Finite	Predicator	Complement	Adjunct
	Mood				
Textual meaning	Theme	Rheme			

Figure 1.7 Three-strand analysis of the clause in example (5)

It is important to note one important distinction to be made in this presentation of SFL. In both examples above, the meanings represented are those interpreted by the analyst as having been selected by the speaker. As analysts, we deduce the selection of options based on the instance presented. The description given in these diagrams is a kind of visual labelling of the functions of the various parts of the clause – it doesn't help us to identify these parts and this is precisely the goal of this book, to equip the reader with the tools and strategies for analysing and segmenting the units. For example, how do we know that *the new Jamie Oliver recipe book* constitutes a unit? How do we know what the subject is?

What we need to be able to do is look at the internal structure of these units and determine confidently where the internal boundaries are within the clause. We also need a clear sense of how the group units work so that we can recognize their structure.

1.4 THE GOAL OF GRAMMATICAL ANALYSIS

Everyone reading this book will have different reasons for wanting to get better at grammatical analysis. It might just be for fun. Playing around with language is fun and can be a bit like solving a tricky puzzle. For others it might be to improve their own language use, maybe to write better essays or be a better journalist. Some may be involved in teaching grammar and/or reading and writing skills. Perhaps you work with people who have difficulty with communication and want to develop your understanding of how grammar works so you can help them better. Those who carry out research on language (media texts, political commentary, etc.) may want to develop critical analytical skills in working with language. The goal of grammatical analysis will always depend on the purpose of the investigation. Ultimately, however, the goal of functional grammatical analysis is to gain a deeper understanding of language in use and an insight into language use that would not be possible without this kind of in-depth analysis. As Halliday (1973: 57) explains, 'the essential feature of a functional theory is not that it enables us to enumerate and classify the functions of speech acts, but that it provides a basis for explaining the nature of the language system, since the system itself reflects the functions that it has evolved to serve'.

Regardless of the particular goals a researcher may have, the approach and process are the same. Of course the selection of the data or texts is also dependent on the research goals but grammatical analysis itself does not rely on a particular objective. It is important, however, to know what problem or question you want to answer as this will lead the focus of the research. As previously stated, the goal of this book is to develop the skills and procedures for general grammatical analysis within a functional framework.

1.4.1 The organization of the book

The organization of this book is intended to build up the approach to grammatical analysis being presented here. In Chapter 2, the focus is on identifying the main units of the clause and on recognizing groups and lexical items. Chapter 3 offers a description of the nominal group, analysing simple structures at first and then moving to increasingly challenging complex expressions. Then Chapter 4 contributes to the knowledge gained in the previous chapters by considering the clause as a whole. It deals specifically with the problems of analysing experiential meaning in the clause. The topic of Chapter 5 is understanding how the clause is used in interactions. It concentrates on the verbal system in English and how to identify the Subject and verbal elements of the clause. Chapter 6 covers the textual functions of the clause, discussing how to identify thematic elements in the clause including constructions that are more challenging. Having completed the internal view of the clause, Chapter 7 explains how to segment text into clause units by recognizing the boundaries of the clause within a text. Chapter 8 presents a complete step-by-step guide to analysing language. It is essentially a summary of the previous chapters, listing the steps for the analysis of an individual clause. Finally Chapter 9 demonstrates how the analysis of clauses reveals the meanings in the text. The answers to all exercises are given in Chapter 10.

1.5 EXERCISES

Exercise 1.1

Clause recognition exercise

The two texts below, Text 1.1 and Text 1.2, are reproduced here without any punctuation. Your job is to punctuate them as best you can, trying to identify individual sentences. In doing so, you will be indicating where you think the clause boundaries are. What this exercise will do is access your unconscious knowledge about the main grammatical units of language. It may help to read it aloud. Once you have finished, try to answer these questions. How did you know where to put punctuation? What criteria did you use? Was one text easier to punctuate than the other? What can you tell about the social context of each text? How were you able to recognize this?

Text 1.1

hello there how are you how are you managing with work school and the boys are you finding time for yourself at all again sorry I have been so long in getting back to you work has been crazy too I always feel like I am rushing so now when I feel that I try and slow myself down I also have the girls getting more prepared for the next morning the night before and that has seemed to help the mornings go more smoothly I will be glad when we don't have to bother with boots hats and mitts the days are getting longer so hopefully it will be an early spring

---

Text 1.2

this module aims to offer an introduction to a functionally oriented approach to the description of the English language and to provide students with an understanding of the relationship between the meanings and functions that are served by the grammatical structures through which they are realized the major grammatical systems will be explored through a functional framework at all stages the description and analysis will be applied to a range of text types by so doing we will be able to explore both the meaning potential that speakers have and how particular choices in meaning are associated with different texts

Exercise 1.2

Consider the two statements given below. Compare the underlined sections in statement A and statement B. Do you feel each speaker is saying approximately the same thing? If so, how are they similar and, if not, in what ways do they differ?

A

Tony Blair, Special Conference (Labour Party). 29 April 1995.

I wasn't born into this party. I chose it. I've never joined another political party. I believe in it. I'm proud to be the leader of it and it's the party I'll always live in and I'll die in.

B

Nick Clegg, Liberal Democrat Party. 19 October 2007.

Like most people of my generation, I wasn't born into a political party. I am a liberal by choice, by temperament and by conviction. And when I talk to the people I represent, I become more convinced every day that only liberalism offers the answers to the problems they face.

1.6 FURTHER READING

On the functions of grammar:

Fawcett, R. 2008. *Invitation to Systemic Functional Linguistics through the Cardiff Grammar: An Extension and Simplification of Halliday's Systemic Functional Grammar.* 3rd edn. London: Equinox.

Halliday, M.A.K. 1994. *An Introduction to Functional Grammar.* 2nd edn. London: Arnold.

Other relevant introductory textbooks:

Bloor, T. and M. Bloor. 2004. *The Functional Analysis of English: A Hallidayan Approach.* 2nd edn. London: Arnold.

Coffin, C., J. Donohue and S. North. 2009. *Exploring English Grammar: From Formal to Functional.* London: Routledge.

McCabe, A. 2011. *An Introduction to Linguistics and Language Studies.* London: Equinox.

Thompson, G. 2004. *Introducing Functional Grammar.* 2nd edn. London: Arnold.

On grammatical structure:

Fawcett, R. 2008. *Invitation to Systemic Functional Linguistics through the Cardiff Grammar: An Extension and Simplification of Halliday's Systemic Functional Grammar.* 3rd edn. London: Equinox.

Fawcett, R. 2000c. *A Theory of Syntax for Systemic Functional Linguistics.* Amsterdam: John Benjamins.

Morley, D. G. 2000. *Syntax in Functional Grammar.* London: Continuum.

On system networks:

Fawcett, R. 2008. *Invitation to Systemic Functional Linguistics through the Cardiff Grammar: An Extension and Simplification of Halliday's Systemic Functional Grammar.* 3rd edn. London: Equinox.

Halliday, M. A. K. and C. Matthiessen. 2004. *An Introduction to Functional Grammar.* 3rd edn. London: Hodder Arnold.

Chapter 2: The units of language analysis

2.1 INTRODUCTION

In the previous chapter, a distinction was made between structural and functional descriptions of grammar. It was suggested that a complete analysis must take a functional–structural view of language since these two components work together and are normally inseparable. Grammatical structure, including lexical structure, is what allows the functions to be expressed. So with this relationship between function and structure in mind, this chapter will take a deeper look at structure and offer some descriptions of the main grammatical units we will be working with.

This chapter offers a general overview of the clause and its internal composition. It also introduces the basic terminology and notation that will be useful for our exploration into analysing English grammar. The main idea presented here is that when a speaker says something about something, they are using language to describe (very loosely) a situation, and that this situation is represented in language by a structure called the clause. For now we can think of this structure as being very similar to our understanding of sentence in written language, as was explained in Chapter 1. The entities (the 'something') we want to say something about are seen as participating in the description of the situation. In this chapter we will begin to explore the relationship between the functions involved in the situation and the structures that these functions typically take.

2.1.1 Goals and limitations of the chapter

In my view, the nature of grammatical analysis is complex and it is this complexity that makes analysing grammar so challenging and interesting. Each chapter in the book tackles a different area of the grammar so that, as we go through the book, we will be progressively building up our view of analysing grammar. In doing so we will be piecing together the puzzle. This approach itself can be challenging because it means that it may leave you with a feeling of not seeing the big picture until we get to the end. From experience, by developing an approach to analysing grammar in stages, the methodology and strategies needed to work through the complexities of analysing grammar will become clearer and easier to do. As is always the case, we have to start somewhere, and in analysing language we have to impose an order to what we do and how we do it. This implies that there are different ways to do this and all analysts need to find the best way for them. However, a full analysis can't really be done until a full view of the clause has been developed within the functional framework being presented here. I think we all experience some degree of frustration when learning a new analytical method because it is tempting to want to know everything all at once, but this would actually make things even more difficult. Instead, by working through the methodology in stages, the full view will be built up gradually. Consequently, some concepts and terminology may need to be mentioned before being fully explained at a later stage. This is especially true in this chapter because it attempts to provide a general overview of the clause and the main grammatical structures we will be working with, but without going into enough detail to really get a good understanding of them. However, this will come as we progress through the chapters.

2.1.2 Notation used in the book

It is standard practice in linguistics to use the asterisk, *, to indicate an unacceptable or ungrammatical structure. This practice is adopted in this book, and where an asterisk is used at the beginning of an example it will indicate that the example is not considered grammatical.

As stated in Chapter 1, certain specific terms will be written with an initial capital letter to mark that they differ in meaning and use in this specific context from more general meanings of the word in its common use. These include all of the functional elements of the clause. Structural units will not be capitalized nor will any other terms since this would become quite distracting, as there are so many words that have both a general and specific sense within functional grammar. For example the word 'text' as used in this book means any instance of language in use – or, in other words, the output from the language system, regardless of whether it is in print, electronic or spoken form. To note each specific term with a capital would almost certainly lead to far too many words being capitalized, so an effort is being made here to reduce the use of capitals.

The relationship between function and structure was introduced in Chapter 1 and explained as one of realization or expression: function (or meaning) is realized or expressed through linguistic structure. This section will introduce notation for referring to this relationship. In diagrams, this will be noted by a horizontal bar, – (as is used in written fractions), and in written form, for ease of typography, it will be noted by a vertical line, | (e.g. 'function' | 'structure'). It is simply a way of indicating that a particular unit of linguistic structure is serving to express one or more functions.

One of the difficulties of dealing with a functional–structural approach to analysing grammar is learning the distinctions being made when wanting to focus on one or the other, because this means there is a need for terms to refer to the functions of grammar and different terms to refer to the structures of grammar. So, for example, in Chapter 1, the term 'clause' was used to describe the main (or largest) grammatical structure in English, and 'situation' was used to describe its functional or semantic role. Because there isn't a one-to-one relationship between function and structure (e.g. a given structure may be used for a variety of functions), it is important to be able to discuss relevant features in either strictly structural terms or strictly functional terms, or even both at the same time.

This chapter also introduces the notation used in this book for tree diagrams which represent the functional–structural analysis of English grammar. In addition to the bar mentioned above to indicate the relationship of function and structure, the slash (a diagonal line), /, is also used to show cases where more than one function is mapped onto a particular structure. For example Subject and Theme, which are two functions that will be introduced later in the book, very often map onto the same structure, as is shown in Figure 1.6. The notation used to indicate this would be as follows: Subject/Theme. This will be discussed in more detail in Chapter 5.

Tree diagrams are used in this book because they most accurately illustrate the complex relationships within the clause. In SFL, box diagrams are frequently used (as shown in Figures 1.6 and 1.7) but they often do not clearly identify the relationships between function and structure nor do they readily describe some of the interesting and sometimes complex relations within the clause. Many people find drawing tree diagrams useful from the analytical perspective because it forces you to actually work out the internal workings of

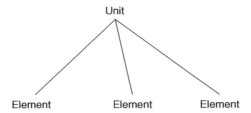

Figure 2.1 Basic principles of a tree diagram

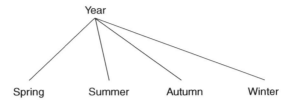

Figure 2.2 The components of the year as a tree diagram

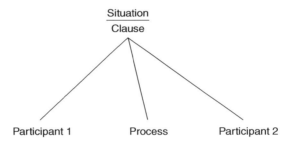

Figure 2.3 Example of a general description of the clause as a situation

the clause. There are two main principles of drawing tree diagrams. One is the use of nodes to indicate a single unit of structure and the other is the use of branches to indicate membership within a unit. This is shown in Figure 2.1, where the node is indicated by the point made where the branches (lines) join. All nodes are labelled by the unit being represented. Each branch is labelled with the elements which are being expressed in the unit of language being analysed. The structure and components of units will be presented later in this chapter and throughout the remaining chapters of the book.

The principles of tree diagrams can work with almost anything. Figure 2.2 illustrates how a tree diagram could represent an analysis of the concept of <year> by segmenting it into its main components (seasons). Using tree diagram notation, this diagram is saying that there is a unit called 'year' and it has four components (elements), labelled spring, summer, autumn and winter respectively. To show even more detail for the representation of the year, each season could also become a node itself and branches would include the potential components for each season (e.g. the months for each season).

The main components of the clause can be represented in a similar way, using tree diagrams as shown in Figure 2.3. Due to the multifunctional nature of the clause, it is

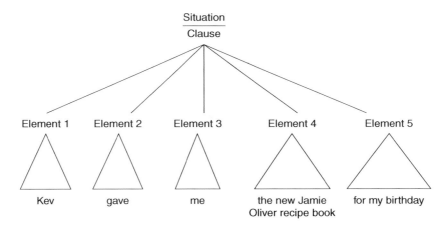

Figure 2.4 Use of triangle notation to replace branching in tree diagrams

difficult to represent its structure without having first considered the various functions that it expresses; however, for illustrative purposes here, we can take a very general view of one function to show how the clause can be described in terms of its main components. Using the terminology we have developed so far, the diagram is saying that the clause has three components: one process and two participants. This very basic, generic structure is representative of the most common configuration of the English clause. For example, this could be the clause configuration for something like *[the girl] [kicked] [the ball]* or *[the dog] [chased] [the cat]*.

Finally there is one last symbol which is used in this book as notation. There are instances where the structural detail within the tree diagram is not being shown for some reason (e.g. further detail is not necessary for the current purposes or reducing the amount of detail is more appropriate to save time). In these cases, a triangle, Δ, is used rather than a line notation and it replaces all branching beneath the given node. This is illustrated in Figure 2.4, which shows example (4) from Chapter 1. Here the triangle notation is used rather than branching from each element (component) of the clause because at this point the detail has not yet been developed. By the end of Chapter 7, all detail in the analysis of the clause will be able to be included.

The notation presented above is just a starting point; more detail and notation will be added throughout the remaining chapters as needed. The rest of this chapter focuses on providing a general view of the clause and the various units involved in its composition.

2.2 THE CLAUSE: ELEMENTS AND UNITS

Language can't be analysed whole; it has to be segmented in some way to make it manageable. This could be as individual words, as a section of speech, as sentences or even longer stretches of language. For grammatical analysis, most linguists agree that there is a unit of language called the clause, which corresponds roughly to the unit of sentence in written language. If this is true, you might be wondering why we aren't interested in studying the sentence. The sentence in English is generally accepted as an orthographic convention, something that has developed in the writing system along with punctuation. There is no equivalent marked unit in spoken English, where recognizing the units of grammar is challenging and requires some understanding of tone patterns and pausing as well as grammar. So it is problematic from an analytical perspective to rely on the sentence as the core unit of interest because it restricts us to written texts and it does not help us when we are interested in texts without punctuation, such as spoken language or some forms of electronic language.

If we come back to the idea that the sentence is close to a core grammatical unit, we begin to get a sense of the unit we are trying to describe. But our main problem is that it is nearly impossible to define a clause. To the best of my knowledge, there is no existing (satisfying) definition. The challenge is due to the fact that while there is considerable regularity in the main components of the English clause, there is also considerable variation. Consider the following short text, which is an email from an adult daughter to her mother.

Text 2.1 Personal email text

Hi Mom,

We'll be going to Scotland from March 30 to April 2nd. We'll go to London April 14th. It's a nice day here too. John has taken Tom to the dentist for a check-up, we'll see if he agrees to open his mouth!!

This short text has four sentences which are clearly recognizable by the punctuation (if we exclude *Hi Mom*). Almost every one of these corresponds to a single clause as we will see shortly, but we first need to know what a clause is before we can identify it. A full description of the clause is not going to be developed until much later in the book. So in the meantime we need some working guidelines in order to begin the analysis. The clause can be thought of as a structural grammatical unit that expresses a given situation. A situation can be thought of as similar to the everyday meaning of the word: 'a set of circumstances; a position in which one finds oneself; a state of affairs'.[1] In functional terms, it describes or relates a particular process (what is going on) and particular participants (one or more individuals or objects that are involved in the process). This description of situation will be presented in more detail in Chapter 4.

The sentences in the text are listed below as examples (1) to (4). The first two sentences in the text above, shown in (1) and (2), each express a situation where someone (*we*) is going somewhere (*Scotland* and *London*). In (3) the situation is one of something being something (i.e. 'today is a nice day'). Sentence (4) is more challenging because it is difficult to determine what the situation is because of the number of verbs. Although we would all agree this is one sentence based on the punctuation, there seems to be more than one situation being expressed.

    (1) We'll be going to Scotland from March 30 to April 2nd

    (2) We'll go to London April 14th

    (3) It's a nice day here too

    (4) John has taken Tom to the dentist for a check-up, we'll see if he agrees to open his mouth!!

We might argue that in fact if we replaced the comma with a full stop after the word *check-up*, we would have two sentences. This is true and certainly this would work as shown in (5) and (6) below. However, this only solves the problem for the new sentence (5) and we still can't be sure about the situation being expressed in (6). This is because two processes are being described: seeing and agreeing.

(5) John has taken Tom to the dentist for a check-up

(6) We'll see if he agrees to open his mouth!!

There is a subordinate clause in example (6), namely, *if he agrees to open his mouth*. However, the tools needed to confidently determine the clause boundaries have not yet been developed (i.e. whether sentence (6) is in fact one clause or two). This isn't something we can resolve now because we need more information about how to determine clause boundaries. We will come back to this later in the chapter once we have developed some initial strategies for identifying a situation.

What we want to focus on here is an understanding of what we mean by a clause. For our purposes, we will define clause as the linguistic (grammatical) resource for expressing a situation, which describes who or what is involved and what kind of relation or activity is involved (a process and the participant(s) it involves). This is still somewhat vague but we will have developed a better view of the clause after reading through Chapters 4 and 5. The core elements of process and participant can be illustrated with example (1) above. This clause represents a particular situation: in other words, someone is going somewhere. The entities (who or what) participating in any situation are referred to as participating entities or simply participants. A participating entity (or participant for short) in this sense includes any entity (person, object, place, idea, concept, etc.) that *participates* in completing the process. In example (1), although we do not know who exactly is involved, we do know that the 'someone' who is going is the speaker and some others, which is indicated by the use of the pronoun *we*. We also know that the 'somewhere' participant (a location) is given as *to Scotland*. The relation or activity represented in the situation is referred to as the process. In example (1), as we have already said, the process is one of 'going'. We can now begin to describe the situation in example (1) as a process of 'going' with two participants. This leaves us with a bit of language left over: *from March 30 to April 2nd*. Clearly, in the context, this information is very important to the speaker and addressee. It is within the boundaries of the clause and offers an additional description to the situation, namely when precisely the event will occur. This kind of descriptive information is considered optional in functional grammatical terms because the only parts that are expected within the language for this particular situation are the process and two participants: one participant who is the one who is going and a second participant which is the location of where the first participant is going. The other information included in this situation doesn't have to be there in order to meet the expectations of the language (in other words, no speaker will find it missing any content if it isn't included). For now we put this to the side temporarily so that we can focus on the core elements of the clause, and we'll come back to it briefly throughout this chapter and in detail in Chapter 4.

In this discussion I have been switching back and forth between functional elements and structural units. This is because they are expressed simultaneously. In other words, there can be no expression of a functional element without some structure. Each situation is realized through the unit of the clause. We can represent this using notation to show this relationship by using a straight line (either vertical or horizontal) as follows.

situation | clause

situation
clause

The linear form (the first one above using a vertical bar) will be used when referring to this relationship in text: situation|clause. The second form is used in diagrams following conventions in SFL. This will become clear as the notation is used in examples.

Each clause is a constellation or configuration of component parts which express various functional meanings, which will be referred to as elements, and these component elements are realized or expressed through various different structural units. These structural units will be described in section 2.3 below. As we saw in Chapter 1, the clause expresses three main functions (called metafunctions), and these will be discussed in detail in Chapters 4, 5 and 6. For now, we want to think of the clause as the linguistic realization of the situation that the speaker wants to express, and that the clause is made up of component parts that fit together.

So far, the only parts we have mentioned are the very general functional labels of process and participant. In this chapter, we will not describe the functional elements in any detail since, as stated above, this will be covered in Chapters 4, 5 and 6, each detailing one of the three main metafunctions of the clause. The focus here will be on the structural units which give the clause its shape. Functional elements are usually realized through group structure (i.e. a group of words). There are some cases where a particular functional element is realized by a single word (lexical item) rather than a group. For example, let's consider the clause in example (7) below, which is just an invented example for the purposes of illustration.

(7) but the boy doesn't know the answer

This clause relates a particular situation and it is composed of four parts as follows: *but / the boy / doesn't know / the answer*.

The clause is representing a situation of someone knowing (or not knowing in this case) something. There are two participating entities: *the boy* and *the answer*. Each of these expressions consists of more than one word which work together to express the Participant. We can prove this by asking questions about this situation. If I asked 'Who doesn't know the answer?', someone would reply 'The boy'. So we can be confident that these two words work together as a group to express the first participant in this situation. This is also true for the second participant, and I could ask 'What doesn't the boy know?' and the reply would be 'The answer'. In fact, the segmentation of the clause into four parts shows that, most of the time, each part includes more than one word working together in this way. However, the first section of the clause has only one word, the conjunctive word *but*. Its function can be seen primarily as linking this clause with another part of the text since the use of *but* in English always assumes a connection to something already said. This function will be described in Chapter 6. In this example, we would say that *but* is not seen as a group because there are no other words in the language that can work with it, so it does not have the potential to expand to a group. Instead this first element is seen as being realized by a single lexical item (i.e. not a group or phrase).

2.2.1 Units of the clause

When we talk about the units of the clause, we are referring to the grammatical structures which combine to form it. The challenge in analysing grammar in a functional framework is working out the relationship between the functional elements and the structural units. As we saw in Chapter 1, the approach to the clause in SFL is multifunctional; in other words, the clause itself and its elements may express more than one function at the same time. These different functions can be considered as different views of the clause (as in Chapter 1, section 1.3).

In analysing a clause, the first job for the analyst is to segment the clause into identifiable units. The main grammatical units found within the clause are described in section 2.3 below. At this point, a few basic notions will be covered before moving on to the individual groups.

Basic notions
- Every text contains at least one clause.
- The clause is made up of units.
- Each clause has one and only one main verb.

These are very useful guidelines for the analyst. If the main verb can be identified, then finding the clause boundaries is much easier. The main verb is the key to understanding how the clause works because it expresses the main process represented in the situation. As we will see in section 2.4, once we have worked out what the process is, we can use some tests to determine what participants are included in the situation. This in turn will help us to identify the relevant structural units expressed in the clause.

The main problem is that finding the main verb can be challenging, and this is due in part to the way the verb system works in English. Chapter 5 will describe the verb system in detail, but for now it is enough to continue with our discussion of the clause and its composition. In this section, I want to point out the main complexity in working with English grammar, which is the frequent use of embedding. Embedding simply means that the language lets us insert units inside other units and this is what makes it so difficult to identify them. To better understand this, we'll take a look at a famous example from a children's story, 'The House that Jack Built'. In this story, a funny tale is told by playing around with embedding. The story starts off with a very simple clause and each successive clause embeds something from the previous clause in the story. I won't retell the whole story but, just to give you an idea, here's how it begins (although there are many different versions of this tale).

The House that Jack Built
This is Jack.

This is the house that Jack built.

This is the malt that lay in the house that Jack built.

This is the rat that ate the malt that lay in the house that Jack built.

This is the cat that chased the rat that ate the malt that lay in the house that Jack built.

This is the dog that scared the cat that chased the rat that ate the malt that lay in the house that Jack built.

The kind of embedding shown in this text is very common in English but it can make analysing language very challenging at times. In each of the clauses listed above in the 'House that Jack Built' story, a different entity is being identified: first it is a person named Jack, then a particular house, and then some malt, and so on. If we take for example the clause which is introducing a dog and consider the different ways in which this could be done by the speaker, we should get a sense of the slots or components involved in expressing one particular situation. All the clauses listed in Figure 2.5 represent the same situation but they differ in terms of the grammatical structure and

(8) This is [the dog]

(9) This is [a nice dog]

(10) This is [my dog]

(11) This is [the dog that chased the cat]

(12) This is [the dog that chased the cat that scared the rat that
ate the malt that lay in the house that Jack built]

Figure 2.5 Simple clause, *this is [<dog>]*.

the description of the second participant (*the dog*). This is illustrated visually with an arrow, which is meant to indicate *this is* and a photograph of a dog to represent the actual referent being talked about.

Examples (8) to (12), shown in Figure 2.5, illustrate some of the different ways the dog in question can be referred to. Examples (8) to (10) would be considered relatively simple expressions but (11) and (12) involve embedded units. In these two cases we find clauses inside the expression used to refer to the dog and they serve to offer a full description of the dog (so it's not just any dog but the one that chased the cat, for example, and not just any cat but the one that scared the rat, etc.).

The last example in Figure 2.5, example (12), illustrates the problem of identifying the main verb in a given clause. It is easy to do in (8), for example, because there is only one verb in that clause and this is the verb 'be' (*is* in this case). However, in example (12), there are a total of six verbs: *is, chased, scared, ate, lay* and *built*. There are ways to reduce the complexity in these cases. For example, the entire expression used to refer to the dog in example (12) (i.e. *the dog that chased the cat that scared the rat that ate the malt that lay in the house that Jack built*) can be replaced by *it*. This should eliminate some of the challenges because it shows that all of the verbs in that section of the clause are there to describe which dog is being talked about and consequently they are not there to express the process. Section 2.3 below presents a brief overview of lexical classes, which will help to remind readers how to recognize verbs. Chapter 5 will discuss the verbal system in some

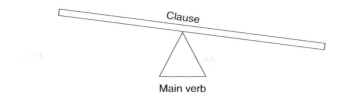

Figure 2.6 Main verb as pivotal element of the clause

detail, providing the information required to be able to confidently recognize main verbs and clause boundaries.

When beginning to analyse a clause the key is to be able to identify the main verb because so much of what is expressed within the clause is organized around it.

The main verb expresses the process (i.e. what's going on). In addition to the process, the clause may also contain participants (who or what is involved). It may also include other descriptive information called circumstances (for example information about how or why the process is taking place) – see Chapter 4. The clause is the central unit in analysing grammar because it is the grammatical resource for expressing a particular situation. The key point of entry to identifying the clause is by its required main verb, which links it to the situation that is being represented by the clause.

When we say that the clause has only one main verb, this does not mean that each clause has only one verb. A clause can combine verbs in various ways. For example, I could say: *I might have been sleeping*. This clause is almost exclusively expressed by verbs and they are underscored in the example. Nevertheless this situation is about someone sleeping and the main verb is 'sleep'. The remaining verbs contribute towards the meaning of the process in terms of when in time the participant was sleeping and also the degree of certainty about the process. The way verbs combine in English is another reason why working with grammar can be so challenging. It can be very difficult to confidently identify the main verb in a clause; it takes practice. Words alone are not enough, as shown in examples (13) and (14).

    (13) Time flies like an arrow

    (14) Fruit flies like apples and bananas

Each of the clauses in (13) and (14) expresses a situation. The first step to analysing the clause is by locating the main verb. In a sense the main verb is the pivotal element of the clause, as illustrated in Figure 2.6. The analysis of the clause hinges on the main verb since it is by identifying the main verb that the process can be determined, and then the rest of the analysis unfolds from this.

In (13) the main verb (the only verb) is *fly* and in (14) the main (and only) verb is *like*. Consequently each verb expresses a different process and we can describe each clause very generally as follows. The clause in (13) expresses a situation of flying where *time* (participant) is flying and this process of flying is being described as happening in the same manner as an arrow flies. The clause in (14) expresses a situation of liking where *fruit flies* (participant) are said to like *apples and bananas* (participant).

There is a trick to working through these two clauses because the same two adjacent words (*flies* and *like*) appear in each clause and it isn't immediately obvious which one of these is the verb in each case. In the next section, groups and word classes are presented. This includes an overview of the main word classes such as noun, verb, preposition and adjective as well as the different types of groups (grammatical word groups) which we will be using in the description of English grammar.

2.3 WORD AND GROUP CLASSES

In some analytical frameworks a distinction is made between two types of unit: a phrase and a group. This is a theoretical distinction and not everyone is in agreement on the distinction. For Halliday and Matthiessen (2004: 311), the terms phrase and group are not equivalent: 'a group is an expansion of a word, a phrase is a contraction of a clause'. In this view, the clause is considered a full phrase rather than a group since it is not based upon the expansion of a particular word or class of word. The special status of the clause as compared to other types of unit is generally accepted. The notion of group centres on the concept of headedness – in other words, each group is based on a pivotal element, such as a noun, a verb or an adjective. Halliday's notion of expansion is important. For each type of head – whether a noun, a verb or whatever – there is the potential for expansion through modification (modification in this sense can be thought of as an elaborated description).

In the previous section, I mentioned that finding the main verb in a clause is difficult because verbs are combined in English to modify the core meaning of the verb as in the example given above, *might have been sleeping*. However, it is clear that these verbs are working together as a unit, or group, in order to alter the meaning of 'sleep' as the event in a particular situation.

Before explaining the concept of group and how it is used in this book, the next section provides a brief overview of word classes for those who want to be reminded about nouns, verbs, adjectives and other word classes. Having a good understanding of this kind of classification is important because, in general, the concept of group and group structure is based on word categories.

2.3.1 Lexical categories (also known as word classes)

Certain types of words behave similarly enough to be grouped in the same word class. These classes are not strict with clear boundaries since some words in a given word class may not behave identically to all other members of that class. For every word class there tends to be a typical member of that class that can be thought of as the prototypical member, which displays all the important features of the class. There will also be members that only share some of these features. Before giving an overview of the main grammatical groups, we will review the main word classes. For many readers this will be familiar ground.

Let's start with a little experiment about words.

Say the first word that comes to your mind.

What word did you think of first?

Psycholinguistic research shows that if you ask most people to say the first word they think of, they will usually say a word that is a noun. Noun is perhaps the word class that most people can identify with most easily. It is often the easiest class of word for children to learn as they begin to speak. In school most of us were told that a noun is a person, place or thing. This is a very vague definition but it works as long as you can understand that 'thing' can mean anything whether it is real or imaginary, including feelings, thoughts and abstract concepts such as *jealousy*, *happiness* or *love*.

In analysing language, it is convenient to be able to group words in this way so that we can use a term, such as 'noun', to refer to a set of words that are similar in most ways and that have similar properties. This does not mean that this is how words are organized in the language system or indeed in our brains. In fact, we are pretty sure that they are not organized by classes but rather in networks that connect the meaning and forms (e.g. sound form or written form) by various types of associations. So the terminology used in this section is more a matter of convenience and we are not attempting to describe the way language is really organized in the brain.

2.3.1.1 Nouns

Nouns are words used by speakers to denote objects in our world, including ones that are real, imaginary, concrete or abstract. Nouns can be sub-classified based on features such as mass or count, which explains distinctions between nouns such as *flour, sand* or *water*, which are mass nouns, as compared to nouns such as *egg, shovel* or *pin*, which are all count nouns. These two sets of nouns behave differently in the grammar. For example in English it is acceptable to say *I need flour in the recipe* but not **I need egg in the recipe*. Similarly, with a non-specific or indefinite reference such as in *I have a shovel*, the indefinite article, *a*, is required for count nouns but with mass nouns the indefinite article is not acceptable, **I have a sand*.

There is also a distinction to be made between what is called common and proper nouns. Proper nouns are actually names and these are used by speakers to refer to a specific person or place, such as *John, Toronto, Buckingham Palace*. Common nouns are all other nouns. Most often, there are grammatical differences between proper nouns and common nouns because proper nouns (since they are names) are not usually modified or described in any way. For example, it would sound very odd indeed to hear someone say **I went to a nice Toronto for two weeks*. In this sense, proper nouns are much more like pronouns than common nouns. However, you might hear someone say something like *you aren't the John I know*. In this case, the speaker isn't using *John* as a proper noun to name and refer to a particular person. *John* is being used here as a common noun. What we mean by common noun is a word that is recognized by speakers to denote a particular class of entity. So, in this particular use of *John*, the speaker isn't referring to a particular person named John, but rather a class or set that includes all the possible Johns. A similar thing happens when we talk about 'keeping up with the Joneses'.

In some cases, a noun has been derived from a verb. This process is called nominalization. These derived nouns are abstract common nouns and they function the same way as other common nouns. However, they seem to retain much of the meanings from the associated verb. For example, the noun *evaluation* carries with it the meaning that someone evaluated something. While these types of noun can be significant in certain kinds of analyses, as a lexical item, they behave as normal common nouns and display the same features as summarized below.

In discussing what it is for a word to be a noun, we've also seen examples that illustrate how nouns behave. There are three main ways in which we can readily identify a noun.

1. Nouns are the only kind of word in English that are affected by quantities – they can be made plural or singular (e.g. evaluation – evaluation**s**).
2. Nouns are affected by definiteness – they can be made definite or indefinite by different determiners (e.g. **the** apple – **an** apple).
3. Nouns can be modified in their description – they can be extended into a group, most often by an adjective (e.g. the **juicy** apple – the **red** apple **in the fridge**).

2.3.1.2 Pronouns

Usually the class of pronouns is included in the word class of noun but this hides a major difference in how they work in the language. Clearly, there are significant similarities in terms of how they are used by speakers but pronouns are not simply another kind of noun. In fact, the similarities between pronouns and names (proper nouns) are considerable and there are some good reasons for grouping these two categories together. It isn't so important how they are grouped but it is important to be able to recognize a pronoun.

You may have been told in school that a pronoun replaces a noun. This isn't actually true. This point will be made clearer in the next chapter but for now a simple example should illustrate what I mean. If someone wanted to tell you something about a particular dog, they might say something like this (the nouns are underscored): *That black dog came into my house yesterday*. If I wanted to say more about this dog and include what it did in my yard, I would say something like the following, where the pronoun is double underscored: *and it knocked over my plant*. However, if the pronoun *it* were to really replace the noun *dog*, the clause would have to become: *and that black it knocked over my plant*. What this shows is that, when a pronoun is used, it does not simply replace a noun. A pronoun is used to replace the full expression being used to refer to some object. In technical terms, a pronoun functions in the same way as a group and not as a word. This is the main difference between nouns and pronouns. Nouns do not actually refer to an object in and of themselves; they denote (or represent) objects in the language system. They must be incorporated into an expression (a nominal group) that a speaker uses to refer to an object. Pronouns, on the other hand, work differently. They have no inherent meaning of their own; their meaning is always by reference to something said elsewhere in the text or by reference to something known (for example by pointing at a person and saying *he* as in *he looks bored*).

Like nouns, there are various types of pronoun and each type fits into the grammar in a slightly different way.

Personal pronouns Personal pronouns are used to refer to living things with the exception of the special pronoun *it*, which can refer to anything at all in the singular. Recognizing personal pronouns is easy because we don't have very many of them. They are further grouped by sex and number as shown in Table 2.1.

I've used the terms 'subjective' and 'objective' to refer to the distinction between grammatical uses of the personal pronouns. Many use the terms 'nominative' and 'accusative' but I think these are not as transparent as 'subjective' and 'objective'. These terms are used to indicate the distinction for example between *I* and *me*, which has to do with the grammatical position of the pronoun in modern English. Subjective pronouns are used in the Subject position of the clause whereas objective pronouns are used in Object (or Complement) position in the clause. Where the first person (or self-reference) pronouns are concerned, there is currently considerable variation in use and it has become relatively common to hear objective pronouns in Subject positions, especially with conjunctions (e.g. *John and me went out last night*). This variation does not happen with third person pronouns in standard English (the second person pronoun forms are identical so there would be no difference to notice). Table 2.1 is not a strict description of how speakers use personal pronouns but rather a description of the different classes of personal pronouns; different varieties of English may distribute the pronouns differently.

Possessive pronouns mark a relationship of possession, ownership or association between two objects (referents): e.g. *Does Steven like his teacher?* In this example, *his* refers to <Steven> and it marks the relationship between *Steven* and *teacher*. This is not strictly

Table 2.1: Personal pronouns in English

		Subjective	Objective	Possessive		Reflexive
1st person (self-reference)	singular	I	me	determiner	my	myself
				absolute	mine	
	plural	we	us	determiner	our	ourselves
				absolute	ours	
2nd person (addressee reference)	singular	you	you	determiner	your	yourself
				absolute	yours	
	plural	you	you	determiner	your	yourselves
				absolute	yours	
3rd person (other person reference)	singular	she/he/it	her/him/it	determiner	her/his/its	herself/himself/itself
				absolute	hers/his/its	
	plural	they	them	determiner	their	themselves
				absolute	theirs	

possession, of course, but these pronouns always mark some kind of possessive relationship between two referents, which determine the object which is being referred to (e.g. *his teacher*). As indicated in Table 2.1, there are two sub-sets of possessive pronouns: possessive determiners (e.g. *my*) and absolute possessive pronouns (e.g. *mine*). The distinction made between the two different forms has to do with what function they serve in the full nominal expression. The possessive determiner works like other determiners in English such as the article *the*. Its role is to modify a noun so that it is definite or specific. It works just like the grammatical possessive morpheme, *-'s* (e.g. *I have met my son's teacher*). The second form, called the absolute possessive pronoun, functions as a true pronoun and replaces a full nominal expression: e.g. *that money is mine*.

Relative pronouns Relative pronouns have a double duty to perform: part pronoun and part conjunction. They work as pronouns in the sense that they refer to some object (person or thing) that has already been mentioned in the text, except that with relative pronouns the referent is mentioned within the same clause. They are also like conjunctions because they serve as a link between a main clause and an embedded clause by marking the introduction of the embedded clause. This is illustrated in example (15), where the relative pronoun is underlined.

(15) It was just a thought <u>that</u> crossed my mind

The most common relative pronouns are *who*, *that* and *which*, but the full set includes: *that*, *which*, *who*, *how*, *whose*, *whom*, *where* and *when*. These pronouns show up in different places in the grammar. For example *that* is also a demonstrative pronoun and *who*, along with all the other so-called 'wh' words (including *how*), is an interrogative pronoun (e.g. *How are you? Who are you? Where are you?*). It is important to be able to recognize how the word is functioning depending on what it is doing in the clause.

Deictic (demonstrative) pronouns There are four deictic pronouns in English: *that*, *this*, *these* and *those*. A deictic word is a word that gets its meaning from a shared context. If I were to say, for example, *that is beautiful*, it would be impossible to know what I was talking about unless the person I was speaking to could figure out what *that* meant or what the referent for *that* was (e.g. something I am pointing at). This use of these words sees them working as true pronouns since they replace the full expression. For example, if I had been referring to a particular table when saying *that is beautiful*, then I really would have been saying *that table is beautiful*. Note that in this last example, *that* in *that table* has the same function as the article *the*. Once again, this shows that word classes are not fixed groups; words vary in the ways that they can be used.

Indefinite pronouns The words that are grouped under the heading of indefinite pronouns are varied and include words that have no specific referent, such as *anyone* or *somebody*. In a way this is a catch-all category for words that are used to refer to vaguely specified or unspecified objects (e.g. *something*) or to unspecified amounts or quantities (e.g. *all*, *many* or *everything*). Many of them include both kinds of meaning: non-specific reference and non-specific amount. It is debatable whether or not they are truly pronouns in the way we have been discussing them here. Most of the indefinite pronouns are historically noun bases which over time fused to form one single word (lexical item), e.g. *some thing* → *something*; *any body* → *anybody*. So they are not really pronouns in the strict sense of the word, although some would argue that these forms have become grammaticalized as pronouns. There is considerable variation with these forms and, as with many of the kinds of words we have been discussing, some of them can work as nouns: for example *a nice little something*. They border the two word classes of noun and pronoun because, on the one hand, they tend to be substituted for a full description and they tend not to be altered by plural, modifiers or determiners (e.g. **I haven't seen the anybody*). However, this may well be because plurality and definiteness (or indefiniteness) is encoded in these words already. For example, *anybody* was originally *any* + *body*. The word *any* includes meanings of indefiniteness (non-specific) and amount (unspecified amount but greater than zero). There is a difference though between *nobody* as a noun and *nobody* as an indefinite pronoun; the meanings of *nobody* are different in each case. The word *nobody* can be used as a noun as in *a silly nobody like him*, where it denotes a person who is insignificant. It can be used as a pronoun as in *nobody was here*, where *nobody* could replace a full expression such as *your friends* (i.e. *your friends weren't here*). Even as pronouns, these words have considerably more semantic content than other types of pronouns. Usually the use of pronouns requires reference to information that is either already known or information that can be retrieved from the situation or context. In this sense they are stand-alone forms with respect to meaning.

2.3.1.3 'One'

The lexical item *one* is listed separately here because traditionally it is included among the pronouns but it has uses that make it slightly different from the other pronouns. As a true pronoun, *one* is an indefinite pronoun because it does not refer to a specific person (i.e. *one* meaning anyone). This form is dropping from use. It is rare to hear someone say something like *one shouldn't eat too much meat*. It would be more common now to say *you shouldn't eat too much meat*. So *you* has largely replaced *one* as an indefinite pronoun.

It also has another use which is very much like a pronoun but which differs from all others in the sense that it actually does replace a noun. It is like a pronoun in the sense that its meaning is recovered by making the link to something already said in the text or something known from the context or situation. In example (16), it is clear that *one* is substituted for *medication*. What is different here as compared to pronouns is that in this example the speaker is referring to two different objects (i.e. two completely different medications) and not the same object as would be the case with a personal pronoun. This distinction is shown in example (17), where *it* and the expression *the new medication* refer to the same object.

(16) I haven't started on the new <u>medication</u> as I will use up the old <u>one</u> first

(17) I haven't started on the new <u>medication</u> but I will start <u>it</u> tomorrow

Although nouns and pronouns do share some features, the distinction isn't always clear and some of the classification problems discussed above demonstrate that clear-cut boundaries around word classes are rather artificial. We should expect the boundaries to be fuzzy at best.

2.3.1.4 Verbs

The class of verbs includes words that express an event (i.e. a relation or happening). This can be an event which is very active such as *he kicked the ball* or something that expresses a relation, as with the copular verb, *be*, as in *he is a lawyer*. The range of types of event is very broad and the various types will be covered in Chapter 4. These words differ from other word classes because they have different forms for past and present: for example, *the dog chases the cat regularly* [present] vs. *the dog chased the cat regularly* [past]. This can often be the distinguishing feature between words that look identical to verbs, as in the case of *love*: *he loves her* [verb] vs. *his love for her was not strong enough* [noun]. We can be certain that in the first instance *love* is a verb because the verb would change forms in the past: *he loved her*.

There are various ways to sub-classify verbs and perhaps the most essential distinction is between auxiliary verbs and what are commonly called main verbs, or lexical verbs to be more technical. Main verbs express the type of event and carry the meaning of the event, whereas auxiliary verbs work in support of the main verb to express different meanings related to the event. For example, auxiliary verbs can be used to express a particular aspect of the main verb in terms of its duration in time, regardless of whether the reference point is in the past, present or future (e.g. *he is meeting a client now* vs. *he is meeting a client tomorrow*). Auxiliary verbs can also be used to express doubt or certainty with respect to the main verb. It is important to understand how verbs combine in English because in many cases it is through certain combinations that these various meanings are expressed (this will be explained in detail in Chapter 5). For any such combination, there can only be one main verb although there may be several auxiliary verbs. Auxiliary verbs never appear on their own; they always work with a main verb. However, *be*, *have* and *do* can be both main verbs and auxiliary verbs (*will* and *get* also have this variation but for different historical reasons). Recognizing the distinction will be explained in Chapter 6 although, given the properties of auxiliary verbs explained below, it should be fairly straightforward to recognize whether one of these verbs is being used as an auxiliary verb or a main verb. The important thing to understand about auxiliary verbs is that they adhere to very specific rules in English, which is explained briefly in the following list of the standard auxiliary verbs.

Progressive auxiliary verb There is only one verb in English which can be used as a progressive auxiliary verb and this is the verb *be*. It is often referred to as the 'be + -ing' form because any verb following the progressive auxiliary, *be*, will be in the progressive form (or the present participle) – in other words, this verb will end in '-ing'. It doesn't matter whether the verb following the progressive auxiliary is another auxiliary or a main verb: *I was going to Spain, I might be going to Spain, the boy was being bitten by ants*. The use of the progressive auxiliary is generally used to represent the event as ongoing or in progress, such as *I am eating my lunch*, which means that the event of eating is ongoing and not completed.

Perfective auxiliary This perfective auxiliary is always expressed in English by the verb *have*. As with all auxiliary verbs, the perfective auxiliary determines the form of the following verb and forces it to take the past participle form, which can be referred to as the '-en' form of the verb because of the '-en' suffix on irregular verbs such as *eat* (*eaten*). In other words whenever *have* is used as an auxiliary, the next verb following it will always be in past participle form. This means that we can retrieve the past participle form of any verb simply by placing *have* before it. Being able to recognize the past participle is also important in the formation of passive verb constructions, as we will see with the passive auxiliary below. The *have* auxiliary combines with another verb to express the speaker's perspective on the event in terms of having been completed with respect to some point or period in time, such as *I had eaten my lunch before you arrived*. Perfective forms are usually seen in contrast to the progressive. However, they can combine in both past and present forms or with modal auxiliary verbs (see below), as in *I had been sleeping when the alarm went off*.

Passive auxiliary verbs There are two passive auxiliary verbs, *be* and *get*. The use of this auxiliary is slightly more complex in some ways than the progressive auxiliary. This is because its use changes the voice of the clause from active to passive and as a consequence the grammatical structure and meaning of the clause shifts. In the example given above involving *ants*, the main verb in the clause is *bite* but notice that in the clause, *the boy was being bitten by ants*, the Subject, *the boy*, is not the participant doing the biting. We know that, in this case, the ants are biting the boy. The active form would be: *ants were biting the boy*. There are two auxiliary verbs in the passive example (*the boy was being bitten by ants*) and they are both *be*, but the first one is the progressive auxiliary and we can tell this because the following verb is in the progressive form (*being*). The second auxiliary is the passive auxiliary *be*. It is this auxiliary that tells us that the boy is not doing the biting but rather he is being affected by the event of biting (by the ants). The form of the main verb *bite* is the past participle form of the verb. This is always true of the passive auxiliary; the following verb will always be in the past participle form, irrespective of whether it is another auxiliary verb or the main verb.

Support auxiliary verbs English has a special auxiliary verb, *do*, which supports the main verb to form interrogatives (e.g. *Do you like pizza?*), negatives (e.g. *you don't like pizza*) and tag questions (*you like pizza, don't you?*) or to express emphasis (e.g. *but you do like pizza*). The *do* auxiliary verb cannot occur with any other auxiliary verbs; in a sense it replaces all others.

Modal auxiliary verbs Modal auxiliary verbs are distinct from other verbs since they only have an auxiliary use and they do not have the same range of forms as do all other verbs (e.g. there is no past participle form for modal verbs). However, they overlap with *do* in the sense that they can be used to form interrogatives and negatives. The set of modal auxiliary verbs includes: *can, could, shall, should, may, might, will, would* and *must*. The modal verbs express a range of meanings that relate to the speaker's view or opinion about the event. Traditionally these meanings are divided between epistemic meanings (probability related) and deontic meanings (obligation related). The modal auxiliaries can combine with all other auxiliary verbs except *do* in expressing the event, as is shown in example (18).

(18) I might[mod.] have[perf.] been[prog.] being[pass.] tricked[main verb] by that guy

2.3.1.5 Adjectives and adverbs

The classes of adjectives and adverbs have been grouped together here because of how very similar they are and the fact that historically adverbs in English were inflected forms of adjectives. Both are used as properties to describe or modify things and events. The distinction between the two relies on whether the properties concern a noun or a verb. Adjectives can be seen as properties of nouns, whereas adverbs generally modify verbs (although they are used for other purposes as well). In some cases there are adjective plus adverb pairs which are distinguished by the morpheme '-ly', as in *quick – quickly* or *happy – happily*. For both classes, identifying members is usually done by testing the word for the main properties of this word class. There are two main tests:

- Can the word be modified by *very*, as in *very quick* or *very quickly*?
- Can the word be made comparative, as in *quicker, happier, faster, more quickly*?

2.3.1.6 Prepositions

Prepositions are words that typically indicate direction of some kind usually in relation to a nominal group, such as *in the box*, *on the table*, *behind the chair*, *around the tree*. They sometimes appear on their own without the nominal group to indicate the direction or location: for example, *I'll take this coffee up to my father now*. Prepositions combine with other words such as nouns and verbs to create new words, such as *upstairs, back-up* or *understand*. Prepositions can be recognized generally by whether or not the word *right* can modify it; in general only prepositions can be modified by *right* in standard English (cf. the colloquial usage of *right* meaning *very* as in *He was right pleased about that*, which has a different sense). For example, *right* could appear before each of the prepositions given in this paragraph: *right in the box*, *right on the table*, *right behind the chair*, and *right around the tree*.

2.3.1.7 Articles and numerals

The word items that fall under these two categories always work with a noun of one kind or another. They tend to function as determiners within the nominal group, as will be explained in Chapter 3.

Traditionally English has only two articles: definite article, *the*, and indefinite article, *a*. These words are often called determiners (which they are) but since there are many other kinds of words and groups that also function as determiners (e.g. demonstrative pronouns and indefinite pronouns), using the more traditional label of article seems more appropriate for this presentation. Inherent in the meanings associated to *the* and *a* is the notion of number (singular or plural) and definiteness (definite or indefinite). The differences between these two words could suggest that they should belong to different lexical classes. *The*, for example, is used with both singular and plural nouns but it always indicates that the object being referred to is already known or that it is a particular object (i.e. definite). For example, in the email text given earlier in this chapter, the speaker said: *John has taken Tom to the dentist for a check-up*. With the use of *the*, it is clear that it is a particular dentist, whereas if *a* had been used (*John has taken Tom to a dentist for a check-up*), then no particular dentist would be being referred to. The indefinite article *a* is always used with a singular countable noun (e.g. *a dog* but not **a sand*) and it is used with the noun to indicate an indefinite (or non-specific) referent. Historically, it derived from the word *one* (the indefinite article was originally *an*) most probably due to influence from Norman French since Old English – like modern Welsh, for example – did not have an indefinite article. It is this quantity specification (i.e. one or single) that separates *a* from *the* and makes it reasonable to include it with the numerals.

The class of numerals includes words which express specific quantities (i.e. numbers). They are commonly listed within the adjective word class since they typically describe or modify nouns in terms of quantity. Numerals can also be considered as determiners of quantity since they specify the quantity (e.g. *one dog, two dogs, five dogs*). There are many other kinds of words which are used to express quantity (e.g. *a cup of coffee, a bunch of bananas, a few trees*), and in a functional sense numerals could be grouped with these words and groups (generally, nouns or adjectives and their groups).

2.3.1.8 Conjunctions

The class of conjunctions forms a relatively small set of words which serve to link or connect words, groups and clauses. They all work and behave in a very similar way. They always indicate a connection between two parts of language (e.g. to group together as with *and*, or to contrast or exclude as with *or*) as in the following examples.

- Conjoining words: I like [dogs] and [cats].
- Conjoining groups: I only read [historical novels] or [trashy magazines].
- Conjoining clauses: [I like John] but [he doesn't like me].

As conjunctions, these words are fixed forms and, in general, they do not take any affixation (e.g. suffixes) as is possible with nouns, verbs, and adjectives and adverbs. However, new conjunctions can be formed by compounding two words, typically where one of the words is a conjunction (e.g. *even if, on the grounds that*). The most common examples of conjunctions are: *and, or, but, so, if, because, since, although, while, unless*.

2.3.1.9 Other lexical categories

It is impractical if not impossible to do justice to the topic of lexical classification in this book. There will always be words that do not fall neatly into these categories and some that may seem impossible to identify. I include in this section some of the ones that were not covered above, but if you are unsure about the nature of a particular word it is always good to consult an in-depth and comprehensive source (such as Quirk, Greenbaum, Leech and Svartvik, 1985).

Interjections and exclamations are really formulaic (or idiomatic) expressions that we have learned to slot in for certain contexts such as greetings or gratitude. They don't work as words in the sense we have been discussing. They are fixed expressions. Examples of these include: *hello, goodbye, what!, thanks* and so on.

The English language, as with most languages, is full of such fixed expressions and idiomatic sayings. An expression such as 'break a leg', which has the meaning 'good luck', cannot be understood by knowing the meaning of each word. It is a fixed expression that is equivalent to a single word. No one would say 'break your right leg', and if they did they would actually mean for your right leg to get broken.

I have been using the word 'word' throughout this section because it is familiar, but most often when we think of what it means we think of an orthographic word which is marked in written language by spaces. It is a problematic term in linguistics because there are many examples where we find multi-word expressions such as 'break a leg' which really are single items. We also find some expressions are written as a single orthographic word and some as two or more. For example, 'tea towel' is written as two orthographic words whereas 'cupboard' is written as one, but each constitutes a single noun. So to avoid any ambiguity, the term 'lexical item' is preferred since it does not imply any particular number of orthographic words and lets us talk about a particular lexical item without concern for its orthographic representation (i.e. whether written as one single orthographic word or as two or more).

Many of the multi-word lexical items in the English language will be difficult to classify. For example, 'kick the bucket' would be difficult to classify as a verb even though it expresses an event. Sometimes these formulaic expressions are not fixed word for word as is the case for 'kick the bucket'. If *the bucket* were to be replaced with anything else, the idiomatic meaning would be lost (e.g. *He kicked the stove*). In a saying such as 'drop your guard', which means to stop being cautious, the expression is considered semi-fixed because the verb can change (e.g. 'lower' or 'relax') and the reference of the pronoun (*you*) can vary (e.g. *my*, *his*). Identifying such expressions is difficult because it implies that the expression works at the level of the word rather than at the level of the group; in other words, the question is whether the multi-word expression has been built up through the grammar (compositional) or whether it is a single lexical item (non-compositional). Resolving this is beyond the scope of this textbook but it is a fascinating area of study. When analysing language, if in doubt, it is probably safest to analyse the expression as compositional and work out the group structure rather than assuming a formulaic expression without evidence to support it.

The overview of lexical classification presented in this section has been necessarily brief and selective. See Section 2.7 for suggestions for further reading on this topic.

2.3.2 Groups and group classification

In a book about grammar, even functional grammar, space is not often given to words and word classes. A brief overview, such as the one given in the previous section, is necessary because our understanding of grammatical structure is largely based on lexical categorization. There is also an underlying premise that these items behave sufficiently similarly that the units of structure which develop from the items (usually through modification) can be described in more or less fixed or regular terms. Consequently, for most of the lexical classes discussed above, there is a corresponding group structure associated to it. This section will briefly present the basic concept of the group as a structural unit and the general considerations that are needed to describe and represent group structure. Specific groups will be discussed throughout the next few chapters, where they will be introduced as required.

Written language has imposed upon us the notion of unit. We generally recognize word, sentence, paragraph, and perhaps text as units of language. Language description must be broader than a specific kind of language use (e.g. written language). In linguistics we tend to think of language units in terms of levels or ranks either from smallest to largest units or vice versa. If we ignore sound units (phonemes), the smallest unit is the morpheme, which is generally accepted as the smallest unit of meaning. A morpheme can correspond to a single word, as in *dog*, or combine within a single word, as in *dogs* (dog + plural, 's'). The highest grammatical structure we can recognize (at least in terms of a generic structure) is the clause. However, between these two levels, there are intermediate units where words are grouped together. As Halliday explains (1994: 180), 'describing a sentence as a construction of words is rather like describing a house as a construction of bricks, without recognizing the walls and the rooms as intermediate structural units'.

This can be illustrated with the following humorous example from a newspaper headline, which for one reading at least suggests a highly dexterous cow that is able to wield an axe.

(19) Enraged cow injures farmer with axe

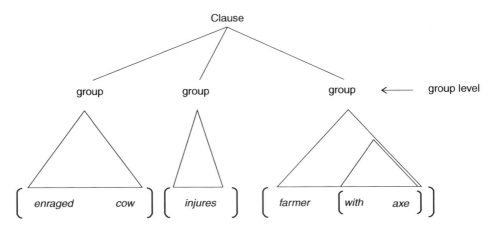

Figure 2.7 Level of group structure

If we were to ignore the internal boundaries marking the intermediate structural units between the word and clause levels, we would probably struggle to make sense of this clause. The structural ambiguity presented here is identical to the Groucho Marx example, *I shot an elephant in my pyjamas*, which was discussed in Chapter 1. If, as illustrated in examples (20) and (21), the structural boundaries (shown by enclosed boxes) within the clause are interpreted differently, we get a completely different meaning.

    (20) &boxed;Enraged cow&boxed; &boxed;injures&boxed; &boxed;farmer&boxed; &boxed;with axe&boxed;

    (21) &boxed;Enraged cow&boxed; &boxed;injures&boxed; &boxed;farmer with axe&boxed;

In (20), the cow used an axe to injure the farmer but in (21) the farmer had an axe with him when the cow injured him. Speakers recognize these group structures without really being aware of them, and the humour in examples such as this one and the Groucho Marx joke is proof of this. They show that there is a level at which a set of grouped words act like a single unit. The intended meaning, as given in (21), is illustrated in Figure 2.7.

All recognizable units have an internal structure that can be described (although these descriptions are often the subject of theoretical debate). The notion of structure implies that it is something that has some kind of framework and boundaries (as for a house, for example). There is a difference to be made between the generic structure of a particular group and the structure realized in a particular clause. In the former, the generic structure is a generalized description of a particular group which represents the full potential of the group (i.e. it includes everything that is possible). In the latter, the description of a particular clause will only include a representation of the structures that were actually expressed in this particular instance. As we will see for example in Chapter 3, the description of the nominal group will present the full range of possibilities for this group.

2.3.2.1 Classification of groups

There are two main types of structural unit which are generally used in the literature on grammar: phrase and group. The distinction between these two terms is somewhat contentious and, without entering into this theoretical debate, I would like to make clear how they are being interpreted in this book.

For many these two terms refer to the same thing; that is, a grammatical unit which is seen as operating at a level between the word and the clause. However, for Halliday there is a distinction to be made and he claims that a group is an expansion of a word whereas a phrase is a contraction of a clause. Amongst the various structural units that have been identified, some do seem to be structured based on a particular word class which can be modified or expanded. Others do not and yet they maintain a regular structural pattern as a unit. Following Halliday, a distinction will be made between units which work more as a group and those which operate more as a phrase. However, it wouldn't be unreasonable to use either phrase or group as a more general heading for these units without specifying any distinctions.

Groups are units which are based on a head element which may be modified by other elements; the head element is the only required element of a group, with all other elements being optional. This is a relatively standard or common head + modifier type of structure, where the head is based on a particular word class (e.g. noun or verb) and the way in which the head can expand, through modification, to form a group is captured by the full generic description of the particular group. In this book, the main groups included for the English language are: nominal group, verb group, adjective/adverb group and quantity group. Each group will be presented and described in detail in the appropriate places throughout the book. For example, the whole of Chapter 3 is devoted to the nominal group, including other related groups and phrase units (e.g. adjective group and prepositional phrase) as needed, and the verb group is presented in Chapter 5.

Phrases are those units which are based on a pivotal element which must be completed by one or more elements. This is in contrast to the head + modifier relationship found in groups; even though the head element of a group is a kind of pivotal element, there is no requirement for a modifier to be expressed. With a phrase, it is the combination of the pivotal element and the completing element(s) that define the phrase. In other words, one is not seen as a modification of the other but rather as a completion or Complement. Therefore, in a phrase, at least two elements are required: the pivotal element and the completing element(s). Examples of phrases include: clause, prepositional phrase and genitive phrase.

One central concept concerning the clause has been repeated throughout the book so far: the clause is multifunctional. Every clause serves several different functions at the same time; the structure of the clause is defined by the configuration of these functions. Furthermore, any individual constituent of the clause is also multifunctional in the sense that 'in nearly all instances a constituent has more than one function at a time' (Halliday, 1994: 30). Identifying the constituency and structure of the clause is made quite challenging because of its multifunctional nature. As Halliday (1994: 35) explains, 'the clause is a composite entity. It is constituted not of one dimension of structure but of three, and each of the three construes a distinctive meaning.' Each dimension has associated to it particular functional elements. As a result of the three dimensions (relating structure and meaning), the clause is best described in terms of the full set of functional elements. This is why the presentation of the clause is given in stages throughout the book.

2.4 AN INITIAL VIEW OF THE CLAUSE: REPRESENTING FUNCTIONS AND STRUCTURES

The clause has been described so far as a structural unit which expresses a given situation. In Chapter 1, the multifunctional nature of the clause was briefly presented, and the concept of metafunctions was introduced. The metafunctions each construe different and distinctive meanings, and each has its own structural configuration of elements. This means that the clause is a complex entity and one which has integrated the metafunctions simultaneously such that separating them and isolating them is an artificial exercise. However, this is, to a certain extent, what we must do in practice because analysis is relatively linear and it is generally done in steps. Different analysts will find it preferable to begin the analysis of the clause from different starting points. In this book, the preferred starting point is the clause as representation – the experiential metafunction, which involves identifying and describing the process and any participants involved. In this section, a very general view of this metafunction will be presented as a starting point, which will then lead into more detailed analysis in the following chapters. Specific detail about the analysis is given in Chapter 4.

We can rely on the basic principle of the clause, which is that it will have one and only one main verb. The main verb expresses the process, and so if we can identify the process and main verb it should be a good starting point for teasing out the rest of the analysis. As we saw earlier in this chapter, this can prove rather challenging when a clause has more than one verb. To make things simple for our current purposes, we will analyse a short text with relatively simple clauses; the *This little piggy* nursery rhyme, given below as Text 2.2.

Text 2.2 This little piggy

This little piggy went to market.

This little piggy stayed home.

This little piggy ate roast beef.

This little piggy had none.

And this little piggy went all the way home.

The first step in analysing text is to identify the clauses. Since the text above is written and includes punctuation, we can assume that each sentence has at least one clause. Therefore, each sentence becomes a potential clause and must be examined further before it can be determined that the clause boundaries have been correctly identified. In order to do this, all verbs in each potential clause must be identified, and if more than one verb is found then further investigation is required. A set of guidelines on how to do this is developed in Chapter 7. In this case, the text is a fairly simple text with only one verb in each sentence. We can therefore rely on each orthographic sentence in the text as one single clause.

The analysis of Text 2.2 will begin by listing all the clauses in the text and then working through the initial analysis in general terms using the process test (see below). Basic tree diagrams are provided to illustrate the analysis at this stage.

Here is the list of clauses, with the verbs underlined:

[1] This little piggy went to market

[2] This little piggy stayed home

[3] This little piggy ate roast beef

[4] This little piggy had none

[5] And this little piggy went all the way home

The main verb of each clause expresses the process, and it is the process which determines what participating entities are expected within the situation. The term participating entity or participant needs to be seen in the sense given in section 2.2 above and not in its common meaning of person. There is a test that can be used to help work out the participants. The process test (see Fawcett, 2008) relies on what speakers know about how a particular verb works to express a process. The test itself is a way of generalizing the particular situation I clause being analysed so that the number of participants involved can be determined, and so that the participants may be identified in the clause. The process test is given below and, to use it, simply replace the word 'verb' with the actual verb being tested and see which participant(s) are naturally expected to complete the process. The process test implies that every situation|clause will have one process and at least one participant. It is sometimes difficult to know whether or not there is a second participant, and this will be discussed in Chapter 4. The second and third participants are represented in parentheses in the test since different verbs have different configurations of participants, and not all of those listed will need to be used. Every verb has at least one Participant but some have two or even three. I cannot think of any example of a process with four or more participants. The process test is written to accommodate these configurations in very general terms.

Process test

In a process of [verb-]ing, we expect to find someone/something [verb-]ing (someone/ something) ((to/from) someone/something or somewhere).

The next step in analysing the clause is to apply the process test. The test assumes that the main verb in the clause has already been identified (see above). This test will help identify the participants since, based on the outcome of the test, we simply need to replace the pronouns in the wording of the test by the actual Participants in the clause. It is import- ant to note that the process test should be done in abstract terms rather than by focusing on the clause in question so that the result is based on how the language has organized the use of the verb. The process test will not help identify any other elements of the clause so it should not be surprising if there are bits of language left over once the process and participant(s) have been identified. These remaining bits do have functions within the clause but not as a process or participant. The results of the process test for each of the clauses are given below, along with a tree diagram showing the elements identified within the clause so far

 [1] This little piggy went to market
Process test: In a process of going, we expect to find <u>someone</u> going <u>somewhere</u> ⇒ two participants, see Figure 2.8.

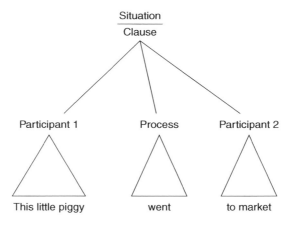

Figure 2.8 Process and participants for *This little piggy went to market*

[2] *This little piggy stayed home*

Process test: In a process of staying, we expect to find <u>someone</u> staying <u>somewhere</u> ⇒ two participants, see Figure 2.9.

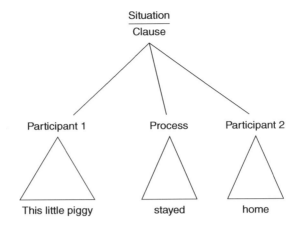

Figure 2.9 Process and participants for *This little piggy stayed home*

[3] *This little piggy ate roast beef*

Process test: In a process of eating, we expect to find <u>someone</u> eating <u>something</u> ⇒ two participants, see Figure 2.10.

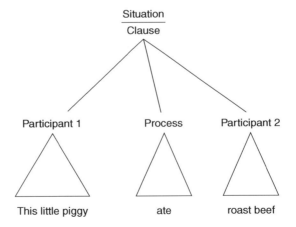

Figure 2.10 Process and participants for *This little piggy ate roast beef*

[4] *This little piggy had none*

Process test: In a process of having, we expect to find <u>someone</u> having <u>something</u> ⇒ two participants, see Figure 2.11.

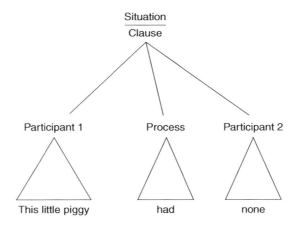

Figure 2.11 Process and participants for *This little piggy had none*

[5] And this little piggy went all the way home
Process test: In a process of going, we expect to find <u>someone</u> going <u>somewhere</u> ⇒ two participants, see Figure 2.12.

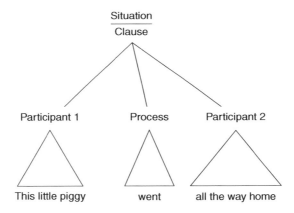

Figure 2.12 Process and participants for *This little piggy went all the way home*

Note that it is possible to interpret this process as a one-participant process, as in: In a process of going, we expect to find <u>someone</u> going.

This basic and very general view of clause structure provides a starting point for exploring its potential for construing meaning. The terms used here (i.e. participant and process) are far too general to explain the differences amongst, for example, the clauses as described in Figure 2.8 to Figure 2.12. The tree diagrams and functional elements are identical. The specific framework for analysing experiential meaning in detail will be given in Chapter 4. However, before we get to this, Chapter 3 takes a close look at the main structure which expresses or realizes the participant element; the nominal group. It is important to understand how this unit works before starting a detailed analysis of experiential meaning because it gives us the structural framework (like the walls and rooms in Halliday's house metaphor) which will enable us to more confidently determine the boundaries of the functional elements of the clause.

2.5 SUMMARY

This chapter has provided some of the foundation needed for understanding the functional–structural analysis of English which is being developed in this book. It introduced some of the basic terminology and notation that will be used in the remaining chapters. The basics of tree diagram notation were also presented, and these will be developed as the chapters progress. As was shown, tree diagram notation allows us to represent both functional elements and structural units in the analysis.

In the general overview of the clause given in this chapter, a distinction was made between functional elements and structural units (groups and phrases). The relationship between these two has been described as that of expression or realization; in other words, structural units serve to express one or more functions. The process test was introduced, which is useful in one of the early steps of the analysis. The identification of the process (in terms of its lexical expression) is significant because it represents the pivotal element of the clause. From this, any participants involved in the process can be readily identified. This provides a very general description of the clause as a starting point for the analysis. In Chapter 4, a more detailed account will be given which explains the specific functions within the experiential metafunction.

Some of the examples presented in this chapter show that language is complex. We have only begun to touch on the reasons for this complexity, but it is unavoidable when analysing real texts. In later chapters, we will revisit embedding and verb complexes. The next chapter presents a detailed look at the lexicogrammar of things: how speakers refer to the things they want to talk about (i.e. referring expressions) and the structural resources available to speakers in order to do so (i.e. the nominal group).

2.6 EXERCISES

Exercise 2.1 Word class recognition

Identify the word class for each word in the text below:

How are you? How are you managing with work, school and the boys? Are you finding time for yourself at all again? Sorry I have been so long in getting back to you. Work has been crazy too. I always feel like I am rushing. So now, when I feel that, I try and slow myself down. I also have the girls getting more prepared for the next morning the night before and that has seemed to help the mornings go more smoothly. I will be glad when we don't have to bother with boots, hats and mitts. The days are getting longer, so hopefully it will be an early spring.

Exercise 2.2

List the clauses in the text below. Try to work out the process and participant(s) for each clause.

Jack Sprat

Jack Sprat could eat no fat. His wife could eat no lean. And so between the two of them, they licked the platter clean. Jack ate all the lean. Joan ate all the fat. The bone they picked it clean. Then they gave it to the cat.

Exercise 2.3 Ambiguity

Ambiguity in a clause can sometimes be quite funny, as for example with the Groucho Marx joke about the elephant and the newspaper headline about the cow.

Try to identify the ambiguity in each of the following sentences. For each case, use word class and groups to explain the different meanings.

1. He gave her dog treats
2. She saw the man from the store
3. He painted the canvas in the bedroom
4. The girl teased the cat with the ribbon

2.7 FURTHER READING

On lexical items and classes:

Jackson, H. and Zé Amvela, E. 2007. *Words, Meaning and Vocabulary: An Introduction to Modern English Lexicology*. 2nd edn. London: Cassell.
Morley, D. G. 2000. *Syntax in Functional Grammar*. London: Continuum.

On phonology and intonation:

O'Grady, G. 2010. *A Grammar of Spoken English Discourse*. London: Continuum.
Tench, P. 1996. *The Intonation Systems of English*. London: Cassell Academic.

On the clause and grammatical units:

Bloor, T. and M. Bloor. 2004. *The Functional Analysis of English: A Hallidayan Approach*. 2nd edn. London: Arnold.
Halliday, M. A. K. 1994. *An Introduction to Functional Grammar*. 2nd edn. London: Arnold.
Thompson, G. 2004. *Introducing Functional Grammar*. 2nd edn. London: Arnold.

Chapter 3: The grammar of things: the nominal group

As speakers, the first grammar we learn is most often the grammar of things. The vocabulary of young English speaking children typically will include nominal expressions such as *ball, mamma, dadda, cat, dog, juice, water*, and so on. There is considerable variation of course but these word forms are used to communicate; that is, to ask for things or to tell someone something. They provide a basis upon which to build up the grammar of the language. The grammar of things is precisely what this chapter will describe.

As was shown in the previous chapter, many of the main word classes form the basis of the main structural units of the clause. The most important of these is the unit of the group, which is considered as an extension of the word. Chapter 2 also introduced some terminology and notation that will be helpful for the exploration into analysing English grammar presented in this book.

This chapter is the first detailed look at one particular part of the grammar. It begins with an introduction to referring expressions and then moves on in section 3.2 to describe the nominal group, which is the main linguistic resource for these expressions. The nominal group is a complex unit which expresses a range of meanings. Once this description is complete, some guidelines are presented in section 3.3 which offer help in recognizing nominal group boundaries. As a summary, 3.4 provides a worked example of nominal group analysis.

3.1 INTRODUCTION TO REFERRING EXPRESSIONS

You might be wondering why the nominal group is being given prominence in this book. After all, it is the subject of our first detailed look at analysing language. It is being presented before any details about the clause or any other unit of language. This reflects the belief I have that, in the English language at least, entities (i.e. things, people, objects, ideas and concepts) are more relevant and salient than anything else. When we use language, we generally want to say something about something or someone. If we group all the kinds of things we can say something about into one category, it will make it much easier to say something about these things. So we will use the term entity to refer to anything that we can say something about and the term will include things, objects, persons, living things, abstract things, concepts, and so on.

As discussed in Chapter 2, when a speaker says something about one or more entities, they are describing (very loosely) a situation, and this situation is represented in language by the clause. Once included in the situation, we will refer to the entity or entities as participating entities or participants because they participate in the situation in some way. In the next chapter we will take a close look at the various ways in which participating entities can function within the situation. Before moving on to an example, it may be useful at this point to clarify some of the terminology that is used in this chapter.

Entity:	a term used to categorize a distinct thing in the speaker's world, including living things, non-living things, places, concepts, ideas, phenomena, etc. (e.g. *dog, chair, woman, climate, unicorn, president, wind, ghost, love, happiness, sand, feeling, emotion, puddle*…)
Referent:	something outside the language system (i.e. non-linguistic entity) that the speaker wants to refer to; in other words, something that is brought into focus or attention by the speaker. It is a concept in the mind of the speaker rather than an object in the world (e.g. in *I like my neighbour's new car*, the speaker has a mental image or concept of what he or she wants to refer to).
Refer:	a process created by a speaker who uses a linguistic expression to indicate or identify a referent for the addressee.
Participating entity (participant):	an entity which is included (participating) as a referent in a situation and is therefore completing a process.
Referring expression:	the linguistic representation of a referent (i.e. a linguistic expression used by a speaker to refer to a referent). This is most commonly expressed as a nominal group.

To illustrate what these terms mean and how they are used, consider Text 3.1 below. It is a short excerpt from an interview[1] with Rick Falkvinge, who is a strong advocate of the legalization of file sharing. In this brief text we will focus on one particular referent: <proposal>; recall that a referent is a non-linguistic thing (or object or concept) that is brought into focus by the speaker. The entity involved is some kind of proposal, and two different referring expressions are used by the speaker to refer to this referent: *a mass surveillance proposal for wiretapping every communication crossing the country's border* and *it*.

Text 3.1 Excerpt from an interview with Rick Falkvinge
A mass surveillance proposal for wiretapping every communication crossing the country's border was introduced in 2005, then [it was] retracted because it had received too much attention. It was reintroduced by the new administration and [it] is pending a new vote this summer.

For now we will ignore the complexity of the first referring expression other than to say that it is a very detailed and descriptive expression. The speaker could have simply said either *a surveillance proposal was introduced in 2005* or *a proposal was introduced in 2005*. The referent of these expressions is significant in this excerpt and it is clearly an important feature since it is repeated five times in this short text. In each case, the referent is a participating entity because the speaker has included it in specific situations. These situations include processes of *introducing, retracting, receiving, reintroducing* and *pending*. The entity (i.e. the referent) is participating in each of these processes and consequently each instance constitutes a participating entity. The specific function of each participating entity will differ in relation to different processes and this will be discussed in Chapter 4.

As stated above, then, we can define a referring expression as a linguistic expression that the speaker uses to refer to an entity which is a participant in the situation he or she is describing. The organization of these expressions is not random; there is a pattern or a grammar to them. Languages have resources to govern this organization. The most common or frequent linguistic resource in English for doing this is the nominal group. The nominal group gives linguistic structure to this part of the language – the part that lets speakers refer to the entities they want to say something about.

Consider a simple sentence such as *My neighbour is nice*. The referent is the person who lives next door to the speaker and the referring expression is a nominal group (*neighbour* is a noun and *my neighbour* is a nominal group). This type of sentence can be used generally to help us recognize these referring expressions. Any referring expression should be able to fit into the X slot in the generic sentence: X is/are Y, provided that Y is giving us some information about X (i.e. a description). In the invented examples from (1) to (7), the expression in the X slot is underlined.

(1) <u>A man</u> is an adult human male
(2) <u>The house</u> is beautiful
(3) <u>Those two apples</u> are organic
(4) <u>Unicorns</u> are real
(5) <u>Love</u> is free
(6) <u>The man in the moon</u> is scary
(7) <u>The leather bag that I saw in Marks and Spencer</u> is expensive

It is clear from this list of examples that some expressions are longer than others. In fact, there is no theoretical limit to the length of a referring expression as we will see later in this chapter. However, they all have some things in common and this relates to how the words combine to function as a group. The trick is to be able to recognize when a series of words is working together as a group to serve some function in the clause or in another group and to be able to identify where the boundaries of this group are. If a referring expression is a linguistic expression which is used by a speaker to refer to some referent, then it will have a function; in other words it will be doing something for the speaker. We will come to a better understanding of the various functions it can have in later chapters. For the moment we will concentrate on how to recognize these types of expressions by considering the structure of the nominal group. The way in which words group together to form a referring expression is regular enough that we can talk about it generically. In the next section we will take a detailed look at the nominal group.

3.2 THE NOMINAL GROUP

So far the nominal group has only been mentioned in passing. All that has been said up until now is that it is the main linguistic resource speakers have for referring to a referent. By linguistic resource I mean that it is a group of words which is organized by the language system. This idea of organization is important since the language system doesn't often allow any random arrangement of words; the grouping of words fits a particular pattern. What we want to do now is describe this pattern; in other words, we want to describe the way in which words can group together to enable a speaker to refer to a referent. In Text 3.1, the most frequent referring expression used to refer to the referent (<proposal>) was *it*. This is a very simple nominal group and, as we saw in the previous chapter, it is the role of personal pronouns to express the full nominal group. This is because they are complete referring expressions, unlike nouns, which denote entities and must be incorporated into a nominal group in order to function as a referring expression (compare *dog chased cat* and *the dog chased the cat*). In the case of personal pronouns, the nominal group has only a single element (one word).

The first referring expression in Text 3.1 is a complex nominal group which clearly has more than one element: *A mass surveillance proposal for wiretapping every communication crossing the country's border*. The length of this nominal group shows how important it is to be aware of group boundaries and to know how to identify where a group begins and ends. The expression gives us quite a bit of information: the entity being referred to is a *proposal* (it isn't something else like a letter or a book); there is only one proposal involved (rather than more than one or an unspecified number of proposals); the expression describes what kind of proposal is being referred to (*mass surveillance*); and it describes the proposal in terms of what it will be used for (*for wiretapping every communication crossing the country's border*). In very general terms, there are four different kinds of information included in the referring expression and, as will be shown below, these correspond to particular elements of the nominal group.

In this section, we will describe the potential of the nominal group – in other words, its generic structure. To do so we will consider the range of possible functional elements. It should be said here that coverage of the full range of the potential of the nominal group would be beyond the limits of this book. The goal here is to present a thorough but basic approach to analysing language. Once the concepts, functions and structures presented here are mastered, further exploration in more detailed literature will help complete the full picture.

As part of our language system, we know what resources we have available to enable us to talk about things or objects. Children work this out very early in their language development. My son, at age two years ten months, had no trouble saying things like *that's the same book we saw at the shop yesterday*, which is a very complex way to refer to a particular book. A speaker just somehow knows how to construct an expression that will enable an addressee to identify what it is that he or she is referring to. As effortless as it may seem to do this, it can be quite challenging for the analyst to sort out the ways in which language is grouped and how it functions.

There is a very strong relationship between referring expressions and the structure of the nominal group. This isn't really surprising because referring expressions are used to refer to a referent. Something most of us were taught from a very early age is that a noun is a person, place or thing, which is a very restricted view. Nouns are the words used in the language system to represent (or denote) entities in the non-linguistic world (i.e. things that are real or imaginary, whether living or not including concepts). In other words, nouns are the way we classify the things we want to talk about (e.g. 'cat' classifies all entities that we consider similar enough to belong to this class). Derived nouns (nominalizations), such as *evaluation*, work in the same way except that the noun is classifying the process behind the derived noun (i.e. as represented by the root verb) as a kind of entity. For example, *evaluation* denotes the process of evaluating or the result of evaluating and, as a process or a result, *evaluation* is a kind of entity. This is true for all nominalizations regardless of whether the verbal qualities are transparent or not (e.g. *cancellation* may immediately evoke the verb *cancel* but *revolution* is not transparent and does not suggest the verb *revolve*, although it is debatable whether or not such borrowed items should be considered nominalizations).

As discussed in Chapter 2, groups are formed by the patterns of structures which support the expansion of a particular word class. Therefore the nominal group can be thought of as the structure of the words that group around a noun. We need to ask two important questions in order to understand the nominal group: What is the context of nouns? How do they function? We will focus on the first of these two questions in this chapter. The functions that the nominal group realizes in the clause will be explored in Chapter 4 when we consider the clause in more detail. As a summary of the main features of nouns (which were presented in Chapter 2):

- Nouns can be determined either by number or amount or by whether the referent is already assumed to be known to the addressee:
  - *one cat* vs. *five cats*, or *the sand* vs. *some sand*
  - *the cat* vs. *a cat*
- Words which have this kind of determining function in relation to nouns are called determiners. The most common word classes associated to this function are articles, demonstratives and numeratives.
- Nouns can be modified in order to give more descriptive or identifying detail to the referring expression:
  - *nice cat*, *bad cat*, *fat cats*, *the cat with stripes*
- This is different from the determining functions of the nominal group. The modifier function describes the entity (noun). As we will see below, there are two ways nouns can be modified. One is in the position immediately before the noun; a pre-modifier. The other is immediately following the noun; a post-modifier. The most common word class associated to the function of pre-modifier is the adjective class (*nice*, *bad*, etc.).

These generalizations about how nouns work can be used to test whether or not a given word is indeed a noun in a particular context or whether it is something else (for example a verb or an adjective). This is relevant for recognizing nominal groups and their boundaries given the principle of group structure.

The description of the nominal group (Ngp) presented here is adapted from Fawcett (2000c), which offers a very detailed account of this structure. The nominal group has four main types of element: determiners (d), modifier (m), thing (th), and qualifier (q). Each of these will be presented in detail in the sections below. The most basic structure of the Ngp can be described by the following elements: {determiner + modifier + thing + qualifier}.

Not all elements in the nominal group are obligatory. In fact, as we saw in the examples above, some nominal groups have only one element (e.g. *unicorns*). The thing element is the only element which must be present in the nominal group. It is an essential element because its role is either to denote the entity being referred to or to refer directly to the referent by reference (i.e. the use of a pronoun such as *she*). There are instances, as we will see later, where the thing element is not actually expressed and is left empty (ellipsis), but in these cases it can easily be recovered. We will leave this exception for the moment. If the thing element is the only obligatory element then all other elements are optional. Furthermore, there can only be one thing element but it is possible to have more than one determiner, modifier or qualifier. This can be expressed using notation, where an asterisk, *, after the element means 'can be repeated' and the parentheses mean the element is optional, as follows: {(d)* (m)* th (q)*}.

This states that the nominal group must include the thing element and it may optionally include a determiner and/or modifier and/or qualifier. It also states that there can be more than one determiner, modifier and/or qualifier.

Each element represents a function within the expression. If, as we stated above, the expression is being used to refer to some entity, then we should expect to find a representation of that entity within the expression. Above, it was pointed out that in English we tend to use nouns for this purpose. Nouns are words that are used to denote an entity (e.g. *car, flour, house, love, kindness*). If I want to refer to a particular house, I may use the noun *house* to denote what kind of entity I am talking about. In addition to this, I may want to further classify the referent by the expression *the red house*. In doing so, I sub-classify the referent in the sense that the expression excludes all non-house and all non-red entities. The main function within the nominal group then is the thing element, which is the linguistic classification or representation of the entity being referred to. Frequently, this is the only element of a nominal group. In examples (1) to (7) above, there are two such instances: *unicorns* and *love*. In each nominal group, there is only one element and it is the thing element. However, as shown in the remaining examples, the nominal group may contain other elements (e.g. *the man in the moon*) and, for each example given, the other elements can be described in terms of the four main types of elements introduced above.

This section will explain the basic structures with a few examples of each nominal group element and then move on to analysing full nominal groups. The generic organization of the nominal group is given in Figure 3.1, which shows the order in which the elements occur: determiners occur before modifiers, modifiers occur before the thing, and qualifiers always occur after the thing.

The nominal groups from examples (1) to (7) above have been represented as tree diagrams in Figures 3.2 to 3.8. Figures 3.2 and 3.3 show examples of a nominal group with thing as the single element. Figures 3.4 and 3.5 each show an example of a nominal group with a determiner + thing. Figure 3.6 illustrates two determiners preceding the thing element. In

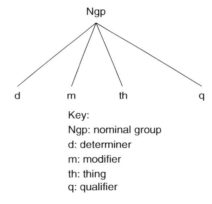

Key:
Ngp: nominal group
d: determiner
m: modifier
th: thing
q: qualifier

Figure 3.1 The basic organization of the nominal group

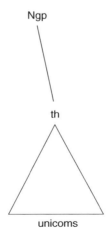

Figure 3.2 Example 4, *unicorns*

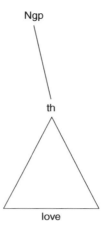

Figure 3.3 Example 5, *love*

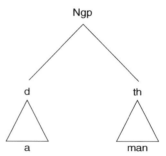

Figure 3.4 Example 1, *a man*

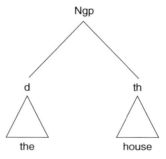

Figure 3.5 Example 2, *the house*

the section below on determiners we will come back to this type of example because there is much more to say about these determiners. Each of the two determiners has a different type of determining function. In Figure 3.7 the nominal group structure is that of deter-miner + thing + qualifier. Here *in the moon* is describing *man*. Qualifiers are interesting because this type of description involves another referring expression, and you might have

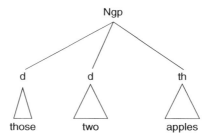

Figure 3.6 Example 3, *those two apples*

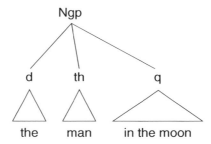

Figure 3.7 Example 6, *the man in the moon*

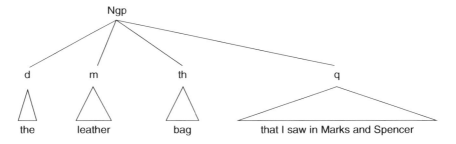

Figure 3.8 Example 7, *the leather bag that I saw in Marks and Spencer*

noticed *the moon* as another nominal group within the nominal group *the man in the moon*. This will be discussed in detail in the section on qualifiers. Finally in Figure 3.8 we see an example of a nominal group with all four main elements represented.

The remainder of this section presents a description of the main elements of the nominal group.

3.2.1 Determiners

There are many types of determiner but all of them have a similar function. The following three types of determiner will be discussed in this section: deictic determiner (dd), partitive determiner (pd), and quantifying determiner (qd). The deictic determiner may be more familiar in some ways than the other two. As will be discussed below, the partitive determiner and the quantifying determiner sometimes require the addition of an extra element in the nominal group called the selector element, which is represented in notation by 'v' and which is always expressed by the preposition 'of'. This element provides a structural link between the determiner and the head of the nominal group. The principle of selection does not always require the presence of the selector element ('of') and sometimes it is not expressed. If we consider the examples in (8) and (9), the thing element for both is *apples*. However in (8) the nominal group expresses a quantifying determiner and thing, whereas in (9) the quantity is being expressed as a selection from a set.

(8) five apples

(9) five of those apples

There are some very tricky areas related to the selector, specifically concerning the use of 'of' in nominal groups. There are references in the section on further reading at the end of this chapter which would be of interest to those wanting more information about this construction. The selector element of the nominal group is particularly significant in instances of selection involving the quantifying determiner or the partitive determiner, and this will be discussed in the relevant sections below.

In the description of the nominal group given above, we saw that determiners were optional and that they could repeat. In other words, it is possible to have more than one. In fact, it is possible to have more than one determiner but it so happens that, in English at least, specific types of determiner don't repeat. So while we may have a deictic determiner and a quantifying determiner (i.e. more than one determiner), we won't have more than one deictic determiner or more than one quantifying determiner. This is an important distinction.

The order of occurrence of the determiner elements is more or less fixed, so we can now revise the basic structure of the nominal group from {(d)* (m)* th (q)*} to {(pd) (v) (qd) (v) (dd) (m)* th (q)*}.

However, these two statements are saying the same thing. One is simply more specific than the other.

3.2.1.1 Deictic determiners

The use of a deictic determiner (dd) includes an implicature of definiteness or uniqueness in the sense that they specify or identify the referent in some way. For example, if when shopping with a friend in a furniture store I say 'this table is really nice', then my friend will know exactly which table I am referring to, not by its description but by the way I identify it with respect to the context by the use of a deictic determiner. So this type of determiner has the function of making the referent a particular referent. The use of a deictic determiner in a nominal group implies that the speaker believes he or she can presume that the referent can be identified by the addressee. This category includes what have been called definite articles, demonstrative pronouns and possessive phrases (including possessive pronouns).

> **Examples of deictic determiners (dd)**
> *a, the, this, that, those, these, my, his, their, John's, my neighbour's, my friend's mother's, the nice man's*

3.2.1.2 Genitive phrases

If you look closely at the examples of deictic determiners given above such as *my neighbour's* or *the nice man's*, you might notice that some look suspiciously like nominal groups

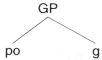

Figure 3.9 The generic structure of the genitive phrase

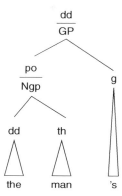

Figure 3.10 Genitive phrase expressing the function of deictic determiner

themselves, and to a certain extent this is right. However, this kind of expression is not a group because it is not based on a lexical head word. There are two required elements in this structural unit: the entity involved (the possessor) and the marker of the possessive relations (the genitive marker). The name of this unit is the genitive phrase (GP). When a nominal group includes this type of phrase, it is always being used to express a determiner function. Within the genitive phrase, the two main elements are called the possessor (po) and the genitive element (g). In the possessive examples given above, some have a suffix, the genitive marker, which indicates who or what the possessor is. This isn't always necessary, as is shown by the genitive pronouns (*my, his, their*, etc.). In these cases the genitive marker has been incorporated into the pronoun (compare: *I, me, my* for example). Both the possessor and the genitive marker are obligatory elements of this cluster. The function involved here is in relation to the thing and not to any other element within this cluster. When a genitive marker is present, it cannot really be seen as having a modifier function with respect to the possessor element or vice versa. It is rather a structural (inflectional) marker. Figure 3.9 shows the basic structure of the genitive cluster and its relationship to the deictic determiner in the nominal group. An example of this is shown in Figure 3.10. When the deictic determiner is realized by a possessive pronoun, then the relationship between the linguistic form and the function can be simply noted as in Figure 3.11, which shows the deictic determiner as directly expressed by the item *his*. The use of the possessive pronoun in this case is very similar to the definite article.

3.2.1.3 Quantifying determiners

The function of the quantifying determiner (qd) is to indicate the quantity or amount of the thing being referred to (Fawcett, 2000c). The quantity may be very specific, as in *three sandwiches*, or non-specific, as in *some sandwiches*. We can recognize a quantifying determiner because it will answer the question 'how much?' or 'how many?'.

dd

his

Figure 3.11 Deictic determiner directly expressed by a possessive pronoun

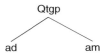

Qtgp

ad   am

Figure 3.12 The structure of the quantity group

Examples of quantifying determiners (qd)

a, some, many, one, two, six hundred, almost fifty, very few, about seven, two cups, a handful, a pinch

As with the deictic determiner (e.g. *the*, *this*, *my*, *John's*), which is most frequently realized by *the*, sometimes the quantifying determiner (e.g. *two*, *some*, *a teaspoon*) is expressed by a single item such as *five* and sometimes it is realized by a group such as a nominal group (e.g. *two cups of coffee*) or a quantity group (e.g. *nearly five people*). The article 'a' is included among the quantifying determiners as well as in the set of examples above for deictic determiners because it has both the function of a determiner and the function of specifying an amount. Unlike *the*, which can be followed by a quantity (e.g. *the five men*), 'a' takes up both functions and there cannot be both a deictic determiner and quantifying determiner (e.g. *a man* but **a two men* and **the a man*). Note that examples such as *a couple (of) people* is not an instance of deictic determiner plus quantifying determiner preceding the thing element but rather only quantifying determiner, since *a couple* expresses the quantity (in this case the quantifying determiner is expressed by the nominal group *a couple*).

The quantity group (Qtgp) organizes the structure of quantities and amounts (see Fawcett, 2000c). The main element of this group is called amount (am). In addition to this, it is also possible to have an adjustor (ad) element. The basic structure of this group is given in Figure 3.12. Whether a quantifying determiner is expressed as a nominal group or a quantity group is determined by what type of lexical item is conveying the amount. If it is a noun, as in *a cup*, then it will be expressed by a nominal group. If it is numerative, such as *five*, then it will be expressed by a quantity group. The distinction is based on the lexical class of the head element of the group – that is, whether it is a thing element (a nominal group) or an amount element (a quantity group).

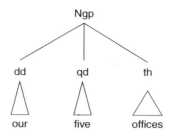

Figure 3.13 Example 10, *our five offices*

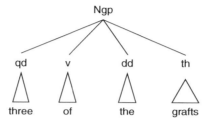

Figure 3.14 Example 11, *three of the grafts*

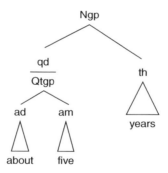

Figure 3.15 Example 12, *about five years*

Examples (10) to (12) illustrate the various ways in which the quantifying determiner is realized. The tree diagram for each underlined nominal group is shown in Figures 3.13 to 15.

(10) We are relocating our five offices

(11) The blood is going through three of the grafts

(12) I hadn't seen him in about three years

3.2.2 Partitive determiners

The partitive determiner (pd) is much less frequent than deictic determiners and quantifying determiners. Its function is to indicate that the referent is a part of the entity being referred to (Fawcett, 2000c), such as in *I'm painting the top of the desk* (cf. *I'm painting the desk top*). Clearly in this example what is being painted is the desk. Therefore the thing

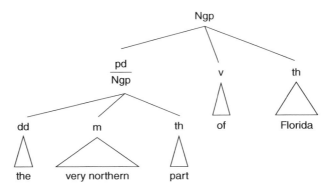

Figure 3.16 The partitive determiner as expressed by a nominal group

being referred to has been classified as *desk*. Partitive determiners always require the selector element (v) (note the use of 'of' in the examples in the box).

> **Examples of partitive determiners (pd)**
> *the top* (*the top* of the desk), *the back* (*the back* of the house), *a part* (*a part* of the book), *the arm* (*the arm* of the chair), *a section* (*a section* of the room)

The examples given above are all nominal groups. This is the only realization for the partitive determiner. Therefore there is no particular group associated to the partitive determiner as there is for the quantifying determiner and the deictic determiner.

The implication here is that being able to identify the thing element is critical to the analysis of the nominal group. Consider examples (13) to (15) given below, where the nominal groups of interest have been underlined. If we were to select the first noun in each case, we would be forced to see it as the thing element. This would mean that the classification of the entity being referred to would be *part*, *area* and *rest* respectively. The consequence of this is that it forces the analyst to treat the remainder of the nominal group as a qualifier (i.e. as a post-modifier of the thing element). Of course we can't be certain of the speaker's real intentions, but from the analytical perspective it seems more reasonable to consider *Florida*, *mill* and *mill* as the entities being referred to. This lets us recognize the determiner function of *the very northern part*, *an area* and *the rest*. The tree diagram for example (13) is given in Figure 3.16 to illustrate the associated structure for the partitive determiner in this example.

    (13) she is in the <u>very northern part of Florida</u>

    (14) the green end is <u>an area of the mill</u>

    (15) the remaining three supervisors had responsibility for <u>the rest of the mill</u>

We'll discuss the role of the thing element again in the section below on qualifiers. For now, let's just accept that the key to understanding the nominal group is through the identification of the thing element (which represents the entity being referred to) and working through the functions of the remaining elements to find a 'best fit' analysis.

3.2.3 Modifiers

There is a distinction to be made between determiners on the one hand and modifiers (m) and qualifiers (q) on the other hand. In very general terms, determiners signal the referent by the specification of the entity (i.e. definiteness, quantity and/or possession). Modifiers and qualifiers function differently since they are more like descriptions. They typically contribute to the classification of the thing. For example, *red* in *a red car* does not express a meaning which could identify specifically the entity being referred to but it does describe it in such a way that it says something that further specifies or sub-classifies the car. As with all other elements, there are many things to consider in analysing modifiers and qualifiers. The discussion of these two elements will be kept as simple as possible, but for those wanting more detail the section on further reading at the end of this chapter lists relevant literature on these topics.

There are two main functions of modifiers within the nominal group: classification and description. A classification modifier (cf. Classifier, Halliday, 1994) has the function of classifying the referent as being a member of a sub-set of the class to which the entity belongs (e.g. *the bus station*, where *bus* sub-classifies *station*). A description modifier (cf. Epithet, Halliday, 1994) functions to describe the entity with more descriptive detail (e.g. *a cool breeze*). As was stated above, modifiers always occur immediately preceding the thing element, although generally classifying modifiers occur immediately before the thing element after any describing modifiers.

Examples of modifiers (m)
red, wooden, sharp, wet, kind, ugly, beautiful, leather, brick, colourful, very smart, really black, extraordinarily intelligent, easy

The examples of modifiers given in the box show a pattern in the type of word or words that realize this type of meaning. Some words should look familiar since they are nouns (e.g. *leather, brick*). You might recognize now that this means that modifiers can be expressed by nominal groups. Most of the other words in the list are adjectives. Adjectives are the most common form of modifier. What might also be clear now is that some adjectives have words grouped with them and these are examples of the adjective group. This is indeed what we find, except that there is a kind of duplication since this type of group works in the same way for both adjectives and adverbs. Some academics combine these groups into one and others only consider the adverb group. We won't consider the case of adverb groups now since they are not directly relevant to the nominal group and they will be discussed in Chapter 4. However, we will take a look at the elements of the adjective group now and consider how it works within the nominal group.

3.2.3.1 The adjective group

The adjective group (Adjgp), as with all groups, has a particular class of lexical item as its head; in this case it is the adjective. The description of this group is based on work done by Tucker (1998) and his terminology for the elements of this group has been adopted. The head element of the adjective group is called the apex (a). It is always expressed as an adjective (in the case of the adverb group, the apex is expressed as an adverb – see Chapter 4).

The basic organization of the adjective group is illustrated in Figure 3.17. The main element as stated above is the apex (a), and it is the only obligatory element. However, as with all groups, it is possible to modify the head. In the case of adjectives, such modification typically serves to temper the degree to which the adjective applies. So for example the quality of *happy* can be intensified or reduced as in *very happy* or *somewhat happy*. Therefore there is a need for an element within the adjective group for this function. This

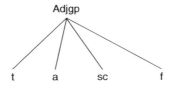

Figure 3.17 Basic structure of the adjective group

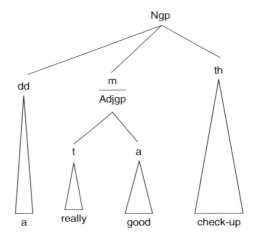

Figure 3.18 An adjective group expressing a modifier in a nominal group

element is called a temperer (t). There are two other elements in the adjective group. These are scope (sc) and finisher (f); both are post-modifiers. The scope element has the function of post-modifying the head of the adjective group, for example, *I am happy to see you*, where the scope element is underscored. The finisher element is also a post-modifier but, unlike scope, it is an obligatory element which depends on the lexicogrammatical requirements of the head element (apex). Its function is to complete (or finish) the lexicogrammatical requirements of the comparative structure determined by the apex. The organization of all four elements is shown in Figure 3.17, with examples of specific instances following in Figures 3.18 to 3.20.

Perhaps the most common adjective group is of the type shown in example (16) and illustrated in Figure 3.18, where the adjective group is composed of the apex element and a temperer element (*really good*).

(16) she had a really good check-up

When an adjective group expresses a modifier in a nominal group and it has a scope (sc) and/or a finisher (f), then these two elements will generally be separated from the apex by the thing element of the nominal group. This is shown in invented examples (17) and (18) (accompanied by Figures 3.19 and 3.20 respectively). In both cases the group of words after the thing element in the nominal group contributes meaning to the meaning of the apex rather than the thing element. For example *for the job* functions as scope because it limits or specifies the range of coverage of the adjective, *good*; in other words, *she* is not being said to be a 'good' person generally, but rather a person who is *good for the job*. In example (18),

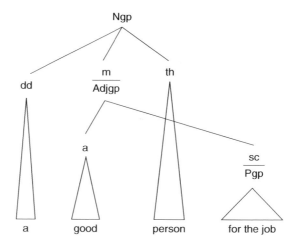

Figure 3.19 Example of discontinuous scope within the adjective group

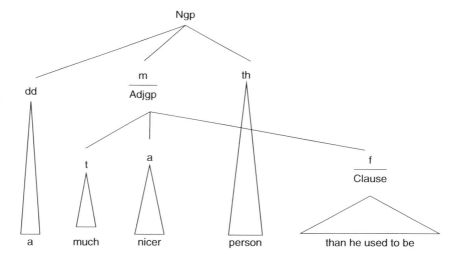

Figure 3.20 Finisher element separated from apex in adjective group

the finisher, *than he used to be*, is an obligatory element which completes the conditions of the comparative structure set up by the apex, *nicer*. It is not a qualifier element of the nominal group.

(17) She is a good person for the job

(18) He is a much nicer person than he used to be

To end this brief presentation of modifiers, consider the invented example given below in (19), which is illustrated in Figure 3.21. It illustrates the representation of cases where a nominal group, rather than an adjective group, realizes the modifier element in a nominal group.

(19) She is a career person

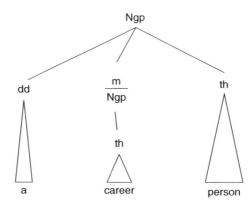

Figure 3.21 Modifier realized by a nominal group

3.2.4 Qualifiers

The last element of the nominal group that we will consider is the qualifier element (q). It is similar in function to the modifier element in the sense that it adds to the overall description of the referent. There are two main structural differences between modifiers and qualifiers. The first is that modifiers occur before the thing element and qualifiers occur after it. The second is that, while modifiers are typically realized by an adjective group or a nominal group, qualifiers are most often expressed by prepositional phrases or clauses. It is possible for a qualifier to be expressed by a nominal group or an adjective group but this is relatively uncommon. The examples given below illustrate the four types of structure which express this function in English.

Examples of qualifiers (q)

Sue (as in *my best friend Sue*), *in the corner* (as in *the table in the corner*), *that lives across the street* (as in *the dog that lives across the street*), *special* (as in *nothing special*)

The functional differences between modifiers and qualifiers are less obvious. The qualifier extends the nominal group in a way that isn't possible with the other elements. From the perspective of referring, the qualifier introduces another referring expression. In this sense, referring expressions which are realized by a nominal group having a qualifier are complex referring expressions since they always involve an additional (secondary) situation which is different from the one in which the entity is currently involved. This may be a difficult concept to comprehend without some examples. Example (20) should help clarify this.

(20) He was one of the guys that found him

In (20), the nominal group of interest has been underlined. Whenever a nominal group is being analysed, the first task is to identify the thing element (which is the head of the group). In this case, the thing element is *guys*. How do we know this? The thing element must be a noun or a pronoun and in this example there are only three possibilities: *one*, *guys* and *him*. If we try to establish what entity the speaker is referring to (sometimes it helps to try to visualize this), then it should become clear from the context. In this case, one particular male person is the referent that the speaker has in mind. We can then be confident that *guys* is expressing the thing element and is therefore in the head position

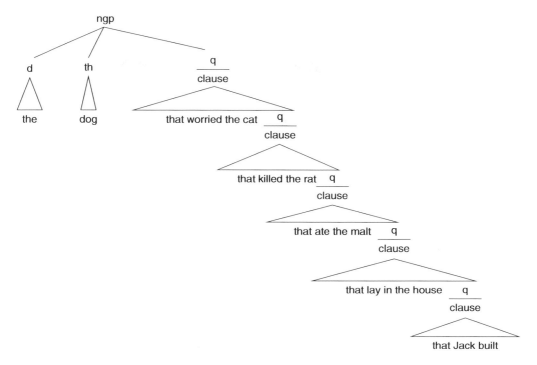

Figure 3.22 The 'House that Jack built' example

of the nominal group. Once this has been determined, it is relatively easy to sort out the remaining elements. This nominal group also expresses a quantity (*one*), the selector element (*of*) and a deictic determiner (*the*).

In this nominal group, up to and including the thing element, we find: qd + v + dd + thing. The rest of the nominal group, following the thing element, tells us which guy (or guys) is being referred to. In a sense the qualifier gives us more information, detail and description about the entity being referred to. The entity is involved in the main situation (i.e. in a process of being, *he was one of the guys*) and it is also involved, through the qualifier, in a secondary situation (i.e. in a process of finding, *[the guys] found him*). This secondary situation is created by the speaker for the purposes of referring to the referent.

The qualifier area of the grammar is complex due to the great potential for embedding in this part of the nominal group. As we saw in Chapter 2, there is a very famous example of this kind of embedding in the last line of the 'House that Jack Built' example, which is repeated here in (21). The nominal group of interest to us here has been underlined. Clearly, this shows the potential for complexity that is incorporated into the qualifier element. The first level of analysis of the nominal group would show only three elements: dd + th + q. The tree diagram for this nominal group is shown in Figure 3.22. The triangle notation is used here since we have not yet covered the detail on the functions and structures of the clause. We will come back to qualifiers in later chapters once we have considered the clause in sufficient detail.

> (21) This is <u>the dog that worried the cat that killed the rat that ate the malt that lay in the house that Jack built</u>

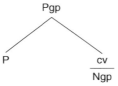

Figure 3.23 Completive element expressed by a nominal group, as in *in the woods*

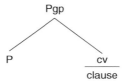

Figure 3.24 Completive element expressed by a clause, as in *by closing the bar*

3.2.4.1 The prepositional phrase

There is one final group that we need to discuss before completing the presentation of the elements of the nominal group. The prepositional phrase (PP) is an important unit for the nominal group for two main reasons. The first is that it is by far the most frequent type of qualifier. So, when a nominal group includes a qualifier, it is most likely that the structure realizing the qualifier will be a prepositional phrase. The second is that the prepositional phrase is similar to the nominal group in the sense that it will very often be used to introduce a new referent. The main element of the prepositional phrase (PP) is a prepositional element (p). This element is almost always expressed by a single preposition (e.g. *in, on, with, for, by*). However, there are times when the preposition is modified, and in these cases the prepositional element is expressed by a preposition group (e.g. *right on the table*). In addition to the prepositional element, the prepositional phrase has another element, which is called a completive (cv). The completive is most often realized by a nominal group (see Figure 3.23), although it is also possible for it to be expressed by an embedded clause (see Figure 3.24) or even a prepositional phrase (see Figures 3.25 and 3.26). The distinction between the units of phrase and group was discussed in Chapter 1 and, as explained there, groups are based on a head word plus modifier relationship between elements whereas phrases are based on a relationship of completing. In this sense, the prepositional phrase is more closely related to the composition of the clause than any group unit. Finally, although the prepositional phrase most frequently expresses both the prepositional element and the completive element, it is possible for the completive element to be omitted. There are several references listed in the further reading section at the end of this chapter which will be useful for the keen reader who wishes to explore the theoretical concerns related to prepositions and the prepositional phrase.

3.2.4.2 Some examples of qualifiers

In the following two examples, each nominal group includes a qualifier which is post-modifying the thing element. The qualifier is realized in example (22) by a prepositional phrase and in example (23) by a nominal group. The analysis for these is given in Figures 3.25 and 3.26 respectively.

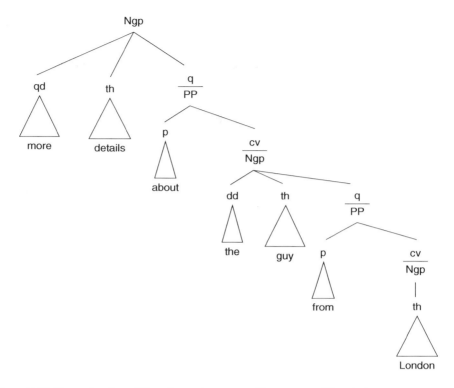

Figure 3.25 Example of qualifier element expressed by a prepositional phrase

(22) do provide <u>more details about the guy from London</u>
(23) <u>Bob the neighbour from across the street</u> is golfing with John

This completes the presentation of the structure of the nominal group in this chapter. As we have seen there are some areas that are complex, especially when embedding is involved. One consequence of the role of the qualifier element is that it can be difficult to know where the nominal group ends. There are strategies that can be used to help identify the limits of the nominal group. The next section will explain some of the tests that can be used to help determine the boundaries of groups within the clause.

3.3 TESTS FOR RECOGNIZING NOMINAL GROUP BOUNDARIES

> This morning, I shot an elephant in my pyjamas ...
> How he got in my pyjamas, I'll never know!
>
> (Groucho Marx)

This Groucho Marx joke was discussed in Chapter 1 to illustrate how playing with language this way reveals our understanding of grammatical structure. At the first reading, there would be no grammatical association between the elephant and the speaker's pyjamas. However, the humour comes retrospectively with the second sentence when it becomes clear that *in my pyjamas* can be interpreted as a qualifier which describes the referent (<elephant>). The joke is dependent on getting people to recognize the ambiguity and therefore recognize two different functions and structures related

63

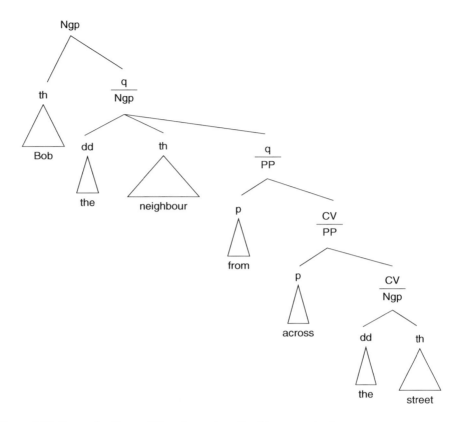

Figure 3.26 Example of a qualifier element realized by a nominal group

to the nominal group *an elephant* and the prepositional phrase *in my pyjamas*. The different structures and functions are shown in the tree diagrams in Figures 3.27 and 3.28. Figure 3.27 shows the reading that is obtained after the first sentence (i.e. the speaker is in his pyjamas when he shoots the elephant). Figure 3.28 shows the re-analysed humorous reading that is obtained at the end of the joke (i.e. the elephant is wearing the pyjamas).

In what follows, we will consider tests that help to identify where the boundaries are for the nominal group. These tests do not help if a clause is ambiguous because the result will be that two different structural representations are possible. However, they can be used effectively when there is uncertainty about the boundaries around a nominal group.

3.3.1 Pronoun replacement (or substitution) test

This test helps you to identify group boundaries, including boundaries around embedded clauses. The test is based on a fundamental principle of personal pronoun use. Personal pronouns do not replace nouns, they replace entire nominal groups. We can use this principle to our advantage to test where group boundaries are (including boundaries around embedded clauses). In theory any participating entity can be replaced by a pronoun (there may be some exceptions to this).

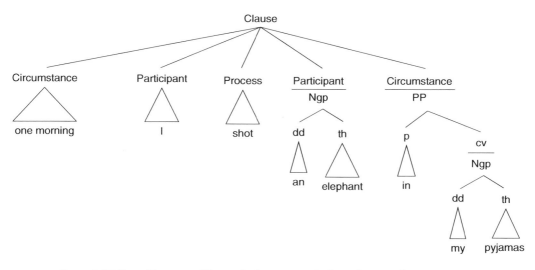

Figure 3.27 Tree diagram with *an elephant* separate from *in my pyjamas*

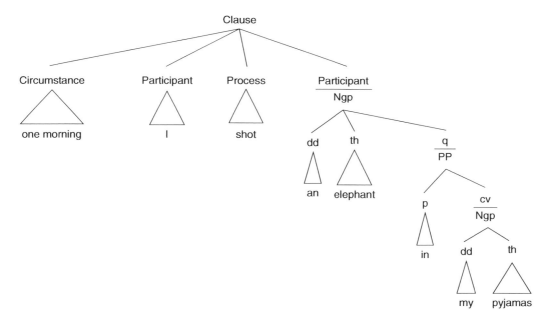

Figure 3.28 Tree diagram with *an elephant in my pyjamas* as one group

To use this test, consider example (24). The pronoun replacement test will be used to see where the nominal group boundaries are.

(24) I saw an expert on Tolkien on TV

Since the clause begins with a pronoun, we can be reasonably confident that this is a nominal group; there is no need to replace a pronoun with a pronoun. However, everything following the verb *saw* could potentially be one nominal group with one or two qualifiers or one nominal group followed by two prepositional phrases. The question is whether *on Tolkien* is part of the referring expression and therefore expressing the function of qualifier in the nominal group or not. The first step is to attempt to replace the nominal group *an expert* by a personal pronoun. The result given in (24′) shows that it doesn't work and therefore *an expert* cannot function as a separate group from the words that follow. The test doesn't end here because we still don't know where the end of the nominal group is. The next candidate is *an expert on Tolkien*. The results for replacing this group of words with a pronoun is given in (24″) which shows that *an expert on Tolkien* is a single nominal group and *on TV* is a separate unit. Within this nominal group, *on Tolkien* has the function of qualifier; it is modifying *expert* (i.e. what kind of expert? a Tolkien expert). The prepositional phrase *on TV* has no direct involvement in the referring expression – it has a function related to the process of seeing (i.e. where the expert on Tolkien was seen).

(24′) *I saw him on Tolkien on TV

(24″) I saw him on TV

Therefore *an expert on Tolkien* will have one function and *on TV* will have a different function with respect to the clause. Within the nominal group, *an expert on Tolkien*, we find the following elements: dd + th + q. It is certainly possible for *on TV* to be included within the nominal group, as would be the case for an example such as *I know an expert on news reporting on TV*, where *news reporting on TV* is a nominal group within the prepositional phrase *on news reporting on TV*, which functions as a qualifier in the nominal group, *an expert on news reporting on TV*.

This test can be used in most instances where it is necessary to verify or determine group boundaries.

3.3.2 Movement test

The movement test is similar to the replacement test in the sense that it relies on a principle of how groups work. This principle is that groups can be moved by rephrasing the clause in question. The corollary to this is that generally speaking one part of a group cannot normally be isolated from the rest of it. As with the replacement test, the movement test can be used to help you to identify group boundaries. It can be useful in helping to determine whether a group is realizing a qualifier (in a nominal group) or is a separate group (and therefore has a different function). However, there are instances where, in certain contexts, a qualifier element can be separated from the thing element in the nominal group without sounding odd (see example (25′), for which the movement test does not provide a clear result).

To try out this test, consider example (25).

(25) Send me information about where you will be

The problem we are faced with is how to sort out the internal units of the clause. After the verb *send*, the first word we come to is *me*, which is a personal pronoun, so we can be reasonably confident that this is a separate group. Next we have a noun (*information*) and a preposition (*about*) and then an embedded clause (this will be covered in Chapters 5 and 7). We know that prepositions often introduce a prepositional phrase so it is likely that *about where you will be* is a prepositional phrase. This can be tested by attempting to replace *where you will be* with a preposition such as *that* or *it*. If we do so, we have *send me information about that*, which shows that the unit in question is indeed a prepositional phrase. However, what needs to be decided is whether *information about where you will be* is one nominal group, or *information* is a single nominal group with a separate prepositional phrase, *about where you will be*, in an adjacent

3.4 Worked example of the nominal group analysis

position. We could also apply the pronoun replacement test to see whether a pronoun could replace *information*. In the movement test, we want to see whether *information* could be moved elsewhere in the clause. If so, then this indicates *information* is a group which is separate from *about where you will be*. If not, then this suggests *information* is part of another group. There are a number of ways we can move things around in a clause. One is to rephrase the clause in the passive voice. Another way is to rephrase the clause as a cleft sentence. Passivization will only work if the clause in question is in the active voice. The cleft test relies on fitting the units into the grammatical frame 'It was X that Y', where X is a single unit (group or phrase) and Y is the remainder of the clause.

These reformulations are given in (25′) and (25″) below.

(25′) ?information was sent about where you will be

(25″) *It was information that was sent about where you will be

The result of this test using the passive structure is not as conclusive as the result from the use of the cleft sentence. By combining the results from both attempts, it seems clear that *information* does not constitute a group of its own. However, for the sake of completion, we should continue with the tests until we have a satisfactory result. In this case, we need to test whether *information about where you will be* does constitute a single nominal group.

(25‴) information about where you will be was sent

(25⁗) it was information about where you will be that was sent

The results from this application of the movement test seem clear; *information about where you will be* constitutes a single nominal group. The constituency of this group is: th + q. The prepositional phrase *about where you will be* is realizing a qualifier within the nominal group.

The individual tests may not work on every clause and sometimes a combination of tests is needed to determine the unit boundaries. As we will see throughout this book, these tests are important tools in analysing language. Part of the analyst's job is to work out relations and functions, and doing so involves being able to manipulate the language under analysis in order to feel confident about the results.

3.4 WORKED EXAMPLE OF THE NOMINAL GROUP ANALYSIS

To summarize this chapter on the nominal group, this last section will work through the analysis of nominal groups in a clause. This will consolidate everything we have discussed so far. Upon completion of this section, you should be ready to work on some analysis of nominal groups on your own. You will find exercises at the end of this chapter in section 3.5 and then the answers can be found at the end of this book in Chapter 10 – but of course it is best if you don't look until you have tried to complete the exercises yourself.

The clause that will be analysed is given below in example (26). It is from an email written by an adult woman to her friend. Since we have not covered how to analyse the clause yet, we will avoid any discussion of details that are not particularly relevant to the nominal group.

(26) A friend from John's lacrosse team met a woman that way

The first thing to do is look for all the nouns in the clause. This follows on from the principle that where there is a noun there is a nominal group. As we saw in the section above, if we find a pronoun, we will have most probably found a nominal group (except for possessive pronouns, of course, which will always be expressing a determiner function within the nominal group, e.g. *my job*). Once we identify the nouns, we need to look around the noun for elements of a nominal group. We can use our knowledge of the nominal group to make educated guesses at the nominal group boundaries and then test this using the test discussed in section 3.3.

We will now work through the analysis for example (26).

- Identify all nouns.

  A friend from John's lacrosse team met a woman that way
- Look for elements typically found in nominal groups.

A	friend	from	John's	lacrosse	team	met	a	woman	that	way
dd	th	p	dd	th	th		dd	th	dd	th
Ngp		PP					Ngp		Ngp	

This shows that the first nominal group begins with *a friend* but that we have not yet determined where this nominal group ends. The next group of words seems to form a prepositional phrase but we don't know yet whether it is a qualifier in the nominal group beginning with *a friend* or whether it is a separate group. Similarly, two nominal groups have been found but it isn't clear whether they combine in a single nominal group or represent two separate groups.

- Use tests to determine group boundaries.

Replacement test: test *a friend* and *from John's lacrosse team*:

  *He from John's lacrosse team met a woman that way

  He met a woman that way

Therefore *a friend from John's lacrosse team* is a single nominal group and the prepositional phrase *from John's lacrosse team* is realizing a qualifier in that nominal group.

Movement test: test *a woman* and *that way*

  A woman was met that way

  *A woman that way was met

  It was a woman that he met that way

  *It was a woman that way that he met

Therefore *a woman* is a separate nominal group from *that way* and they have different functions with respect to the clause.

- Determine the structural organization of the nominal groups using information about the functions of the nominal group elements.

A	friend	from John's lacrosse team	met	a	woman	that	way
dd	th	q		dd	th	dd	th
Ngp				Ngp		Ngp	

- Draw the tree diagram for each noun group (see Figures 3.29 to 3.31).

This approach should work for any nominal group although, as stated above, not every test will work on every clause. The approach will change slightly once we have covered everything needed for analysing the clause. For example there would be no point in drawing tree diagrams for all nominal groups; instead they would be included in the tree diagram for the clause as a whole.

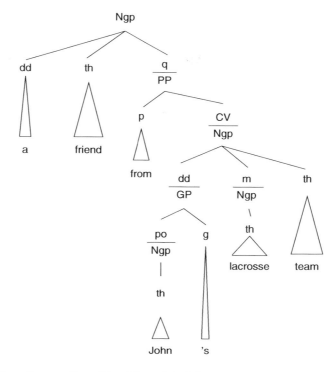

Figure 3.29 Tree diagram for *a friend from John's lacrosse team*

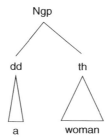

Figure 3.30 Tree diagram for *a woman*

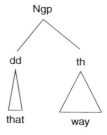

Figure 3.31 Tree diagram for *that way*

Although we have come to the end of the chapter on nominal groups, this is not the end of the discussion about them. We will build on this foundation in the next few chapters as we develop our understanding of the three main metafunctions of the clause.

3.5 EXERCISES

Exercise 3.1

In the following brief text (personal email from 26 June 2010), identify all the nominal groups you can find.

I do have asthma. I'm not getting enough oxygen into my bloodstream. I must find a doctor.

I hope that things are on the mend now for Rowan. It's good that he is being checked out so well. Hopefully the chamber thing will deliver the meds better and get to the problem. Breathing problems are so weird. One of the most important things that I've learned is staying calm. There is an automatic response to get excited when unable to breathe, and the added stress makes it more difficult to breathe.

Exercise 3.2

In the following three clauses, analyse the underlined nominal groups and draw the tree diagram.
1. some symptoms were still present
2. they gave out a couple of awards
3. enjoy the extra hands around the flat

3.6 FURTHER READING

On the nominal group:

Bloor, T. and M. Bloor. 2004. *The Functional Analysis of English: A Hallidayan Approach.* 2nd edn. London: Arnold.

For further reading on modifiers and the adjective group:

Tucker, G. 1998. *The Lexicogrammar of Adjectives: A Systemic Functional Approach to Lexis.* London and New York: Cassell.

On selection and the selector element:

Fawcett, R. 2007a. 'Modelling "selection" between referents in the English nominal group: an essay in scientific inquiry in linguistics', in C. Butler, R. Hidalgo Downing and J. Lavid, eds., *Functional Perspectives on Grammar and Discourse: Papers in Honour of Professor Angela Downing*. Amsterdam: John Benjamins: 165–204.

On the distinction between group and phrase and the differences between prepositional phrases and prepositional groups:

Fawcett, R. 2000c. *A Theory of Syntax for Systemic Functional Linguistics*. Amsterdam: John Benjamins.

Halliday, M. A. K. and C. Matthiessen. 2004. *An Introduction to Functional Grammar.* 3rd edn. London: Hodder Arnold.

Chapter 4: Representing experience

4.1 INTRODUCTION

Functional approaches to language seek to reveal more than structural grammar, they try to tell us something about meaning. One kind of meaning that can be revealed is how speakers represent their experience. This meaning is the focus of this chapter.

The previous three chapters have laid the foundation for our exploration into the functions of English grammar. The first chapter provided a useful overview of the relation between function and structure and introduced the functional–structural view of language. It also provided a brief overview of Systemic Functional Linguistics (SFL). In Chapter 2 more detail was given about the distinction between structure and function and the way in which this will be handled in this book. In doing so Chapter 2 presented a general view of the clause, and this chapter will pick up from this point and provide the first detailed view of the clause. Chapter 3 focused exclusively on a particular part of the grammar: the grammar of things and the structure of the nominal group. In this chapter the focus returns to the clause.

4.1.1 Goals (and limitations) of this chapter

This chapter deals specifically with the problems of analysing experiential meaning in the clause, and so we will take a close look at the ways in which entities participate in the situation.

The view of the clause in SFL is that it represents multiple meanings or functions at the same time. Consequently we need to take a multifunctional view when analysing grammar. As already stated in Chapter 1, this book will only consider the three main functions (or metafunctions): experiential, interpersonal and textual.

The prism was introduced in Chapter 1 as a useful metaphor for how we can look at the clause. As there are three primary colours which make up light, there are three primary metafunctions which contribute to the functions of the clause. Each of these was presented briefly in Chapter 1, and this chapter along with Chapters 5 and 6 will cover each strand in detail. The focus in this chapter is on the experiential strand of meaning.

It is important to note that while there are other meanings, there simply isn't enough space here to cover everything. Furthermore, as there are many existing books which present each metafunction in great detail, the discussion of the metafunctions will be relatively sparse in favour of presenting the functional–structural view, showing how the functions and structures relate, since this is an area that often provides the greatest challenge in analysing the clause.

The goal of this chapter is to introduce the main meanings related to the experiential metafunction and to show how the functions relate to the expressions which realize them. The range of meanings expressed in this metafunction will be covered. The chapter also presents strategies for confidently analysing the functions.

4.2 ANALYSING EXPERIENTIAL MEANING

In order to illustrate the main functional strands of meaning and why we might be interested in analysing these functions, we will look at two brief excerpts from a study

carried out on behalf of Air Canada, an airline company. Communication is vitally important to many companies and organizations but it is especially critical when safety is
involved. Air-travel safety briefings are a particular area of importance because it is
essential that, in the event of an emergency, all passengers respond quickly and appropri-
ately to ensure the safety of everyone on the plane. Many airline companies realize that
they are responsible for passenger safety and, since communication is the only way they
have of transferring safety practice to passengers, the texts used in safety briefings will be
of interest and importance to experts in language and communication. The text excerpts in
this chapter and many of the examples considered were taken from a report written for Air
Canada (Barkow and Rutenberg, 2002). The objective of the report was 'to enhance the
effectiveness of aircraft cabin safety briefings and to recommend improved communication
practices to ensure that the briefings are easily understood by all passengers, including
those with sensory or cognitive impairments' (Barkow and Rutenberg, 2002: 1). Two
excerpts describe the procedure for a high-altitude emergency for particular audiences.
Text 4.1 is the safety briefing for the general public and Text 4.2 covers the same content but
addresses individual passengers who are blind or who have impaired vision.

**Text 4.1 Audio and caption script for high altitude emergencies for the
general public**

In a high altitude emergency, an oxygen mask will drop in front of you from the panel
above. Place the mask over your mouth and nose, straighten out the strap, and pull the
strap to be sure it is tight on your face. After you are wearing it securely, a tug on the hose
will start the oxygen flow. It makes sense to put your own mask on first, before helping
others.

**Text 4.2 Individual audio script high altitude emergencies for passengers with
visual impairment**

During the flight, if the cabin pressure plunges an oxygen mask will drop in front of you
from the panel over your head; it will be at your head height and within easy reach. I can't
demonstrate how that works but it will be easy for you to locate the dangling mask.
Please take the mask that I am now holding in front of you, place the nose part over your
nose and also cover your mouth; pull the rubber strap behind your head and make sure it
fits snugly all around. But the oxygen flow will not start until you give the hose a tug.
If you are trying to help another passenger, please put your own mask on first, just as they
should do if they were helping you.

What might we want to know about these texts? For any safety briefing we may want to
ensure that every passenger knows what he or she must actually do in certain circumstances. The text must clearly state who must do something (e.g. *press an alarm button,
open a window*), what must have something done to it (e.g. *glass must be smashed, door
must be opened*) and if relevant it should also include other important information such as
how something should be done or where something must be done. Of course safety briefings should not include any information that isn't completely relevant either (e.g. how
friendly the pilot is or isn't). In addition to wanting to know whether the safety briefings
are clear and direct, we might also be interested in how essentially the same information

is conveyed to all passengers as a group, compared to how it is conveyed to specific individuals as is the case in Text 4.1 and Text 4.2.

This kind of meaning refers to the content of the text; in other words who is involved, the processes they are involved in, and other information about how, when and where this involvement takes place. We described this in Chapter 1 as the experiential strand of meaning. This metafunction expresses the content of what is being said. Halliday explains it as 'language as the expression of the processes and other phenomena of the external world including thoughts, feelings, and so on' (Halliday, 1978: 48). Experiential meaning is expressed in the clause by a configuration of elements which represent the speaker's experience. These are the processes, participating entities and any accompanying circumstances.

In Chapter 2, a very general description of the clause was given in terms of process and associated participating entities. This was only an introductory presentation of the clause as it is far too general to have any descriptive power. In that description, the main verb was seen as the key item in beginning the analysis. This is because it expresses the event – that is, the means of involvement, such as eating, driving or running. What we have said so far is that we need to be able to identify the main verb since it is the main verb that contributes most to determining the process for any given situation (or clause). The process then determines what the participants are (see the process test presented in Chapter 2). What is being described here is the system of transitivity. In other words, the available choices or options with respect to processes in terms of the representation of experience (experiential meaning) are organized in a system, and this system is called the transitivity system.

4.2.1 The grammar of processes and participants

Transitivity has special meaning in SFL. It is a very important concept, often working as the foundation for any analysis within a SFG framework; that is, from the analysis perspective, it is through the transitivity of a clause that the full analysis is derived. Although many textbooks teaching SFL analysis do not begin with the analysis of experiential structure, they all recognize the strong simultaneity in the relationship amongst the three strands of meaning. Halliday and Matthiessen (2004) begin the analysis of the clause through the textual metafunction, and yet the identification of Theme is determined by locating the first part of the clause to have some kind of experiential function (Halliday and Matthiessen, 2004: 66). This of course cannot be done until an understanding of experiential meaning is gained. The position taken in this book is that transitivity is central to any analysis of the clause.

Traditionally, transitivity is a concept that is associated with the verb; in other words, a verb is either transitive or intransitive (or copular). However, the distinction is always based on the presence or absence of the various roles involving objects: direct object, indirect object, no object and even whether one of these can occur as subject. What this shows is that the relation of transitivity concerns the distribution of objects, whether this means arguments, objects or participants, rather than the status of the verb. These two views of transitivity are really two sides of the same coin.

In traditional syntax, transitivity is determined by the number of arguments that a verb has. Halliday does base his view of transitivity on verbs but he extends it beyond that to include the participants: 'transitivity is the grammar of processes … and the participants in these processes, and the attendant circumstances' (1976: 30). In developing his theory of language, Halliday broadened the traditional notion of transitivity to shift the focus away from solely being placed on the verb. For Halliday, transitivity is instead a notion to be applied to the entire clause, extending beyond verbs and objects and even arguments, given that he also includes circumstances.

Halliday has been clear in his writing that his use of transitivity is a generalization of its traditional uses in grammatical description. He extends transitivity to refer generally to that which 'defines some of the roles which nominal elements may occupy' (Halliday, 2005: 61). It is really from this that we begin to understand that transitivity is about relating participating entities in the clause.

In the two texts given above, it is easy to see that each one is explaining what the passenger must do under certain conditions. For example, a passenger may have to place a face mask over his or her nose and mouth and pull on the strap of the mask. In both texts, the passenger (who is also the addressee) is represented as an active participant – that is, as someone doing something. In these cases, there is often a second participant such as the face mask or the strap, which is not represented functionally as doing something but rather as having something done to it. These activity-based processes are referred to as material processes. This type of process covers the range of processes that express activities of doing, happening, changing and creating. In the two texts above, the following verbs are expressing material processes: *drop, place, straighten, pull, start, put, plunge, demonstrate, take, cover, give, help*. The two main participating entities in material processes have the functions of Actor, the one doing the activity, and Goal, the one impacted upon or affected by the activity. This is illustrated in example (1) with the process *take*, where the Actor is not explicitly expressed but is understood as the addressee (*you*, which is the passenger in this case) and the Goal is expressed by the expression *the mask that I am now holding in front of you*.

(1) Take the mask that I am now holding in front of you

In addition to the two main participants in material processes, there are two other types of participant which can also be inherently involved in the process. These are Beneficiary and Scope. Beneficiary, like Goal, is a participant that is impacted upon by the process, but in this case it is because the participant benefits from the process or is a recipient in the process. Beneficiary typically occurs with verbs such as *give, send, buy*, and so forth.

Scope on the surface is easily confused with Goal. Both can be recognized in traditional grammar as direct objects but functionally they differ considerably. Part of the meaning of Goal is that something was done to it. In contrast, Scope is not affected by the processes but rather it indicates 'the domain over which the process takes place' (Halliday and Matthiessen, 2004: 192). For example, if we were to compare the clauses given in (2) and (3), which are invented for illustration, we'd see that the participant *your violin* does not express the function of Goal in both cases.

(2) He cleaned your violin

(3) He played your violin

Although both clauses express material processes and the first participant in each case is Actor (expressed by *he*), only example (2) expresses a Goal whereas example (3) expresses a Scope. We can use the information given above as a probe to test whether or not *your violin* is a Goal or not (more such probes or tests will be given in section 4.3.2). For a participant to have the function of Goal, it will answer the question 'what happened to it?' If we try this with *your violin*, we get 'what happened to your violin?', and the answer for example (2) will be 'he cleaned it, that's what happened to it'. With example (3), it would be 'he played it, that's what happened to it'. Under normal circumstances, playing an instrument is not something that happens to it; the object is not impacted upon by the process of playing. Of course if someone found their guitar smashed to pieces and the owner asked 'what happened to my guitar?', then perhaps someone might answer 'Pete Townshend played it, that's what happened to it!'. However, in this context, *my guitar* would be expressing the function of Goal as it would be clearly impacted upon by the process of Pete Townshend's playing. In example (3), *your violin* expresses the function of Scope because it serves to indicate the range or domain of the process of playing rather than indicating the participating entity which is affected by the process.

Material processes only represent part of the picture of our experience. In addition to this rather external experience, we also experience the world internally through our senses. As a kind of complement to the active material processes, the sensory-based processes involve the neuro-cognitive system and include processes of knowing, seeing, hearing, and thinking. The label given to this range of processes is mental process. The participating entities involved in these processes express different functions to those involved in material processes. These participants are not actively doing something; they are sensing something (whether through cognition, perception or emotion, for example). The participant that is represented as having the function of sensing is called Senser and the participant that is represented as being sensed is called Phenomenon. Examples of this type of process are given in examples (4) and (5) as expressed by the verbs *recall* and *know*. These two examples are taken from the extract given in Text 4.3, which comes from the same Air Canada report (Barkow and Rutenberg, 2002) as Texts 4.1 and 4.2.

(4) Participants may <u>recall</u> being told not to use electronic devices until after take-off
(5) They may not <u>know</u> whether that includes their wristwatch, heart-rate monitor, pacemaker, hearing aid, and/or their personal-digital-assistant microcomputer

In each case above, the passengers (*participants* and *they*) are represented in the role of Senser. This section of the text is commenting on passengers' ability to understand the safety briefing on the airplane. They are not actively doing something in this representation as they were in Texts 4.1 and 4.2. Similarly the things they are recalling and knowing (or not knowing) are not impacted upon by the process as is the case in material processes; they are rather Phenomena to be experienced or sensed. In terms of the experiential function of the clause, then, examples (4) and (5) can be described as expressing a configuration of Senser – mental process – Phenomenon.

Text 4.3 Excerpt from Air Canada Report (Barkow and Rutenberg, 2002: 1)

This is not, however, a sufficient demonstration of either full comprehension or the likelihood of effective life-preserving behaviour at a much later point in time. For example, participants may recall being told not to use electronic devices until after take-off. But they may not know whether that includes their wristwatch, heart-rate monitor, pacemaker, hearing aid, and/or their personal-digital-assistant microcomputer. They may recall that they should blow into some tubes if their life jacket fails to respond to the pulled tabs, but not be sure where to find those tubes.

Material and mental processes capture two of the three main types of process. The third main process type differs considerably from these two in the sense that, rather than relating the participants through external or internal processes, relational processes relate two participating entities in a more abstract way. The prototypical verb for relational processes is the verb *be*. Examples of this type of process are given in (6) and (7), taken from Texts 4.2 and 4.3 respectively.

(6) It will be at your head height

(7) This is not, however, a sufficient demonstration of either full comprehension or the likelihood of effective life-preserving behaviour at a much later point in time

The process represented here is one of relating; two participants are related with respect to each other. In (6), *it* (i.e. the oxygen mask) is being represented in terms of a particular location (*at your head height*). In this example the second Participant is very close to having a circumstance function since it specifies where a participant is (see section 4.2.2 below). However, the distinction between a participant and a circumstance relates to the degree of attachment it has to the process: participants are inherent to the process because they fulfil an expectation (i.e. they need to be involved); circumstances are attendant to the process but are optional rather than required (see section 4.2.2 below). The specific function of the participants involved in relational processes depends on the type of relational process being expressed. Relational processes will tend to be one of two types: Attributive or Identifying.

Attributive processes attribute some kind of quality to a participating entity. Attributive processes involve two participants. One participant is functioning as Carrier; this is the participant that 'carries' the attribute (quality), as shown in the invented examples (8) and (9), where *the snow* and *my neighbour* express the function of Carrier. The participant which expresses the attribute or quality is called the Attribute. This is shown in examples (8) and (9) respectively as *beautiful* and *a nice person*. In both cases, a relation is set up between the two participating entities.

(8) The snow is beautiful

(9) My neighbour is a nice person

Identifying processes are very similar to Attributive processes in that a relation is set up between two entities, but in the case of Identifying processes the relation is that of assigning an identity rather than attributing a quality. Examples of these are given in (10) and (11), where one participating entity is identified in relation to the other one.

(10) My lecturer is Lise Fontaine

(11) Your cousin is my neighbour

In each of these types of process, one participant will be being identified by the other, so the one being identified is called Identified and the one which is identifying is called Identifier. In (10), *Lise Fontaine* identifies who *my lecturer* is and therefore it is expressing the function of Identifier, whereas *my lecturer* is being identified so it is expressing the function of Identified. The same is true for example (11), where *your cousin* expresses Identified and *my neighbour* expresses Identifier. The main way to distinguish between Attributive and Identifying processes is that, with an Identifying process, the two participants can be interchanged without reducing the acceptability of the clause, whereas this is not the case with Attributive clause. For example, *my neighbour is your cousin* is just as acceptable as *your cousin is my neighbour* whereas *a nice person is my neighbour* is not.

The three process types described above represent the three main ways in which speakers categorize their experience. This is illustrated in Figure 4.1 and Table 4.1, which attempt to show that this description does not represent discrete categories but ones which merge into each other. As with all categorization, some examples are more representative of a category than others and there are instances where it can be difficult to know whether the speaker intended one representation over another. In addition, some clauses express processes which are difficult to label definitively as material or mental, for example.

The degree of detail in representing experience can be refined by considering three additional categories of experiential representation. As Halliday explains, 'we also find

Table 4.1: Summary of Halliday's process types and participant roles (adapted from Halliday and Matthiessen, 2004: 260), participants underscored

Process	General meaning	Participants	Canonical example
Material	*doing, happening*	Actor, Goal, Beneficiary, Scope	John[Actor] hit the ball[Goal] John[Actor] gave the ball[Goal] to Jane[Beneficiary] John[Actor] climbed the mountain[Scope]
Mental	*sensing, seeing, thinking, wanting, feeling*	Senser, Phenomenon	John[Senser] likes Jane[Phenomenon]
Relational	*being*		
Attributive	*attributing*	Carrier, Attribute	John[Carrier] is nice[Attribute]
Identifying	*identifying*	Identifier, Identified	John[Identified] is the lawyer[Identifier]
Behavioural	*behaving*	Behaver	John[Behaver] is laughing
Verbal	*saying*	Sayer, Receiver, Verbiage	John[Sayer] told me[Receiver] a story[Verbiage]
Existential	*existing*	Existent	There was a tree[Existent] near the bench

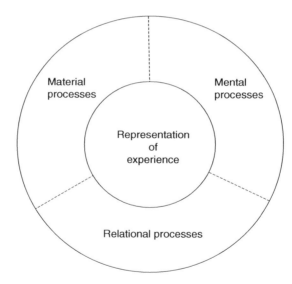

Figure 4.1 Three main processes in the representation of experience (adapted from Halliday, 1994)

further categories located at the three boundaries; not so clearly set apart, but nevertheless recognizable in the grammar as intermediate between the different pairs – sharing some feature of each, and thus acquiring a character of their own' (1994: 107). As shown in Figure 4.2, these additional processes found at the boundaries overlap with the three main process types and they include the more minor processes of verbal, behavioural and existential processes.

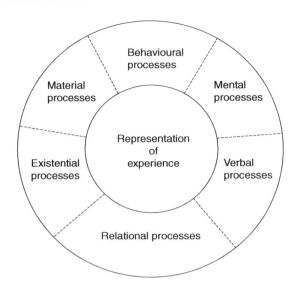

Figure 4.2 The standard six process types in the representation of experience (adapted from Halliday, 1994)

Between material processes and mental processes we find a category called behavioural processes, which 'represent outer manifestations of inner workings, the acting out of processes of consciousness and physiological states' (Halliday, 1994: 107). The participant in this type of process cannot be clearly identified as either Actor or Senser and is instead represented as Behaver – as something in between the two. Examples of verbs expressing behavioural processes include *breathe, cry, laugh, stare, yawn, frown, smile* and *chat*. In these cases, the speaker is representing experience as a kind of combination of material and mental processes since the participant involved is displaying a manifestation of a neurological or cognitive experience. In an example such as *the man is crying* it is difficult to see the participant (i.e. *the man*) as an Actor, as one who is actively doing something. At the same time, this participant is not truly a Senser. The behaviour, which can be thought of as one type of external activity, is the result of something experienced internally.

Verbal processes are seen as covering the border between mental and relational processes. Halliday describes these as 'symbolic relationships constructed in human consciousness and enacted in the form of language, like saying and meaning' (1994: 107). This type of process involves representations of saying and the main participant is that of Sayer, the entity which produces the utterance or message. The utterance or what was said is called Verbiage. Often there is also a participant who receives what was said and this is called Receiver. In the invented example shown in (12), the Sayer is expressed by *he*, the Verbiage is expressed by *the answer* and the Receiver is expressed by *me*.

(12) He <u>told</u> me the answer

Finally, existential processes fall between material and relational processes. They are called existential processes because they are concerned with existence. These processes involve only one participant, called Existent, and they have a particular clause structure. In these clauses the Subject is *there* and the verb is typically *be*, as is shown in example (13). In this invented example, the only participant is *a snow storm*, which expresses the Existent.

(13) There <u>was</u> a snow storm last night

These six types of process provide a model of experience and they categorize the range of experience that can be represented. Although each one has been discussed here in linear order, there is no such order to them. Halliday (1994: 107) describes them as a circular continuum. Figures 4.1 and 4.2 attempt to illustrate this continuum, and they are adapted from the diagram given by Halliday (for example, 1994: 108). What the metaphor is trying to show is that there is overlap amongst the various categories, and within any given category there will be some processes that are more prototypical of the category than others. The distinction among these types of process is related to the type of meaning each represents as well as the associated role of the potential participants for that particular type of process. More often than not, it is the function of the participants that determines the type of process. In section 4.3, some tests for identifying processes and labelling participants are discussed.

A summary of the six process types is given in Table 4.1, where each process type is listed along with its respective participants. Now that we have completed the overview of the process types and their inherent participants, the next section will cover the range of meanings expressed by circumstances.

4.2.2 The grammar of descriptions: circumstances and relevant structures

The process and participants represented in the clause reveal only part of the picture with respect to experiential meaning. As stated above, this strand of meaning covers the range of meanings available to the speaker in representing his or her experience of the world, including processes, participants and circumstances. According to Thompson (2004: 109) circumstances 'encode the background against which the process takes place'. In this sense, they describe the process or situation in some way. This may be related to where the process is taking place, how it is taking place or why it is taking place. There is no expectation involved between the process and any circumstances as there is for participants. Any situation can include additional meaning in the form of an attendant circumstance. This means that circumstances are not part of the core of the clause and they tend to be seen as peripheral elements. In a way, we have already been implicitly working this way because the process test focuses on the process and the expected participants and does not include any circumstances. With the process test, we identify the core elements of the clause and in addition there may be one or more circumstantial elements. Seen this way, circumstances are considered optional elements of the clause even though they may express very important or critical information. For example, when we receive a bill, the statement will tell us what we have to pay. In a process of paying, we expect someone to be paying something to someone but most of us will also want to know exactly when the bill must be paid and we may also want to know where the bill can be paid: e.g. *You must pay us £100 by 1 March 2011*. So although *by 1 March 2011* is not a core element in the sense of being expected by the process *pay*, it is very important information to those involved in the situation. In this case, *by 1 March 2011* indicates when *you* must pay *£100*. This is seen as having the function of Location with respect to time since it specifies a location in time for the process (i.e. when). If the clause had also included information about where the bill can be paid, this would have also been seen as having the function of Location, but this would be a location with respect to place since it specifies a location in space (i.e. where).

In standard SFL, there are nine main categories of circumstance. These are listed in Table 4.2, where each type is illustrated with examples. However, as Thompson (2004: 109) points out, there is a very wide range of meanings which can be expressed as a circumstance. Therefore it is entirely possible that a text will contain circumstances that do not fit

Table 4.2: The nine basic types of circumstantial elements (adapted from Halliday and Matthiessen, 2004: 262)

Type	Sub-type	Question answered	Example
Extent	distance	*How far?*	He ran <u>three miles</u>
	duration	*How long?*	He ran <u>for three days</u>
	frequency	*How frequently?*	He ran <u>every day</u>
Location	place	*Where?*	He ran <u>in Toronto</u>
	time	*When?*	He ran <u>last year</u>
Manner	means	*By what means?*	He saved her <u>with a rope</u>
	quality	*How?*	She saved him <u>quickly</u>
	comparison	*Like what?*	She ran <u>like the wind</u>
	degree	*How much?*	She loved him <u>more than anyone</u>
Cause	reason	*Why?*	She ran <u>because she loved to</u>
	purpose	*For what purpose?*	She ran <u>to raise money</u>
	behalf	*On whose behalf?*	She ran <u>for her sister</u>
Contingency	condition	*Under what conditions?*	<u>In the event of fire</u> leave the building
	default	*Under what negative conditions?*	<u>Without an agreement</u>, the plan will fail
	concession	*With what concessions?*	<u>Despite her help</u>, the plan failed.
Accompaniment	comitative	*Who/what with?*	John ran <u>with Jane</u>
	additive	*Who/what else?*	John wears mittens <u>in addition to his gloves</u>
Role	guise	*What as?*	She spoke <u>as his mentor</u>
	product	*What into?*	He was transformed <u>into a prince</u>
Matter	matter	*What about?*	He warned me <u>about the film</u>
Angle	source	*According to whom?*	<u>According to the lecturer</u>, the class is cancelled
	viewpoint	*From whose viewpoint/ perspective?*	<u>To me</u>, he's an idiot.

one of the nine categories given in Table 4.2. However, the vast majority of cases will fit within the standard categories, which extends to twenty-two categories if the sub-types are counted.

This presentation of circumstances has been very brief, but several of the main issues surrounding analysing participants and circumstances are covered in the next section and specifically in section 4.3.3. Table 4.2 will be a useful reference to have handy for the discussions. Towards the end of this chapter, section 4.4 presents a new structure which is needed for the analysis of circumstances. It also works through the analysis of Text 4.1 by providing step-by-step guidelines for analysing experiential meaning.

4.3 TESTS FOR ANALYSING PROCESSES, PARTICIPANTS AND CIRCUMSTANCES

The difficulty in analysing English grammar is that it will sometimes be unclear what functions are being represented by the speaker. The model of experience described above is meant to cover the range of meanings that the speaker is able to capture with his or her language use. Although some categories are easier to identify and label than others, there is no one-to-one correlation between a particular verb and a particular process. Even the verb *be* does not uniquely identify a particular process type; however, it does reduce the option to either a relational process (e.g. *The weather is beautiful*) or an existential process (e.g. *There was no answer*). Furthermore, some verbs can be used to express a variety of process types, for example *go*, which could express a material (e.g. *he went home*), relational (e.g. *the problem goes back to last summer*) or verbal process (e.g., in informal speech, *then he goes 'you can't have any'*). This section offers some ways in which tests can be used to help identify the functional elements of the experiential strand of meaning.

4.3.1 Processes

There are two main difficulties in analysing processes. One relates to the semantics of a given verb, which often happens with verbs that have a wide semantic distribution or when a verb is not a typical example of a particular category. The other involves the way in which lexical verbs combine in English, which makes it difficult at times to know which verb is expressing the event (and therefore the process).

4.3.1.1 Verb semantics

In cases where the clause has only one verb or clearly only one lexical verb then identifying the process in a general sense is relatively straightforward. In example (14), from Text 4.1, there are only two verbs. The first is a modal auxiliary verb and the second is a lexical verb.

> (14) In a high altitude emergency, an oxygen mask will drop in front of you from the panel above.

Although a detailed account of the verb group will be given in Chapter 5, we can still be confident that the process is expressed by the verb *drop*. The process test can be used here to determine the number of participants seen as inherently involved in this process. The most standard use of *drop* is that of something dropping something. This is where we encounter our first difficulty in working out the specific process type. The problem is that this use of *drop* does not fit this paradigm because in this case *an oxygen mask* is not actually dropping anything. However, it is what is dropping, even though the something that is causing it to drop is not specified. In this sense it is almost as if *an oxygen mask* were simultaneously represented as both Actor and Goal. Halliday and Matthiessen (2004) discuss these types of material processes in detail and argue that, in addition to the transitive analysis we have been discussing, a perspective that is ergative (demonstrates a grammatical pattern where the subject of the clause behaves like the object) is needed to account for these types of clauses. However, for our purposes here we will simply consider that *an oxygen mask* is Goal, since it is affected by the process and since it can be paired with a transitive clause such as *something will drop an oxygen mask in front of you from the panel above*. Section 4.7 details references for further reading on this topic.

In example (15), also from Text 4.1, the main lexical verb is *make*. As will be shown in Chapter 5, the verbs *put* and *help* are not candidates for the main verb of the clause because they are non-finite verb forms. For the current purposes, we can think of them as being without any tense.

(15) It makes sense to put your own mask on first before helping others.

The verb *make* is one that has a wide range of meanings and uses. If we apply the process test, we may end up with: *in a process of making, we expect someone to be making something*. This sense of *make* suggests a material process, since it would involve someone actively doing something. However, when we consider the meanings expressed in example (15) it becomes clear that this clause is not expressing an active process; in other words, *sense* is not being made. This alone does not mean that the process expressed is not material. It is often the case that certain process types can be excluded almost immediately simply because it is clear that they are not being expressed by the clause in question. Example (15) is not expressing an existential process, nor is it behavioural or verbal. This leaves us to work out whether the process is material, mental or relational.

There is one grammatical feature which tends to discriminate between material and mental processes and this is the use of the present progressive (present continuous or, as Halliday [Halliday and Matthiessen, 2004: 346] refers to it, 'present-in-present'). Material processes tend to prefer the present progressive form rather than the simple present, whereas mental processes and some relational processes often seem unacceptable in the present progressive form. If we use this information to test the clause in example (15), we will find the following results.

> *It makes sense to put your own mask on first before helping others*
>
> ?*It is making sense to put your own mask on first before helping others*

Sometimes the clause can sound odd when re-expressed like this so it might be a good idea to reduce it. In this case we could reasonably reduce the clause to: *it makes sense*, which clearly can be expressed in the present progressive (i.e. *it is making sense*). This tells us that the process is not mental. There is a sense of understanding involved, because if something makes sense then it is understood, and this is what may make us think that it is a mental process. However, mental processes must have a Senser and this clause does not include one.

At this point, we have to determine whether the process is material or relational. In section 4.3.2, probes for analysing participants are given which need to be considered in conjunction with the approach discussed here. One solution in these cases is to see whether or not there is a prototypical verb for a given process type which could replace the verb in question. This may help us to see the meanings being represented more clearly. There is only one prototypical verb for relational processes and this is the verb *be*. To test for a relational process, the clause needs to be re-expressed with *be* as the main verb. There is one difficulty as we do this: we can't say **it is sense* but we can say *it is sensible*. Expressions such as *make (no) sense* or *make (no) difference* are idiomatic or formulaic expressions which are difficult to analyse. We need to look to its idiomatic meaning as an expression rather than the individual lexical components. This expression serves to relate two entities by assigning an attribute of 'sense' to some other entity. With this view, it becomes clear that example (15) above expresses a relational process.

4.3.1.2 Multiple lexical verbs

In the two clauses shown in examples (16) and (17), from Texts 4.2 and 4.3, the semantics of the verbs is not the problem. The difficulty here is due to the combination of verbs: *trying to help* and *fails to respond* in each clause respectively.

(16) If you are trying to help another passenger

(17) If their life jacket fails to respond to the pulled tabs

In these cases, the analyst has to determine, as for example in (16), whether the process is one of trying or one of helping, or indeed both. In each of these examples, only one of the lexical verbs is required to maintain the meaning of the clause; the other one is not required for the event to be expressed. Instead it adds meaning by elaborating on the event.

The process test helps identify the expected participants, and in example (16) it can be applied as follows:

- If this is a process of trying, we expect someone to be trying something (e.g. *someone tried the cake, someone tried the lock*); however, we don't find the expected participants (specifically we don't find the entity which was tried).
- If this is a process of helping, we expect someone to be helping someone (e.g. *someone helped that person*).

The movement test (e.g. cleft test: *It was/is X that Y*) can be used to probe the units:

It was another passenger that you were trying to help (*were trying to help* expresses the process)

*It was to help another passenger that you were trying (*were trying* does not seem acceptable as the process)

The results indicate that we do find the participants expected for a process of helping, and the movement test supports the analysis of *help* as the process.

The same approach can be applied to example (17), as follows.

The process test:

- If this is a process of failing (depending on the sense of failing), then we expect someone or something to fail (e.g. the new menu failed).
- If this is a process of responding, then we expect someone or something to respond to something.

The movement test is applied here to clarify the unit boundaries.

It was the pulled tabs that the life jacket failed to respond to

*It was to respond to the pulled tabs that the life jacket failed

In this example, the first lexical verb (*fail*) has an auxiliary-like nature to it, as can be seen if we compare example (17) to (17').

(17') If their life jacket doesn't respond to the pulled tabs

The point is that as analysts we need to have good criteria for the descriptions we provide and this must be done as systematically and consistently as possible. It is also important that we understand the implications of one possible analysis over another.

4.3.1.3 Phrasal verbs

Phrasal verbs pose, in a sense, the opposite problem to the one discussed above with respect to multiple lexical verbs. Phrasal verbs are single lexical items which are composed of more than one orthographic word. They tend to be highly problematic for those learning English as an additional language since they have a meaning that is completely different from that of the root verb. For example, *turn down* means to refuse (e.g. *She turned down the job*) and *turn in* means to submit (e.g. *She turned in her coursework*). In these two cases, the meaning of the phrasal verb has little to do with the meaning of *turn*. These forms can be problematic in analysing grammar because one peculiarity of these multi-word items is that the words can be separated by other parts of the clause. Example (18), from Text 4.2, shows an example of the phrasal verb *put on*, which means *don* or *start wearing*, where the verb and its preposition are separated by *your own mask*. In (18′) the clause has been re-expressed so that the phrasal verb is not separated. These verb forms, whether separated by other words or not, express one verbal meaning and consequently one process; in other words, the morphological description of these forms is that of a free (verb) morpheme and a free (preposition) morpheme combining derivationally to form a new verb. This is in contrast to examples such as (19), where the verb *put* expresses a different function from the preposition *on*; in other words, these two forms are coincidentally in the same clause, but they each have a different job to do. Here, *put* expresses the process on its own and *on* is part of a prepositional phrase which expresses a circumstance.

(18) please put your own mask on first

(18′) please put on your own mask

(19) please put your mask on the shelf

The question for the analyst is how the difference between examples such as (18) and (19) can be identified, since on the surface they look very similar. The movement test will help determine where the unit boundaries are and therefore it can be used to determine whether the preposition in question is part of a prepositional phrase or whether it contributes to expressing the process.

For example, for (18′):

- *It was on first that you should put your mask (on first* is not a prepositional phrase)
- *It was your mask that you should put on first (put on* is a phrasal verb)

For example, for (19):

- *It was on the shelf that you should put your mask (on the shelf* is a prepositional phrase)
- *It was the shelf that you should put on your mask (put on* is not a phrasal verb)

The results indicate that in the case of (18′), the preposition *on* is part of a single lexical item, *put on*, which expresses the process. As a result, *your mask* is a participant expressing the thing that should be put on (i.e. the Goal). In contrast, the results for example (19) suggest that *on* is part of a prepositional phrase, *on the shelf*, which expresses a circumstance of Location (place).

The challenge with phrasal verbs is two-fold: identifying the multi-word nature of these lexical items (a structural problem) and recognizing the semantic value it contributes to the process (a functional problem). However, by considering both the functional and structural perspectives in a consistent and systematic way, the problem becomes much more manageable.

4.3.1.4 Passive voice construction and relational processes

Certain passive constructions expressing material or mental processes can be difficult to distinguish from Attributive relational processes. The reason for this is that verbs in the past participle can form derived adjectives (e.g. *broken*). This is illustrated in example (20) (discussed above as example (17)) with the adjective *pulled* in the nominal group *the pulled tabs*. The invented example shown in (21) gives an example of how the same form is used as a verb in the past participle.

(20) If their life jacket fails to respond to the pulled tabs

(21) They have pulled the tabs

The difficulty arises in cases where it is difficult to tell whether the past participle form is in the clause as a verb or as an adjective because clauses in the passive voice will have the structure *be + past participle* and clauses which express Attributive relational clauses may have the structure *be + adjective*, and some adjectives look identical to past participle verbs. Examples (22) and (23) each contain a word which is identical to the past participle forms of the verbs *wear* and *break* respectively. Both can appear as adjectives or verbs. The question we need to resolve is whether or not these forms express the process or a participant (i.e. Attribute).

> (22) Seat belts must be worn at all times when seated (Barkow and Rutenberg, 2002)

> (23) The seat belts are broken (invented example)

Any word can be identified as an adjective if it behaves like one and this can be determined using the guidelines given in Chapter 2 for adjectives. Adjectives can be intensified by modifiers such as *very* and they can be used to modify nouns. For example, it is possible to say *that is a very broken seatbelt*. To determine whether the forms *worn* and *broken* are adjectives, they should be tested for these two characteristics, as follows.

> **Seat belts must be very worn at all times when seated*
>
> *The seat belts are very broken*

These results suggest that *worn* is not an adjective and that *broken* is. In order to be certain that the form in question is an adjective rather than a verb, there is one further consideration. If the clause is in the passive voice, then it should be possible to re-express the clause by inserting the Actor or Senser that may have been left out, or by re-expressing the clause in the active voice, as follows.

> *Seat belts must be worn by passengers at all times when seated / Passengers must wear seat belts at all times when seated*
>
> *?The seat belts are broken by passengers / Passengers break the seat belts*

These results support the previous results. It seems reasonable to consider *worn* as a verb, which means that it is expressing the process. The evidence for *broken* is less conclusive, but it seems reasonable here to consider *broken* as an adjective, which means that the process in example (23) is relational and *broken* is expressing the Attribute.

4.3.2 Probes for identifying the functions of participating entities

There are already some very good resources available to help with analysing the functions of participants, and some of these are listed in section 4.7 for further reading. In this section, some of the main sources of confusion will be discussed with some strategies for testing participants.

The participant probes presented here have been adapted from Fawcett and Neale (2005). A probe may be a question that is answered based on the clause or it may be a re-expression of the clause in a sentence that forces a particular functional interpretation. The idea is that the probe for each participant type will work only for that particular participant (e.g. Actor, Goal or Senser). If the probe and its response do not fit with the clause being analysed then this suggests that the participant type does not capture the meaning expressed by the participant in question and another probe should be used. For example, if a participant is being probed for the function of Actor, the successful use of the probe will indicate that Actor is a reasonable label to assign to the participant and, if not, then another probe should be used until a match is found. Some of the probes are a bit difficult to follow in the way that they are worded, but the example for each should show how the probes can be used. These probes assume that the process has been identified and the process test has been applied. In some cases, the clause may need minor revision for the purposes of probing the clause more easily.

4.3.2.1 Probes for material processes

Actor

> Probe: What did [participant] do?
> Response: What [participant] did was to...

Example 1:

> *If you are trying to help another passenger*
> In this example, the process is *help* (*try to help*) and the participant in question is *you*.
> Probe: What did you do?
> Response: What you did was to try to help another passenger

> The result of this probe is to confirm *you* as Actor since the probe fits with the function of the participant in question.

Example 2:

> *But they may not know whether that includes their wristwatch, heart-rate monitor, pacemaker, hearing aid, and/or their personal-digital-assistant microcomputer*
> In this example, the process is *know* and the participant in question is *they*.
> Probe: What did they do?
> Response: *What they did was to know whether that includes their wristwatch.

> The result of the Actor probe indicates that *they* is not functioning as Actor in this clause.

Goal

> Probe: What happened to [participant]?
> Response: What happened to [participant] was that... (complete with the rest of the clause being analysed)

Example:

> *If you are trying to help another passenger*
> In this example, the process is *help* (*try to help*) and the participant in question is *another passenger*, which will be re-expressed as *the other passenger* for ease of expression.
> Probe: What happened to the other passenger?
> Response: What happened to the other passenger is that he or she was helped by you.

> The result of the Goal probe is that it is reasonable to assign the label of Goal to this participant.

Scope

> Probe: What was it that someone <verb-ed>? (where <verbed> = the process)
> Response: It was the [participant]
> For example, Probe: *What was it that Jane played?* Response: *It was the piano.*

Note: This probe will help to distinguish between Scope and Goal but it will not exclude the possibility that the participant is a Phenomenon in a mental process. Therefore a positive result for this probe should also be checked against the probe for Phenomenon unless it is already known that the process is material and not mental.

Example:

> *Can technical and ergonomic improvements be made to the airplane?*
> In this example, the process is *make* and the participant in question is *technical and ergonomic improvements*. The clause will be re-expressed as a declarative clause in active voice (rather than the passive voice) for ease of expression: *They made technical and ergonomic improvements to the airplane.*

Probe: What was it that they made?
Response: It was improvements to the airplane.

The result of the Scope probe suggests that the participant *technical and ergonomic improvements* is functioning as Scope. As noted above, the possibility of Phenomenon must be considered. The Actor probe will show that there is an Actor (i.e. *they*) and this means that we can be confident that the clause is material and not mental. However, in order to be certain that this participant is not a Goal, the Goal probe will be applied.

Goal probe: What happened to (the) technical and ergonomic improvements?
Response: *What happened to (the) technical and ergonomic improvements was that they were made.

The result of the Goal probe is that this participant is not functioning as Goal.

We can now feel confident that in this clause *technical and ergonomic improvements* has the function of Scope.

4.3.2.2 Probes for mental processes

Senser The probe for mental processes is based on replacing the verb for a prototypical verb for mental processes. These include: *perceive, know, believe, understand, think, like, dislike,* and so forth. In a sense, then, the participant in question is removed from the clause being analysed and fitted into a known mental clause to see if their function remains the same.

Probe: [participant] <perceives/knows/believes/likes/etc.> something

Example:
Do you know the location of the nearest emergency exit?
The process is *know* and the participant in question is *you*. This clause will be re-expressed as a declarative clause for ease of expression: *You know the location of the nearest emergency exit.* However, given that the clause is already in the probe format (i.e. *you know something*), the participant *you* is clearly functioning as Senser.

Phenomenon The probe for Phenomenon is the same as the one for Senser except that it is put into the mental process frame in the Phenomenon role to see if it carries this function.
Probe: Someone <perceives/knows/believes/etc.> [participant]

Example:
For this study, six target groups of passengers were considered
This clause is in the passive voice so it will be re-expressed in the active voice for ease of expression in applying the probe:
For this study, someone considered six target groups of passengers
Probe: Someone thought about or pondered six target groups of passengers.

The result indicates that the participant, six target groups of passengers, is functioning as Phenomenon.

4.3.2.3 Probes for relational processes

Carrier The probe for the Carrier function is a re-expression test where the clause in question is split up and fitted into a frame that forces the participant being analysed into the function of Carrier.
Probe: [Attribute] is what (or how or who or where) [participant] was/is

Example:

> *Communication on airplanes is often poor*
> The process is expressed by *be* and the participant in question is *communication on airplanes.*
> Probe: Poor is what <u>communication on airplanes</u> is.

The result shows that *communication on airplanes* functions as Carrier for the Attribute *poor.*

Attribute The probe for the Attribute function works in the same way as the Carrier probe but in this case the re-expressed clause forces the participant being analysed into the function of Attribute.

> Probe: The thing about [Carrier] is that it is [participant].

Example:

> *Communication on airplanes is often <u>poor</u>*
> This example is the same as the previous one. The process is expressed by *be* but the participant in question here is *poor.*

> Probe: The thing about communication on airplanes is that it is <u>poor</u>.

The result indicates that the participant, *poor*, is functioning as Attribute.

Identified and Identifier The Probe for the participants in Identifying relational processes relies on the features of this type of process. The first thing to verify is that the process is relational. The main feature of an Identifying process is that the two participants (Identified and Identifier) can be inverted without affecting the acceptability of the clause. Because of this relation, there is no need for two separate probes as one will suffice.

> Probe:
> 1. *Is the process expressed by 'be'? If not, can the verb be replaced by 'be' without loss of meaning?* If 'yes', then the process is likely to be relational and the participant may be Identified. If 'no', then the process is not relational and the participant cannot be Identified and the probe for Identified should stop.
> 2. *Can the two participants be reversed in order, i.e. [participant1] is [participant2] vs. [participant2] is [participant1]?* If 'yes', then it is highly likely that the process is Identifying and one of the two participants is Identified. If 'no' then the process is not Identifying and the Identified probe should stop.
> 3. *Is the participant known (already mentioned) or recoverable from the context?* If 'yes' then the participant in question is Identified and the remaining participant is Identifier. If 'not' then the participant in question is Identifier and the remaining participant is Identified.

Example:

> *<u>Deafness</u> means an inability to discriminate conversational speech through the ear*
> In this clause, the process is expressed by *mean* and the participant in question is *deafness.*

> Probe:
> 1. Is the process expressed by 'be'? If not, can the verb be replaced by 'be' without loss of meaning?

The process is not expressed by 'be' but it can be:

Deafness is an inability to discriminate conversational speech through the ear.

2. Can the two participants be reversed in order, i.e. [participant1] is [participant2] vs. [participant2] is [participant1]?

Yes.

An inability to discriminate conversational speech through the ear means deafness.

3. Is the participant known (already mentioned) or recoverable from the context?

Yes.

The results indicate that the participant *deafness* is functioning as Identified in an Identifying process.

4.3.2.4 Probes for verbal processes

Sayer The prototypical verb for the verbal process is 'say' but this process type expresses a wide range of meanings related to reporting information. The consequence of this is that the role of Sayer is not always a person who can speak but any participant that can relay the information. Once a Sayer has been identified, labelling the remaining participants in the verbal process is straightforward. For this reason, only the Sayer probe will be considered for verbal processes. If there is doubt about the process type, Sayer could be confused with participants in other processes, especially as Senser in mental processes.

Like mental processes, verbal processes can project another clause, and both types of process prefer the simple present to refer to the present. However, there is one way in which these two processes differ and this is with respect to Receiver. Verbal processes can have a Receiver whereas mental processes cannot. The Senser probe relies on these features of verbal processes.

Probe:

1. *Does [participant] report information?*
2. *Can the process project another clause (even if it does not in this particular case)?* If 'no', then it is not a verbal process and the participant is not Sayer but if 'yes' then it may be either a verbal or mental process.
3. *Can/does the clause include a Receiver as a participant (even if it does not include one in this particular case)?* If 'yes', then the participant in question is Sayer. If 'no', then it is not a verbal process and the participant in question is not Sayer.

Example:

Look in the seat pocket in front of you for the safety instruction card. It explains the safety features of this aircraft.

The process in this example is expressed by *explain* and the participant in question is *it* (*the safety instruction card*).

Probe:

1. Does the safety instruction card report information?

Yes it does.

2. Can the process project another clause (even if it does not in this particular case)?

Yes. The safety instruction card explains that this aircraft has safety procedures.

3. Can/does the clause include a Receiver as a participant (even if it does not include one in this particular case)?

Yes. The safety instruction card explains the safety features of this aircraft <u>to</u> <u>you</u>.

The results indicate that the participant in question can reasonably be analysed as Sayer.

4.3.2.5 Probes for behavioural processes

Behaver It is very difficult to probe behavioural processes because they are a border category which represents sensing and saying as activity. In this sense Behaver is very much like Actor in the sense that this participant is to a certain extent doing something. It is also more like material processes than any other process type because it prefers present progressive (present continuous) in present time reference rather than simple present (e.g. *I am sneezing* vs. *I sneeze*). Unlike verbal and some mental processes, behavioural processes cannot project another clause (e.g. *He said you could not attend* vs. *He chatted with his neighbour* but **He chatted that you could not go*). Behavioural processes tend to be single-participant processes with the only participant being the Behaver. However, there is relative lack of volition or consciousness in behavioural processes (*yawn, shiver, sweat, chat, listen*, etc.) as compared to material processes.

The best way to probe for Behaver then is to consider whether or not the participant is represented in an activity and whether there is a mental or verbal aspect to the process. It is also important to check that the process involved is not able to project another clause so that verbal processes can be ruled out.

Probe:

1. Is [participant] involved in an activity? (if 'yes', [participant] may be Behaver)
2. Is there a mental or verbal quality to the process? (if 'yes', [participant] may be Behaver)
3. Can the process project another clause? (if 'yes', [participant] is not Behaver; if 'no' [participant] is most likely Behaver).

Example:

The little dog laughed to see such fun

In this clause the process is *laugh* and the participant in question is *the little dog*.

Probe:

1. Is the little dog involved in an activity? Yes, it is laughing.
2. Is there a mental or verbal quality to the process? Yes, it is sensing pleasure, he likes something.
3. Can the process project another clause? No.

The results indicate that the participant, *the little dog*, is expressing the function of Behaver.

4.3.2.6 Probes for existential processes

Existent There are two parts to this probe:

1. Is the Subject of the clause 'there'?
2. Is the process expressed by 'be'? If not, can the process be replaced by 'be' without loss of meaning?

If the answers to 1 and 2 are 'yes', then the participant in question is an Existent.

Example:

> *There remain some questions about how a noisy environment might degrade comprehension.*
>
> 1. The Subject is 'there'.
> 2. The verb is not 'be' but it can be replaced by 'be' without loss of meaning:
>   *There <u>are</u> some questions about how a noisy environment might degrade comprehension.*

The result of this probe is that the participant, *some questions about how a noisy environment might degrade comprehension*, is functioning as Existent in an existential process.

4.3.3 Circumstances

Circumstances will generally answer the questions which are associated to each circumstance type (see Table 4.2). For example, a circumstance of Location will answer either 'where?' or 'when?'. The questions listed in Table 4.2 can be used to probe the circumstance being answered in order to identify the function it has in a given clause.

As an example, the clause given in example (22) above is given here again as example (24) so that the circumstance can be analysed.

(24) Seat belts must be worn at all times when seated

In this clause, *at all times when seated* is a nominal group. There is something time-related about this expression. However, if we use the questions from Table 4.2 as probes to test the circumstance, we may find that although it seems to answer the question 'when?' it does not specify a point in time as should be the case with a circumstance of Location. If we consider whether any other of these probe questions fit the circumstance, then we find that a circumstance of Contingency is also possible. The function of *at all times when seated* is not about identifying the process in a point in time, it is identifying the conditions under which the process must be carried out. In this clause then *at all times when seated* is a circumstance of Contingency since it expresses the conditions under which the process must occur.

4.3.3.1 Circumstance or participant

One of the difficulties in analysing grammar in a functional framework is being able to determine whether an element of the clause is functioning as a participant or a circumstance. In section 4.3.1.3, phrasal verbs were discussed in terms of the challenges they present to identifying the process (i.e. whether the process is expressed by a single orthographic word or not), and in particular the phrasal verb 'put on' was considered. There is an implicit consequence for determining the difference between circumstances and participants in these cases as discussed in section 4.3.1.3. However, once the process is correctly identified then there should be few challenges in this regard.

There are some instances that raise questions even if the process is correctly identified. In example (25), from Text 4.1, the process is *place* but *over your mouth and nose* is functioning to specify where the process is taking place, which would indicate a circumstance of Location. It is not sufficient to identify the process; the process test allows us to identify the expected participants. By applying the process test for this example, we find: in a process of placing, we expect someone to be placing something somewhere. Note that we would consider not specifying the 'somewhere' as incomplete, and our expectations would not be met, as shown in example (26).

(25) Place the mask over your mouth and nose

(26) *Place the mask

As a result, *place* has three participants: Actor (the participant doing the placing), Goal (the participant being affected by the placing) and Location (the participant specifying where the placing must occur or where the Actor must place the Goal).

In a sense it is irrelevant whether or not *over your mouth and nose* is seen as a participant or a circumstance because its function is the same in terms of the role it has in this particular clause. The main distinction to be made is whether it is an optional, peripheral element (i.e. circumstance) or a central, core element (i.e. participant) of the clause.

4.3.3.2 Circumstance or qualifier within a nominal group

Confidently identifying the internal boundaries of the clause is critical to grammatical analysis. There are occasions where we find a sequence of a noun followed by a preposition which is part of a prepositional phrase. The Groucho Marx example which was discussed in Chapters 1 and 2 showed how comedians can play with the structural ambiguity at the boundary of a nominal group and a prepositional phrase. As was shown in Chapter 3, the qualifier element of the nominal group can be expressed by a prepositional phrase. This potential for ambiguity is what Groucho Marx exploited in his famous joke.

Once the process is identified and the process test has been completed, it is important to verify the internal boundaries of the clause so that the units can be analysed in terms of the functions they express. In example (27), from Text 4.2, the process is expressed by the verb *pull*. If the process test is applied, the result is that in a process of pulling we expect someone to be pulling something.

(27) Pull the rubber strap <u>behind your head</u>

In this example, there are two possibilities concerning the prepositional phrase *behind your head*. The first is that it functions as a circumstance of Location, expressing where the process should take place. The second is that it functions as a qualifier in the nominal group *the rubber strap behind your head*. Some of the ways in which this can be resolved were given in Chapter 3. In this particular case, there is complete structural ambiguity. In other words, all tests will render an acceptable result because both possibilities are possible. In order to test the group boundaries, the clause will be re-expressed with a Subject as shown in (28).

(28) You must pull the rubber strap behind your head

The passivization test will be used here to illustrate this point made above:

> The rubber strap behind your head must be pulled
>
> The rubber strap must be pulled behind your head

Clearly both are acceptable and therefore the clause is structurally ambiguous. However, the important thing to remember is that, as with the Groucho Marx example, the different structural realizations create different meanings. The context of this utterance is extremely important. This is intended to be said to a passenger who is blind and therefore cannot see what exactly they are meant to do. Furthermore the preceding clauses provided instruction on how to correctly put on the oxygen mask in case of emergency. The rubber strap which must be pulled is located at the back of the head and therefore the most likely analysis for this example is that *behind your head* is a modifier of *strap*. It is true that the person wearing the mask and tightening the strap will do so at the back of the head but it is not true that the pulling must take place behind the person's head. The person could remove the mask and adjust the strap and then replace the mask.

Consequently there are no circumstances in example (28), and the prepositional phrase *behind your head* is a qualifier within the nominal group.

4.4 FUNCTIONAL–STRUCTURAL VIEW OF THE EXPERIENTIAL STRAND OF MEANING

In this section, an overview of the functional–structural view of the experiential strand of meaning is given. It will introduce the relevant structural units related to experiential meaning and consider the relationship between function and structure. It provides a summary of everything covered so far by analysing Text 4.1 in a detailed way using a step-by-step approach. Each clause is then analysed as consistently as possible and the specific challenges posed by each clause are discussed in each case.

4.4.1 Structural units expressing experiential functions

This chapter has presented the main functions of the experiential strand of meaning. These are the processes, participants and circumstances which represent the speaker's experience. This book approaches grammar from a functional–structural view, which focuses on the important relationship between function and structure.

In Chapter 3, most of the structures needed to represent participants were covered since the most frequent grammatical resource for expressing participants is the nominal group.

As we have already seen, processes are generally expressed through verbs in English, and the associated structural unit (i.e. the verb group) will be presented in Chapter 5. Consequently, the detail concerning this part of the clause will not be discussed here but we will come back to this in the next chapter.

What is left, then, are the structural units associated to expressing circumstances. Circumstances are typically expressed by the following structural units:

- prepositional phrase (e.g. *I ate my dinner in the kitchen*)
- clause (e.g. *I ate my dinner sitting at the table*)
- nominal group (e.g. *I ate my dinner last week*)
- adverb group (e.g. *I ate my dinner quickly*)

This section will present the adverb group since the remaining structures are covered elsewhere in the book. It will also introduce the co-ordination of units such as *I ate my breakfast and my dinner* in my hotel room, where two nominal groups are co-ordinated.

4.4.1.1 Adverb group

The discussion of adjectives and adverbs in Chapter 2 explained how similar these two word categories are, and in fact the question was raised as to whether or not there was a need for separate categories. The distinction between the two is often made in functional terms rather than in terms of lexical behaviour. In other words, it is generally accepted that for a given adjective–adverb word it is an adjective if it is modifying a noun and it is an adverb if it is modifying anything else.

The similarity between the two word classes carries over to the structural unit associated to it. The adjective group was presented in detail in Chapter 3 and the adverb group has a very similar structure to it with two exceptions. The first is that the head element is an adverb rather than an adjective. The second is that there is only one type of post-modifier rather than two. Since the adverb group is so closely related to the adjective group, which has already been discussed, this section will simply offer a brief presentation of this unit.

The basic structure of the adverb group is shown in Figure 4.3 and structurally it is identical to the adjective group (see Chapter 3). The head element is called the apex (a), which is expressed as an adverb (it is expressed by an adjective in the adjective group). As with all group units there is the potential for modification of the apex. The pre-head

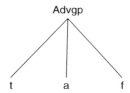

Figure 4.3 Basic structure of the adverb group

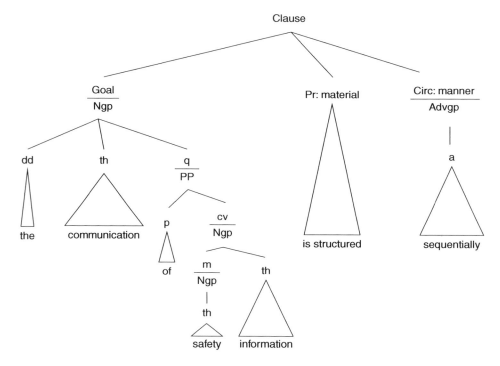

Figure 4.4 Circumstance expressed by an adverb group

modifier element is called a temperer (t). The post-modifying element is called a finisher (f). The finisher element, as in the adjective group, is an obligatory element whose function is to complete (or finish) the lexicogrammatical requirements of the comparison expressed by the apex (as in 'faster') or by the temperer and apex (as in 'more quickly'). An example of a circumstance expressed by an adverb group is given in (29), where the adverb group is underlined. A tree diagram of the clause is given in Figure 4.4.

(29) The communication of safety information is structured <u>sequentially</u>

The adverb group serves a variety of other functions in addition to circumstance. It can express the temperer in an adjective group as shown in (30), where the adverb group is underlined. Here it is modifying the adjective *large*. It also expresses a function which is part of the meanings covered in the interpersonal strand of meaning, which will be discussed in Chapter 5. This interpersonal function concerns the speaker's opinion or judgement of what they are saying such as, for example, the use of *probably* in example (31).

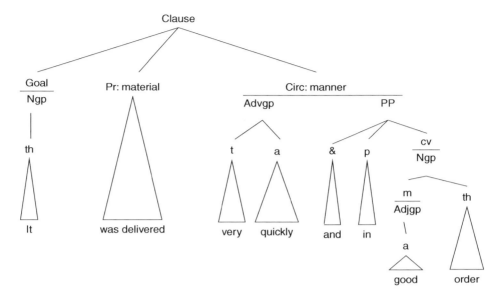

Figure 4.5 Co-ordinated units

(30) It is no small challenge to produce on-board briefings that are understood by an acceptably large proportion of travellers

(31) It probably is a waste of valuable communication time to mention lighting at all

4.4.1.2 Co-ordination

Although co-ordination is not a unit of its own, it does relate to all structural units since they can be co-ordinated. In theory, only the same units can be co-ordinated (e.g. two clauses or two nominal groups) but in some cases the structures co-ordinated are not identical but they share the same function, as shown in (32), where *very quickly* and *in good order* are co-ordinated even though the first unit is an adverb group and the second one is a prepositional phrase. They both express a circumstance function.

(32) It was delivered very quickly and in good order

Clause co-ordination will be discussed in more detail in Chapter 7 but for now the notation used to show unit co-ordination is presented here so that it can be included in the tree diagrams for the text being analysed. The notation itself is relatively straightforward since it simply fits into the existing notation that shows the relation between structure and function. There is one new symbol that is needed to indicate the actual conjunction which indicates the co-ordination. The ampersand symbol, '&', is used to indicate co-ordination (following Fawcett, 2000c). The most common lexical items which express co-ordination are *and*, *or* and *but*. Since these forms do not get modified, there is no associated group for them. There are, however, some conjunctions that can be modified, such as *even if* or *just as* (see Halliday and Matthiessen, 2004: 358). Example (32) is illustrated in Figure 4.5, showing how the conjunction is seen as part of the final co-ordinated unit and the two units are represented as structurally equal and adjacent.

4.4.2 Functional analysis of the clause

This section will walk through the analysis that can be done at this stage. Some parts of the analysis will be omitted since they are only discussed in later chapters (e.g. the verb group). The text analysed here is Text 4.1, which was originally presented in section 4.2.

In a high altitude emergency, an oxygen mask will drop in front of you from the panel above. Place the mask over your mouth and nose, straighten out the strap, and pull the strap to be sure it is tight on your face. After you are wearing it securely, a tug on the hose will start the oxygen flow. It makes sense to put your own mask on first, before helping others.

As stated earlier in this book, one of the main goals is to present a methodology for analysing grammar with a functional–structural approach. Ultimately, in Chapter 8, a full set of guidelines will be developed, offering a step-by-step strategy for analysing the clause. The steps presented here are those that can be done with the information presented so far. Each further chapter will contribute more and more to the picture of the clause and the approach being developed. However, this is not necessarily a linear process in the sense that it is not simply the case that we will add more steps to the end of the list of steps. Instead, as the information becomes available, the steps will be modified in the most appropriate way, which may mean that, for example, what is step 1 now may not be step 1 in Chapter 8.

The steps in the guidelines for analysing experiential meaning are outlined below. After these have been briefly discussed, the clauses in Text 4.1 will be analysed in turn following each step. The approach to identifying clauses within a text will not be covered in this chapter because concepts and understanding must be gained first from Chapters 5, 6 and 7. For example, identifying clauses requires a firm understanding of the verb system and the distinction between finite and non-finite verbs, something that will only be presented in Chapter 5. It also requires an understanding of the various ways in which clauses combine and this is covered in Chapter 7, which relies in part on the textual meaning presented in Chapter 6.

In the analysis of Text 4.1, then, there will be no discussion of the clauses listed (i.e. how the clause boundaries were determined) and they will simply be presented without challenge, since the strategies involved in working this out rely on later chapters. In later chapters, strategies will be developed for working this out. This leaves us with five relatively straightforward steps for analysing experiential meaning, each of which is based on content already covered to this point.

4.4.2.1 Guidelines for analysing experiential meaning

Step 1: Use the process test to show how many participants are expected by the process

This step relies on the process test to identify the number of participants which are expected by the process. It also helps to locate them in the clause. The process Test will reduce the clause to the core experiential elements (i.e. the process and any inherent participating entities). Part of this step includes checking to see if any expected participants have been left out for any reason (e.g. a passive clause such as *The dishwasher was emptied* or perhaps an imperative clause such as *Eat your dinner!*). It may also be important to consider whether the process is expressed by a phrasal verb.

Step 2: Use the replacement test and/or a movement test to identify the internal boundaries of the clause (different elements of the clause)

In addition to the process and any participants there may be other elements of the clause (e.g. perhaps one or more circumstances). This step relates to Halliday's analogy of finding the walls and rooms in the house or the intermediate structural units of the clause (Halliday, 1994: 180). This was discussed in Chapter 2, where its importance was stressed. As a result of this step, the structural units expressing the participant(s) should be clear and, as was discussed earlier in this chapter, it will also help to identify any structural units expressing a circumstance. This step primarily relies on the content from Chapters 2 and 3.

Step 3: Determine the type of process and the participant functions

Completing this step relies on an understanding of the different process types and their associated participants. Various strategies and probes were discussed in this chapter and they must be used here to confidently identify and label the process type and the participant functions. This is not a linear process, and the identification of the process type is often based on the function of the participants.

Step 4: Identify and label any circumstances

This step will probably be quite straightforward if step 2 was done successfully. Table 4.2 lists the most commonly accepted circumstance types, and if the clause under analysis includes a circumstance it is highly likely that it will fit one of these categories. The questions associated to each type should be used as probes in identifying the function of the circumstance.

Step 5: Draw the tree diagram

At this point the tree diagram should be relatively straightforward because the units will already have been identified. It is of course possible that a clause includes structures that have not yet been covered, and in this case the triangle notation introduced in Chapter 2 should be used.

4.4.2.2 List of clauses

The following is the list of clauses in Text 4.1. The process has been underlined in each case.

[1] In a high altitude emergency, an oxygen mask <u>will drop</u> in front of you from the panel above

[2] <u>Place</u> the mask over your mouth and nose

[3] <u>Straighten out</u> the strap

[4] And <u>pull</u> the strap to be sure it is tight on your face

[5] After you are wearing it securely a tug on the hose <u>will start</u> the oxygen flow

[6] It <u>makes</u> sense to put your own mask on first before helping others

Each clause will now be analysed in turn by following the five steps presented above.

Clause [1]

In a high altitude emergency, an oxygen mask will drop in front of you from the panel above

Step 1: Process test

In a process of dropping, we expect something to be dropping.

⇒ 1 participant

Step 2: Find internal structural boundaries

• Pronoun replacement test for *an oxygen mask*:

In a high altitude emergency [*it*] *will drop in front of you from the panel above*

Therefore *an oxygen mask* constitutes a single unit, a nominal group, which is distinct from the remaining units of the clause. Consequently *in a high altitude emergency* is also a single structural unit. It is a prepositional phrase.

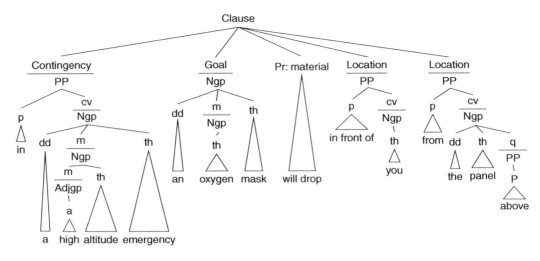

Figure 4.6 Tree diagram for clause [1] from Text 4.1

- Movement test for *in front of you from the panel above*:

  In a high altitude emergency, it will drop from the panel above in front of you

  This shows that *in front of you from the panel above* is not a single structural unit and that *in front of you* and *from the panel above* are distinct units, both of which are prepositional phrases.

  The internal boundaries for this clause are as follows:

  In a high altitude emergency | an oxygen mask | will drop | in front of you | from the panel above

Step 3: Process type and participant functions

Three process types can be eliminated immediately since it cannot be existential, behavioural or mental. The process is not about reporting information so verbal processes can also be eliminated. In fact the process type for this clause was discussed above in section 4.3.1.1, where it was determined that the process is material and that the participant has the function of Goal.

Step 4: Identify any circumstances

There are three circumstances in this clause: *in a high altitude emergency, in front of you* and *from the panel above*. Using the probe questions given earlier in this chapter, the function of each circumstance can be identified as follows:

Under what conditions? *in a high altitude emergency* ⇒ circumstance of Contingency (condition)

Where? *in front of you* ⇒ circumstance of Location (space)

Where? *from the panel above* ⇒ circumstance of Location (space)

Step 5: Tree diagram and box diagram

The tree diagram for this clause can be seen in Figure 4.6.

The same information can be represented in box diagrams but there is often a loss of structural and internal information in doing so. This is illustrated in Figure 4.7. When both types of diagrams are used, it gives a complete functional–structural description of the clause.

in a high altitude emergency	an oxygen mask	will drop	in front of you	from the panel above
Contingency	Goal	Pr: material	Location	Location

Figure 4.7 Box diagram for clause 1 from Text 4.1

Clause [2]

Place the mask over your mouth and nose

Step 1: Process test

In a process of placing, we expect someone to be placing something somewhere.
⇒ 3 participants
Note that the someone doing the placing is not expressed in the clause but it is implicitly understood as the person being spoken to (i.e. *you*, which in this case is the passenger on the plane).

Step 2: Find internal structural boundaries

- Pronoun replacement test for *the mask* vs. *the mask over your mouth and nose*:
  Place ⟦it⟧ over your mouth and nose

Therefore *the mask* constitutes single unit, a nominal group, which is distinct from the remaining units of the clause. Consequently *over your mouth and nose* is also a single structural unit. It is a prepositional phrase. However, if in doubt, this can be tested with a movement test (e.g. passivization or cleft test).

- Movement test for *over your mouth and nose*:
  The mask must be placed over your mouth and nose (passivization)
  * *The mask over your mouth and nose must be placed*
  It is over your mouth and nose that you must place the mask (cleft test)
  **It is the mask over your mouth and nose that you must place*

This shows that *over your mouth and nose* is a single structural unit.

The internal boundaries for this clause are as follows:
Place | the mask | over your mouth and nose

Step 3: Process type and participant functions

Three process types can be eliminated immediately since it cannot be existential, relational or verbal. This clause is representing what someone is doing (or what they will be doing) so it is reasonable to assume the process is material. In order to be certain, the participant probes will be used. The clause will be re-expressed as a declarative clause so that the implicit participant (i.e. *you*, the passenger) is expressed: *the passenger must place the mask over his or her mouth and nose*.

- Probe for Actor:
  Probe: What did the passenger do?
  Response: What the passenger did was to place the mask over his or her mouth and nose.

The result of this probe is that the participant *the passenger* is functioning as Actor. This confirms that the process is material. However, the function of the remaining two participants must be identified. The status of the third participant, *over your*

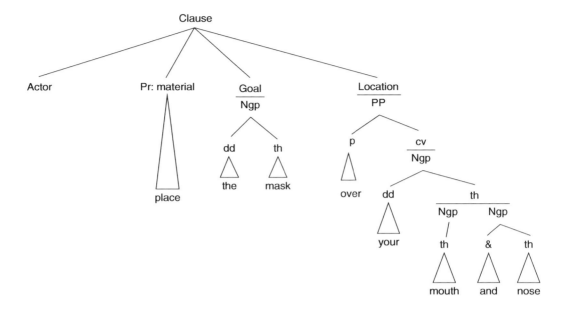

	Place	the mask	over your mouth and nose
Actor	Pr: material	Goal	Location

Figure 4.8 Tree and box diagrams for clause [2] from Text 4.1

mouth and nose, was discussed in section 4.3.3.1, where it was argued that although it resembles a circumstance of Location it has the function of a participant since it is expected by the process. Therefore this participant is labelled as Location. The most likely function of the second participant is that of Goal, but this should be probed so that analysis is conducted in a systematic and consistent way and so that it is justifiable without any guesswork.

- Probe for Goal:
  Probe: What happened to the mask?
  Response: What happened to the mask is that it was placed over the passenger's mouth and nose.

The result from this probe confirms Goal as the function for *the mask*.

Step 4: Identify any circumstances

The function of Location in this clause is an expected participant and it is therefore part of the core experiential meaning of the clause. Consequently it is not a circumstance.

Step 5: Tree diagram and box diagram

The diagrams for this clause can be seen in Figure 4.8.

Clause [3]

Straighten out the strap

Step 1: Process test

In a process of straightening out, we expect someone (or something) to be straightening out something.

⇒ 2 participants

Note that, as with clause 2, the someone doing the straightening out is not expressed in the clause but it is implicitly understood as the person being spoken to (i.e. *you*, which in this case is the passenger on the plane).

Step 2: Find internal structural boundaries

There is no need to test the unit boundaries since the clause expresses only the process and the second participant (*the strap*).

The internal boundaries for this clause are as follows:

Straighten out | the strap

Step 3: Process type and participant functions

Three process types can be eliminated immediately since it cannot be existential, behavioural or verbal. The process of straightening out is very much a physical activity so it is reasonable to assume that the process is material, but as always this must be tested. Before trying the participant probes, the clause will be re-expressed as a declarative clause so that the first participant (*you*, the passenger) is included:

the passenger should straighten out the strap

• Probe for Actor:

Probe: What did the passenger do?

Response: What the passenger did was to straighten out the strap.

• Probe for Goal:

Probe: What happened to the strap?

Response: What happened to the strap is that it was straightened out by the passenger.

The results of the Actor and Goal probe indicate that the process is indeed material and that the two participants are respectively Actor and Goal.

Step 4: Identify any circumstances

There are no circumstances in this clause.

Step 5: Tree diagram and box diagram

The diagrams for this clause can be seen in Figure 4.9.

Clause [4]

And pull the strap to be sure it is tight on your face

Step 1: Process test

In a process of pulling, we expect someone to be pulling something.

⇒ 2 participants

Note that the someone doing the pulling is not expressed in the clause, but it is implicitly understood as the person being spoken to (i.e. *you*, which in this case is the passenger on the plane).

Step 2: Find internal structural boundaries

• Pronoun replacement test for *the strap* vs. *the strap to be sure it is tight on your face*:

And pull [it] to be sure it is tight on your face

Therefore *the strap* constitutes a single unit, a nominal group, which is distinct from the remaining units of the clause. A movement test should be used to test the unit boundaries for *to be sure it is tight on your face*.

101

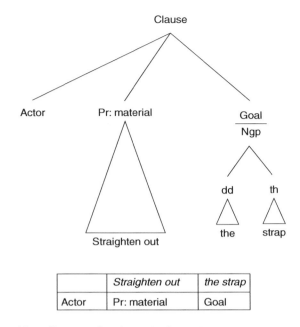

	Straighten out	the strap
Actor	Pr: material	Goal

Figure 4.9 Tree and box diagrams for clause [3] from Text 4.1

- Movement test for *to be sure it is tight on your face* (by fronting):
  to be sure it is tight on your face, pull the strap
- and to test *to be sure* as separate from *it is tight on your face*:
  *to be sure, pull the strap it is tight on your face

This shows that *to be sure it is tight on your face* is a single structural unit (it is an embedded clause; see Chapters 5 and 7).

The internal boundaries for this clause are as follows:
And | pull | the strap | to be sure it is tight on your face

Step 3: Process type and participant functions

Three process types can be eliminated immediately since it cannot be existential, relational or verbal. Because of the second participant, the process is unlikely to be behavioural. The process of pulling is an active physical event which can be observed externally, so the process is most likely to be material and not mental. The participant probes will determine whether the functions of the participants support this analysis. The clause will be re-expressed as a declarative clause so that the implicit participant (i.e. *you*, the passenger) is expressed: *the passenger should pull the strap to be sure it is tight on his or her face*.

- Probe for Actor:
  Probe: What did the passenger do?
  Response: What the passenger did was to pull the strap.

The result of this probe is that the participant *the passenger* is functioning as Actor. This confirms that the process is material.

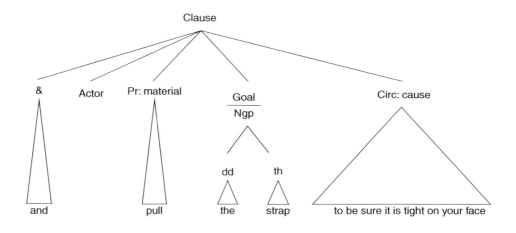

And		pull	the strap	to be sure it is tight on your face
	Actor	Pr: material	Goal	Circ: Cause (reason)

Figure 4.10 Tree and box diagrams for clause [4] from Text 4.1

- Probe for Goal:
  Probe: What happened to the strap?
  Response: What happened to the strap is that it was pulled.

The result from these probes confirms Actor as the function of the person being addressed (i.e. the passenger) and Goal as the function for *the strap*.

Step 4: Identify any circumstances

There is one circumstance in this clause: *to be sure it is tight on your face*.
Following the probe questions for circumstances, this circumstance is expressing why the process should take place and is therefore a circumstance of Cause (reason).

Step 5: Tree diagram and box diagram

The diagrams for this clause can be seen in Figure 4.10.

Clause [5]

After you are wearing it securely a tug on the hose will start the oxygen flow

Step 1: Process test

In a process of starting, we expect someone or something to be starting something.
⇒ 2 participants
Note that the something doing the starting is itself expressing an event (*tug*). However, rather than expressing it as a situation realized by a clause it is expressed as a thing and realized by a nominal group.

Step 2: Find internal structural boundaries

- Movement test to check boundaries of *after you are wearing it securely*
  A tug on the hose will start the oxygen flow after you are wearing it securely
  Although logically this sounds a bit odd, the grammatical structure is fine and so we can conclude that *after you are wearing it securely* is a prepositional phrase. The

103

completive, *you are wearing it securely*, is a clause but it could be replaced with a pronoun, such as 'after that'. Some would argue that 'after' is not a preposition but rather a conjunction introducing a subordinate clause (see Chapter 7).

- Pronoun replacement test for *a tug* vs. *a tug on the hose*:

  *after you are wearing it securely [it] *on the hose will start the oxygen flow*

  after you are wearing it securely [it] *will start the oxygen flow*

Therefore *a tug* does not constitute a single unit but *a tug on the hose* does.

The internal boundaries for this clause are as follows:

After you are wearing it securely | a tug on the hose | will start | the oxygen flow

Step 3: Process type and participant functions

Three process types can be eliminated immediately since it cannot be existential, behavioural or verbal. In addition to this, the participant doing the starting is not sentient so the process cannot be mental. This leaves only two process types: relational and material. We can quickly test for relational by checking to see if the process can be expressed with the verb 'be': **After you are wearing it securely a tug on the hose will be the oxygen flow*. This is clearly not the intended meaning for this clause. Therefore we can be confident that the process is material. The participant probes will be used to determine the participant functions.

- Probe for Actor:

  Probe: What did the tug on the hose do?

  Response: What the tug on the hose did was to start the oxygen flow.

The result of this probe is that the participant *a tug on the hose* is functioning as Actor.

- Probe for Goal:

  Probe: What happened to the oxygen flow?

  Response: What happened to the oxygen flow is that it was started.

The Goal probe seems reasonable and certainly the oxygen flow is affected by the process in this case. Therefore the participant *the oxygen flow* has the function of Goal.

Step 4: Identify any circumstances

There is one circumstance in this clause: *after you are wearing it securely*.

Following the probe questions for circumstances, this circumstance is expressing when the process should take place so is therefore analysed as Location (place).

Step 5: Tree diagram and box diagram

The diagrams for this clause can be seen in Figure 4.11.

Clause [6]

It makes sense to put your own mask on first before helping others

Step 1: Process test

The process for this clause was discussed in section 4.3.1.1 due to the idiomatic or formulaic nature of the expression *make sense*. As a result of the discussion, the process was determined to be relational.

In a process of making sense, we expect someone or something to be making sense.

⇒ 2 participants, where *sense* is the second participant.

It may seem odd to consider that part of what expresses the process is considered as a participant but this is because this slot in the expression can vary (e.g. *make no*

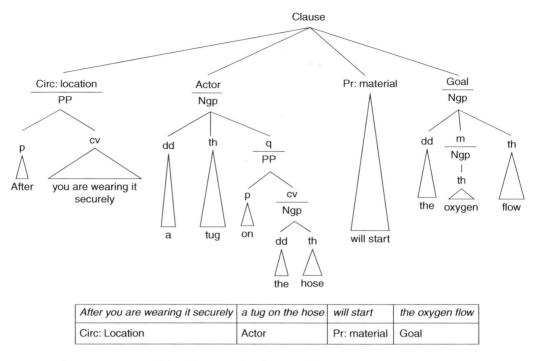

After you are wearing it securely	a tug on the hose	will start	the oxygen flow
Circ: Location	Actor	Pr: material	Goal

Figure 4.11 Tree and box diagrams for clause [5] from Text 4.1

difference or *make no odds*). This will be discussed further in step 3, when the functions of the participants are examined.

Step 2: Find internal structural boundaries

The remainder of the clause needs to be analysed structurally to see if there are any further internal boundaries concerning *to put your own mask on first before helping others*:

• Movement test:

Before helping others it makes sense to put your own mask on first

This shows that *before helping others* is a discrete unit from the remainder of the clause.

The status of *first* is ambiguous since it could be fronted in the clause without changing the acceptability of the clause:

First, before helping others, it makes sense to put your own mask on

However, by moving *first* within the embedded clause *to put your own mask on*, we can show that it is an element of the embedded clause formed by the verb 'put on' rather than the main clause (i.e. *make sense*):

Before helping others it makes sense to first put your own mask on

Therefore the internal boundaries for this clause are as follows:

It | makes | sense | to put your own mask on first | before helping others

Step 3: Process type and participant functions

Three process types can be eliminated immediately since it cannot be existential, Behaviour or verbal. The challenge with this clause is that the process is expressed by an idiomatic expression; in other words, the clause is not about making something. Since it is not about the activity of making, it is not likely to express a material process. This leaves us to consider either a relational or mental process.

If the process is relational, then there will be a relation expressed between two participants (e.g. Carrier and Attribute, where in this case the Attribute is *sense*). The implication here is that *sense* has a role as participant. If the process is mental, then we should be able to test for the participants of Senser and possibly Phenomenon. The implication here is that *sense* expresses the process and does not function as a participant. The probes for these participants have to be considered.

The clause will be re-expressed without the dummy 'it' Subject so that it fits the format of the probes. To use participant probes for relational processes the clause will be rephrased as: *Putting your own mask on first is sensible* (see section 4.3.1.1 for why *sensible* is used here). To use mental participant probes, the clause will be rephrased as: *Putting your own mask on first makes sense*. However it must be noted, as already stated, that analysing idiomatic expressions is challenging and the probes may not work as neatly as they would otherwise.

- Probe for Carrier:
  Sensible is what putting your own mask on first is.

If we accept that the re-expression is reasonable then we can conclude that this interpretation is possible, and therefore *to put your own mask on first* can be seen to function as Carrier. There is no need to test for the Attribute as in this case it would have to be *sense*.

- Probe for Senser:
  Applying this probe is challenging because the expression being analysed does not fit the Senser–Phenomenon frame, as can be seen when the probe for Senser is applied:
  Someone understands something?

The same issue is encountered with the Phenomenon probe:
Someone understands putting your own mask on first?

The meaning of *makes sense* could be seen as cognitive since it does have something to do with understanding; however, it is somewhat of a struggle to interpret the participants expressed as either Senser or Phenomenon. Furthermore it is quite difficult to re-express the clause with a Senser: *Putting your mask on first makes sense to me.* However, *to me* does not seem to express Senser but rather a circumstance of Angle.

It is impossible to be completely confident about what the speaker intended but the evidence here suggests that the process is relational.

Step 4: Identify any circumstances

There is one circumstance in this clause: *before helping others.*

Following the probe questions for circumstances, this circumstance is expressing when the process should take place and is therefore a circumstance of Location (place).

This clause requires a special note since there is a nominal group in the clause that has been left unanalysed. This is a nominal group containing the pronoun *it*. This is in fact a special construction that will be discussed in Chapter 6, but for now we will simply say that *it* is completing the Subject role so that the Carrier can be displaced to a later position in the clause. The pronoun *it* can be seen in this case as

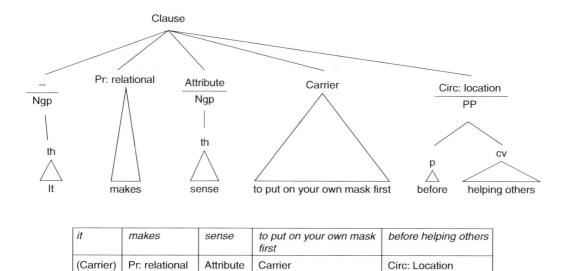

it	*makes*	*sense*	*to put on your own mask first*	*before helping others*
(Carrier)	Pr: relational	Attribute	Carrier	Circ: Location

Figure 4.12 Tree and box diagrams for clause [6] from Text 4.1

coreferential with *putting your own mask on first*. In this view, we could consider that *it* also has the function of Carrier. However, to avoid duplication, Carrier will only be applied once to this participant, which in this case is *putting your own mask on first*. As *it* has no real function in experiential meaning, its function is left blank for now. It has functions in the other two main strands of meaning and these will be discussed in Chapters 5 and 6.

Step 5: Tree diagram and box diagram

The diagrams for this clause can be seen in Figure 4.12.

4.5 SUMMARY

This chapter has provided the first detailed functional analysis of the clause. In addition to the process test and replacement and movement tests presented in Chapters 2 and 3, this chapter has listed various probes and tests for analysing experiential meaning. The guidelines presented here provide a working summary of the steps involved in analysing the clause. These will be supplemented and developed in the next chapter, which explains how to analyse the clause within the interpersonal strand of meaning.

4.6 EXERCISES

Exercise 4.1

Analyse each of the clauses listed below using the steps developed in this chapter and draw the tree diagram. You may need to refer to content from the previous chapters as well, especially Chapter 3 for determining the internal boundaries of the clause and Chapter 2 for the process test. The clauses are taken from a personal email between friends (17 May

2007) about some car trouble they experienced while travelling through the United States. The clauses have been slightly modified from the original.

1. After three more hours of work we discover one of the spark plug cords is frayed.
2. We work for another hour.
3. We notice a cracked bracket.
4. We are sent to a garage for some welding.
5. They send us to a different garage.
6. The people here love our vehicle.
7. Everyone of them used to own one.
8. It's not working optimally.
9. We head to a new garage.
10. The man behind the counter is sweet.
11. He says it will cost approximately $2000.
12. We run back to Mark's garage.
13. We need a new distributor.
14. He orders one.
15. It will be in by noon tomorrow.
16. We love this man.

4.7 FURTHER READING

There are several very good books which cover the experiential strand of meaning in more detail. Perhaps the most obvious one to consult is Halliday's *Introduction to Functional Grammar (IFG)*, which is now published in its third edition, although any edition would be a valuable resource.

Halliday, M. A. K. and C. Matthiessen. 2004. *An Introduction to Functional Grammar*. 3rd edn. London: Hodder Arnold.

There are three books which are seen as more basic introductions to systemic functional grammar. They are often used as course textbooks. Each one has a chapter dedicated to each strand of meaning, including the experiential metafunction. These are:

Bloor, T. and M. Bloor. 2004. *The Functional Analysis of English: A Hallidayan Approach*. 2nd edn. London: Arnold.
Eggins, S. 2004. *An Introduction to Systemic Functional Linguistics*. 2nd edn. London: Continuum.
Thompson, G. 2004. *Introducing Functional Grammar*. 2nd edn. London: Arnold.

The above books are excellent resources for reading about experiential meaning in more depth and breadth – especially *IFG*, which is the comprehensive reference for the subject. There is one book which is highly recommended for those trying to analyse the clause in a systemic functional framework because it provides invaluable guidance in teasing out the kinds of problems discussed briefly in this chapter. It is a workbook with exercises and answers and, since it is a companion to *IFG*, it will refer the reader to the relevant pages of *IFG* where appropriate:

Martin, J., C. Matthiessen and C. Painter. 1997. *Working with Functional Grammar*. London: Edward Arnold.

Chapter 5: Orienting language

5.1 INTRODUCTION

The previous chapter was concerned with exploring how speakers represent their experience through language. This included the various representations of processes, participants and circumstances and how these elements could be configured in meaningful ways. In addition to this, language also has a primary social function; how people interact through language. Most instances of language use will involve both experiential representation and personal interaction. These two functions tend to be so closely connected that it is very difficult to isolate them. In systemic functional linguistics, the main strands of meaning are considered to be created simultaneously. It is therefore artificial to separate the strands completely but we will pursue this and try to keep them isolated in the discussions here in order to gain explanatory power. It is easy to focus on the particular meaning associated to each strand of meaning as we consider each of the three main metafunctions in turn.

Having completed the presentation of experiential meaning in Chapter 4, this chapter concentrates on interpersonal meaning; the meanings created from the speaker's personal 'intrusion' on the language situation (Halliday, 1978: 46) and how the speaker uses language to interact with others. This involves the means by which the speaker's personal views are expressed, such as, for example, degrees of doubt, certainty, ability or obligation. In addition to these more personal meanings, speakers also express meanings that involve interaction more explicitly, such as asking questions, giving instructions or providing information.

To illustrate this, we will take a look at a brief exchange that took place on Sky Sports recently. It was originally a private conversation between two presenters which ended up being broadcast publicly and, because of the controversial content of the conversation, it drew considerable media attention. An excerpt from this conversation is given below in Text 5.1. The two presenters are Mr Keys and Mr Gray, both employees of Sky Sports at the time. As a result of these comments, Mr Gray was fired and Mr Keys resigned. The context for this conversation involves discussion between the two employees before presenting the Liverpool versus Wolves football match on 22 January 2011. They were discussing the female assistant referee who was going to be one of the referees for the match which they were presenting.

Text 5.1 Excerpt from Sky Sports presenters
Mr Gray: Can you believe that? A female linesman. Women don't know the offside rule.
Mr Keys: Course they don't. I can guarantee you there will be a big one today. Kenny will go potty. This isn't the first time, is it? Didn't we have one before?

The brief example in Text 5.1 represents the experience of each speaker. Based on the previous chapter, we should be able to recognize some mental processes (e.g. *believe*, *know*) and relational processes (e.g. *be*, *have*). There are also various participants represented in relation to these processes; for example, Senser (*you*, *women*) and Phenomenon (*that, the offside rule*); Carrier (*this*) and Attribute (*the first time*). However, what is hopefully also clear is that, in addition to the content represented, language is being used to interact as well. The speakers are asking questions and responding to each other. In addition we also get a sense of their opinions.

In this chapter, we want to add to the experiential description of the clause developed in Chapter 4 by incorporating the main functions of the interpersonal strand of meaning. In doing so, the focus will be on the elements of the clause which are contributing to the meanings of personal and interpersonal interaction.

5.2 GOALS AND LIMITATIONS OF THE CHAPTER

Each strand of meaning is expansive and, consequently, the presentation of its features and functions is selective. The goal for this chapter is to explain the main functional elements of interpersonal meaning in terms of their recognition. In other words, keeping in line with the functional–structural view taken in this book, the focus will be on how to analyse interpersonal functions by recognizing their structural form.

This chapter will focus on the core functional elements of interpersonal meaning, including Subject, Finite and Mood. There are many very good textbooks which give considerable detail about other functions such as speech roles (or the role of the clause in the communicative exchange), and a list of suggested reading will be given in section 5.11 as a supplement to this chapter.

The chapter is organized as follows. The next section will concentrate on the Subject element of the clause and consider what its role is and how to recognize it. Then, in section 5.4 the verbal system in English is presented with particular focus on the Finite verbal element of the clause and the distinction between finite and non-finite clauses. Once the Subject and Finite elements have been covered, sections 5.5 and 5.6 will offer a brief presentation of modality and polarity respectively. In section 5.7, an overview of the interpersonal elements of the clause is presented. Following this, section 5.8 will discuss the main mood options of the clause, including indicative and imperative mood choices. Finally a summary of the chapter is given in section 5.9 and this is followed by exercises in section 5.10 and further reading in section 5.11.

5.3 THE ROLE OF SUBJECT AND ITS PLACE IN THE CLAUSE

As mentioned in Chapter 1, one of the main elements of the clause within this strand is that of Subject. It is generally accepted as a well-known term and it is not unique to SFL. In English, the Subject is considered as having a significant role in the clause. Every main clause must have a Subject, whether it is explicitly included or not. In relation to experiential meaning, the Subject most often is expressed by a nominal group that is also expressing a participant, which is usually the first participant. The Subject is also most commonly the first element in a clause, which means it shares the function of Theme in the textual strand of meaning. This was illustrated in Chapter 1 with the example *Kev gave me the new Jamie Oliver recipe book for my birthday*, where *Kev* has simultaneously the functions of Subject, Actor and Theme. The role of Subject is significant, as we will see, because it is a kind of hub of meaning in the clause since, in the most common configuration of the clause, the core meaning from all three strands of meaning conflate at this place. It is the single most concentrated source of meaning in the clause.

In SFL, Subject is seen to play a major part in determining the mood of the clause (see section 5.8). Together with the Finite verbal element, the functioning of the Subject guides the interactional nature of the clause. In Text 5.1, we can identify an alternation in the location of the Subject depending on whether the clause is in the form of a question (interrogative mood) or not. I've relisted certain clauses from that text in order to concentrate on the Subject. In examples (1) to (5), given below, I have underscored the Subject for each clause since we haven't yet covered how to recognize the Subject (this will be done in section 5.3.1).

(1) Can <u>you</u> believe that?
(2) <u>Women</u> don't know the offside rule
(3) <u>They</u> don't
(4) <u>This</u> isn't the first time, is it?
(5) Didn't <u>we</u> have one before?

What we notice is that the Subject is first in the clause most of the time and, when it is not, the clause is in the interrogative mood (in the form of a question, but there is more to say about this later). In these cases, we find an auxiliary verb before the Subject. It is this difference in the Subject location that is a determining factor in both what the Subject is and what the mood structure of the clause is. In this sense, the Subject is the element of the clause that lets the speaker negotiate what he or she wants to do with the clause; for example, is it to tell someone something? Is it to ask someone something? Example (4) is interesting because it seems to be doing both, and indeed it is. The clause itself begins with the Subject and is followed by the verb, which indicates declarative mood; however, at the end a question is added in the form of a tag question where the Subject is ordered after the verb.

In SFL the Subject is seen as having the function of pivoting interaction in the sense that it determines to a large extent what can be said next. As Thompson (2004: 53) explains, the speaker uses the Subject to make a claim about something and the next speaker 'can then accept, reject, query or qualify the validity' of this claim. This is illustrated in examples (2) and (3) above, where Mr Gray makes a claim about women not knowing the offside rule in football and Mr Keys accepts the validity of this claim. If, in his response, Mr Keys had changed the Subject of his clause, he would have had to change the proposition and offered a new claim (e.g. *men know the offside rule* or *men do*). As this example shows, the Subject plays a key role in interaction. It is this functional role that distinguishes Subject as a functional element from traditional notions of subject as grammatical constituent.

In the next section, the Subject will be considered from the analyst's perspective. The main structural units expressing Subject will be discussed and tests for identifying Subject will be presented. More detail about the Subject element and its interaction with the Finite element will be given later in section 5.8, when we consider the Mood element.

5.3.1 Identifying Subject

In the excerpt given in Text 5.1, each Subject was expressed by a nominal group. In fact, this is by far the most frequent structural unit associated to the Subject element. This is not surprising since the unit expressing Subject will most commonly also express a participant and, as was shown in Chapters 3 and 4, the nominal group is the main resource available in English for these functions. Given what we already know about the nominal group and where to expect the Subject, it is relatively easy to find the Subject of the clause. However, as was discussed earlier in this book, clauses can express complex relations through embedding and this can present some challenges when analysing the clause.

There is something inherently nominal about the Subject in English and we can recognize this by the fact that any Subject can be replaced by a pronoun. This may well be a property of association between nominal groups and Subjects or it may simply be the case that, when an embedded clause expresses a Subject function, it is in fact being used to represent a kind of complex entity. For example if we compare *apples* and *eating apples* in examples (6) and (7) the Subject in each case can be replaced by a pronoun, although the pronoun is not the same one since clauses function as singular entities in English.

   (6) apples are good for you (vs. they are good for you)
   (7) eating apples is good for you (vs. it is good for you)

This point about pronoun replacement is important. It is based on the same principles of groups that were discussed in Chapter 3. In other words, whether the Subject is expressed by a nominal group or a clause, it is always expressed by a single structural unit. The pronoun replacement test can therefore be used to help identify the unit which expresses the Subject.

As discussed above, one of the principal functions of the Subject in English is to indicate a distinction between declarative (e.g. *women don't know the offside rule*) and interrogative mood (e.g. *didn't we have one before*). An understanding of the interaction of the Subject and the auxiliary verb can be used to help work out the boundaries of the unit expressing the Subject. Fawcett (2008) refers to this as the Subject test (see below). This test involves taking a declarative clause and re-expressing it as an interrogative clause. In doing so, the Subject will be revealed since it will be the unit which swaps places with the auxiliary verb.

There are two conditions to using this test: (1) the clause must first be in declarative mood and (2) the clause must include an auxiliary verb. Condition (1) can be met even if the clause under consideration is not in the declarative mood because it can simply be re-expressed in the declarative. Condition (2) is necessary because the interrogative structure in English requires a finite auxiliary verb (e.g. *do you eat fish*, or *can you eat fish*) unless the verb is the copular verb *be* (e.g. *are you a fish*). In some varieties of English, *have* can also work this way (e.g. *have you a car* vs. *do you have a car*). If the clause under consideration does not include an auxiliary verb then one must be inserted for the purposes of the test and this can either be a support auxiliary (e.g. *do*), a modal auxiliary (e.g. *can*) or other auxiliary verbs (e.g. *be* or *have*).

The Subject test (adapted from Fawcett, 2008)
   1. Check whether the clause under consideration is in the declarative mood.
   2. Check whether the clause includes an auxiliary verb.
   3. Re-express the clause in the interrogative mood.
   4. Identify the Subject based on the boundaries created by the displacement of the Subject.

In order to demonstrate how this test works, examples have been selected from previous chapters to test for the Subject for each clause. These are given below in examples (8) to (13). The Subject test will be used in each case to identify the Subject.

(8) A mass surveillance proposal for wiretapping every communication crossing the country's border was introduced in 2005

   Subject test:
      1. Is the clause in the declarative mood? Yes.
      2. Is there an auxiliary verb present? Yes.

3. Re-express the clause as an interrogative:
   Was | _a mass surveillance proposal for wiretapping every communication crossing the country's border_ | _introduced in 2005?_
4. The Subject is identified as: _a mass surveillance proposal for wiretapping every communication crossing the country's border._

(9) The leather bag that I saw in Marks and Spencer is expensive
Subject test:
   1. Is the clause in the declarative mood? Yes.
   2. Is there an auxiliary verb present? No, but the verb is _be._
   3. Re-express the clause as an interrogative:
      _Is_ | _the leather bag that I saw in Marks and Spencer_ | _expensive?_
   4. The Subject is identified as: _the leather bag that I saw in Marks and Spencer._

(10) Seat belts must be worn at all times when seated
Subject test:
   1. Is the clause in the declarative mood? Yes.
   2. Is there an auxiliary verb present? Yes.
   3. Re-express the clause as an interrogative:
      Must | _seat belts_ | _be worn at all times when seated?_
   4. The Subject is identified as: _seat belts._

(11) For this study, six target groups of passengers were considered
Subject test:
   1. Is the clause in the declarative mood? Yes.
   2. Is there an auxiliary verb present? Yes.
   3. Re-express the clause as an interrogative:
      For this study, _were_ | _six target groups of passengers_ | _considered?_
   4. The Subject is identified as: _six target groups of passengers._

(12) Pull the rubber strap behind your head
Subject test:
   1. Is the clause in the declarative mood? No. Re-express as declarative: _you pull the rubber strap behind your head._
   2. Is there an auxiliary verb present? No. Add an appropriate auxiliary verb: _you should pull the rubber strap behind your head._
   3. Re-express the clause as an interrogative:
      Should | _you_ | _pull the rubber strap behind your head?_
   4. The Subject is identified as: _you._

(13) Can you believe that?
Subject test:
   1. Is the clause in the declarative mood? No. It needs to be re-expressed as a declarative: _you can believe that._
   2. Is there an auxiliary verb present? Yes.
   3. Re-express the clause as an interrogative:
      Can | _you_ | _believe that?_
   4. The Subject is identified as: _you._

In addition to the pronoun replacement test and the Subject test, there is one additional approach to identifying the Subject of a clause in English. This involves the use of tag questions, such as in example (14) below (originally example (4) as given above). Tag questions attach to declarative clauses and they consist of two parts; a pronoun reference to the Subject and an auxiliary verb, in the same order as in the case of interrogative clauses. In addition to this particular structure, tag questions often reverse the polarity of the clause such that a declarative clause which expresses a negation as in example (14) will usually have a positive tag question.

(14) ***This isn't the first time, <u>is it</u>?***

In this example, the tag question, *is it*, is roughly equivalent to an interrogative expression of this clause (i.e. *is it the first time?* or *isn't it the first time?*). As concerns the identification of the Subject, the most relevant part of these tag questions is the repetition of the Subject of the clause in the form of a pronoun. This property of the tag question can be exploited as a device for identifying the Subject of a clause since in theory any declarative clause can have a tag question attached to it. As with the structure of interrogative clauses, tag clauses require an auxiliary verb except for the copular *be*, which, as shown in example (14), does not require the addition of a supporting auxiliary verb. Basically, then, if we want to identify the Subject of a clause, it should reveal itself when a tag question is added to the clause. As with the Subject test, for this test to work, the clause must first be expressed as a declarative clause.

> **The Tag Question test**
> 1. Ensure the clause under consideration is expressed as a declarative. If it is not, then re-express the clause such that it is.
> 2. If the clause includes one or more auxiliary verbs, use the first one to form the tag question.
> 3. Complete the tag question by adding an appropriate pronoun following the auxiliary verb.
> 4. Identify the Subject by resolving the pronoun reference.

As for the Subject test, examples from earlier chapters will be used to show how the test can be used to identify the Subject of each clause.

(15) ***It was delivered very quickly and in good order***

Tag question test:
> 1. Is the clause under consideration expressed as a declarative? Yes.
> 2. Does the clause include one or more auxiliary verbs? Yes.
> 3. Tag question: *It was delivered very quickly and in good order, <u>wasn't it</u>?*
> 4. The Subject is: *it*.

(16) ***In a high altitude emergency, an oxygen mask will drop in front of you from the panel above***

Tag question test:
> 1. Is the clause under consideration expressed as a declarative? Yes.
> 2. Does the clause include one or more auxiliary verbs? Yes.
> 3. Tag question: *In a high altitude emergency, an oxygen mask will drop in front of you from the panel above, <u>won't it</u>?*
> 4. The Subject is: *an oxygen mask*.

(17) *After you are wearing it securely, a tug on the hose will start the oxygen flow*

Tag question test:

1. Is the clause under consideration expressed as a declarative? Yes.
2. Does the clause include one or more auxiliary verbs? Yes.
3. Tag question: *After you are wearing it securely, a tug on the hose will start the oxygen flow, won't it?*
4. The Subject is: *a tug on the hose.*

This section has presented a foundation in understanding the Subject element, including various criteria for identifying it. In addition to the Subject, the Finite is also a key element in the interpersonal strand of meaning. The next section provides a detailed discussion of the Finite element and how to recognize finite clauses.

5.4 THE FINITE ELEMENT

In the previous section, the focus was on the Subject specifically but it should be clear that it is very difficult to talk about the Subject without discussing its interaction with certain verbal items. This interaction is illustrated very nicely in the 'Argument Sketch' by Monty Python. An excerpt from this sketch is given in Text 5.1 below, where in most cases the so-called argument is reduced and carried through the Subject and a particular verbal item.

Text 5.2 Excerpt from Monty Python's 'Argument Sketch'

Michael Palin:	Is this the right room for an argument?
John Cleese:	I've told you once.
MP:	No you haven't.
JC:	Yes I have.
MP:	When?
JC:	Just now!
MP:	No you didn't.
JC:	Yes I did!
MP:	Didn't.
JC:	Did.
MP:	Didn't.
JC:	I'm telling you I did!
MP:	You did not!
JC:	I'm sorry, is this a five-minute argument, or the full half hour?
MP:	Oh... Just a five-minute one.

As this example shows, the most significant elements governing the interactional and interpersonal elements of the clause concern the Subject and what are called finite verbal operators, as for example in the following instances taken from the excerpt:

I have ↔ you haven't; I did ↔ (you) didn't; is this... ↔ (it is)...

We find here the means of assertion and contradiction are expressed through the Subject and certain auxiliary verbs. This is also true for the expression of the interrogative mood, although the order of the two elements is inverted, as was discussed in the previous section. The functional relationship between these two elements will be discussed below in section 5.8 when clause mood is presented. In this section, the focus will be on the finite verbal operators.

In English, each finite clause contains an element that expresses the finiteness of the clause; this is the part of the clause that enables it to be finite. The distinction between finite and non-finite clauses will be addressed in section 5.4.2.1, but for now we will concentrate on the rather abstract notion of finiteness. The difficulty with the concept of finiteness is that it carries grammatical information rather than lexical and this often makes it difficult to identify. Essentially, the Finite element is what gives the clause a point of reference; it provides a bounded limit to the clause and this is something that speakers recognize. The most common way that this is understood is as inflectional tense (i.e. past or present). In this book, the finiteness is defined as a verbal item which expresses tense, modality or mood. This means that it is not only expressed by tense but includes any inflectional or grammatical morphology that restricts or limits the clause. The result of this is that a clause is considered finite if at least one of the following conditions is met:

- The clause includes a Finite verbal element that can be shown as an inflection for past or present tense (e.g. *he walks* vs. *he walked* or *he is walking* or *he was walking*)
- The clause includes a Finite verbal element in the form of a modal auxiliary verb (e.g. *can* or *should*, as in *I can swim*).
- The clause includes a verbal operator that can be shown to be inflected for grammatical mood (e.g. indicative mood vs. imperative mood, as in *you are happy* vs. *be happy*).

If none of these conditions are met then the clause is non-finite.

5.4.1 Primary and modal auxiliary verbs

While all lexical verbs have the potential to be inflected for tense (e.g. *talks/talked*; *eat/ate*; *run/ran*), there is traditionally a distinction made between the different types of auxiliary verbs. In this book, a very basic distinction will be made between modal auxiliary verbs and what we will call primary auxiliary verbs. In terms of the interpersonal metafunction there are really only two key issues concerning auxiliary verbs. The first concerns the need in English for a Finite element to express mood (as we will see further in the chapter), which is expressed by the first verbal item in a finite clause and might involve an auxiliary verb but not necessarily so. The second involves the speaker's intrusion on what is being said, and one of the main ways of doing this is through the expression of modality. Modal auxiliary verbs have a double function: they express the Finite element of the clause and they express the speaker's modality. Therefore, the basis for the two categories of auxiliary is really a shortcut to facilitate discussion of auxiliaries such that it is convenient to talk about modal verbs on the one hand and all other types of auxiliary verbs (primary) on the other hand.

As was shown in Chapter 2, auxiliary verbs have various roles to play in the clause. In English, temporal, aspectual and modal meaning is often built up by a kind of string of verbs, beginning with the Finite verbal element and ending with the lexical verb (e.g. *I might have been being tricked by that guy*, from Chapter 2).

Before moving on to consider non-finite verbs and clauses, it may be useful to be clear on the use of the term 'tense' in this discussion. Tense refers to grammatical meaning which can be evidenced through inflectional morphology; it concerns the structural form of a verb. However, this is quite different from the functional representation of time from the speaker's perspective. For example, there is no future tense in English. What this means is that there is no inflectional morphology in English to indicate future reference, as there is in some languages such as French. This does not imply that speakers cannot refer to future times in English – they certainly can – but it is done through the use of auxiliary verbs. Most commonly *will* (e.g. *I will call you tomorrow*) is used to refer to a future time-reference point but it is quite common to use the present tense (e.g. *I'm eating lunch at work tomorrow*). Consequently, the temporal reference a speaker makes is not always directly related to the grammatical tense of the verb form.

There is also one other important point to make concerning tense. As stated above, tense is used in its grammatical or inflectional sense and it does not relate directly to the speaker's time reference. English tends towards the use of verb complexes to express time reference and this usually involves a combination of what is generally accepted as tense and aspect. Whereas tense can be identified inflectionally, aspect is much more difficult to define since this kind of meaning has not been grammaticalized in English. What is commonly referred to as aspect in many approaches to grammar is expressed through combinations of verbs in English (e.g. progressive forms such as *has been reading*). The important thing about tense and aspect is that both relate to time reference for a given situation. In SFL, primary tense is used as a term which includes grammatical (inflectional) tense, and secondary tense is used to refer to the time reference achieved through verbal combinations (e.g. *he has been working*). Aspect in SFL is reserved for distinguishing non-finite clauses; in other words, perfective (infinitive forms, e.g. *to work*) and imperfective forms (participle forms, e.g. *eaten*), as we will see in the next section.

In summary, then, there are two main classes of auxiliary verb. One that expresses modality and another that expresses primary and secondary tense. These two classes are not necessarily mutually exclusive, as it is possible for an auxiliary verb to express meaning from both as in the case of lexical items such as *have to*, which express both modality and tense.

5.4.2 Finite and non-finite clauses

Clauses can be either finite or non-finite. Given the discussion above about finiteness, clauses which are limited by tense, modality or mood are finite. Non-finite clauses, by definition, have no Finite element and therefore they are not limited in these ways. In example (7), shown above, the subject is expressed by an embedded clause, *eating apples*. There is no identifiable Finite element that limits this clause in any way. The main or matrix clause, *eating apples is good for you*, clearly is finite because we can contrast the tense or modality: *eating apples was good for you* vs. *eating apples might be good for you*. However, this is not possible with the embedded clause *eating apples*; there is no tense, no modality and no mood within this clause. Perhaps equally significant is the absence of a Subject (although this can often be inferred or recovered by the surrounding context). What this suggests is that non-finite clauses have the capacity to represent a situation in far more abstract terms.

Traditionally, finite status is attributed to the clause as a whole and we tend to talk about finite clauses and non-finite clauses. Because this status is usually identified grammatically by inflectional verbal morphology or by modal auxiliary verbs, there is a strong association between verbs and the Finite element. As will be discussed below in section 5.7, the Finite element is included as part of the verb group, although some would argue that it really is an element of the clause and not the verb group. The remainder of this section presents non-finite clauses in English, including re-expression tests for recognizing finiteness.

5.4.2.1 Three types of non-finite clauses

In English, there are three types of non-finite clauses, and each type is based on the morphological structure of the first verb in the clause: perfective (e.g. '-en' or '-ed' forms); progressive (e.g. '-ing' forms); and infinitival (e.g. 'to + verb' forms). Each type is presented below using examples from the British National Corpus (BNC).

1. Perfective non-finite clauses

In finite clauses, the past participle verb form is always preceded by the perfective auxiliary *have* in the active voice and by the passive auxiliary *be* in the passive voice. In perfective non-finite clauses, we find the past participle verb form in the first verbal position without any preceding auxiliary verb which would predict its occurrence. Examples of this type of non-finite clause are given in examples (18) and (19). Although these examples show the non-finite clause in initial position, they are not restricted to this position in the clause.

(18) Crushed by eight strokes over 18 holes the following day, it was Norman's turn to produce a white towel

(19) Convinced that it was genuine, they decided to find local hosts

2. Progressive non-finite clauses

Progressive (i.e. '-ing') verb forms are always preceded by the progressive auxiliary *be* in finite clauses. In a similar pattern to perfective non-finite clauses, progressive non-finite clauses include the progressive verb form without the progressive auxiliary verb. This type of non-finite clause is illustrated in examples (20) to (22).

(20) Getting married and having a child is better than having a child and getting married

(21) Having left Tony and his Mum at his appointment, I set off in the direction of the A4

(22) Maybe seeing their mother and father in such pain was having a bad effect on the little girls?

3. Infinitival non-finite clauses

This type of clause explicitly marks the fact that it is not finite (i.e. infinite). The verb is in its uninflected form, unlike with the two previous types, and it includes the particle *to*, which marks the infinitival form. The inverse of this is not true since the absence of the particle does not mean that the verb is not in an infinite form; there are many instances where the infinitival verb form does not require the *to* particle (e.g. in imperative clauses such as *be happy!* or *eat your dinner!* or following modal auxiliaries as in *he might be happy* or *the doctor should see you soon*). The difficulty in recognizing this is often due to the fact that English has lost most of its verbal inflectional morphology and most regular verbs appear in a form that looks just like the infinitival form (compare: *I talk, you talk, he talks* vs. *I am, you are, she is*). Like the previous two types of non-finite clause, the occurrence of this verb form is not triggered by any preceding auxiliary verb and there is no Finite element identifiable that would account for the infinitival form. Consequently the clause is non-finite. Infinitival non-finite clauses are shown in examples (23) to (26).

(23) To win the strike on their terms, the unionists would have to shut down not only the union mines, but also the non-union ones

(24) To survive is to dig into the pit of your own resources over and over again

(25) Educating young people <u>to drink responsibly and in moderation</u> is best achieved by parents setting a good example

(26) Information <u>to be contained in personal data</u> shall be obtained, and personal data shall be processed, fairly and lawfully

The examples given above will hopefully illustrate that non-finite clauses are included within clauses in various ways and in various positions. In each case, the non-finite clause is embedded in the situation for some particular use. This may be to express the Subject of the clause (as in examples (20), (22), (24) and (25)) or it may be to express a circumstance (as in examples (18), (19), (21), (23)). There are many functions that these embedded clauses may serve. In Chapter 3, for example, we saw how the qualifier element may be expressed by an embedded clause; we can now expand on this and include both finite and non-finite clauses. Even earlier in Chapter 2, the complexity of the English clause was introduced by the 'House that Jack Built' example, where the amount of embedded clauses is humorous. Recognizing these clauses is a key part of analysing English grammar, and the next section offers some guidance in doing this.

5.4.2.2 Recognizing non-finite clauses

The descriptions given above for non-finite clauses can be used to help identify these clauses. Each type relies on the patterns of the ways in which verbs can combine in English to form certain types of interpersonal meaning such as tense (especially secondary tense), modality and mood. However, the non-finite clauses are recognizable by the absence of key features of interpersonal meaning: notably no Finite element and in many cases no explicit Subject.

There are therefore certain characteristics that can be identified and tested in determining the finite status of a clause. Three characteristics will be used to determine the finite status of a clause:

1. Finiteness: Finiteness can be identified. As discussed above, if a clause is finite then the Finite element must be identifiable and can be revealed by re-expressing the clause. It will be impossible to do this with non-finite clauses since they do not display any tense, modality or mood.
2. Auxiliary morphology: Non-finite clauses display unexpected verb forms since they appear in what is a recognizable form (progressive, perfective or infinitive) but without a finite precedent trigger (e.g. specific auxiliary forms).
3. Pronoun replacement: All embedded non-finite clauses fill a particular function in a higher unit within the clause (e.g. participant, circumstance or qualifier). Therefore in most cases a pronoun should normally be able to replace this unit in expressing the function. It is important to note that this will not be a reliable measure in all instances (e.g. for qualifiers) but it will nevertheless be a useful complementary test.

In order to illustrate how this works, example (22) will be used to determine the finite status of the embedded clauses. However, before the test is begun, the clause must be approached following the steps that have already been identified. First the process must be identified, and this way each verb in the clause is identified. If we find more than one, we need to determine which one is expressing the process.

Maybe <u>seeing</u> their mother and father in such pain <u>was having</u> a bad effect on the little girls?

The verbs have been underlined in the example. There are three verbs but only one will express the process and it must be expressed in a finite clause. Therefore, it is important that we consider the finite status of these verbs.

1. Finiteness. This characteristic should be identifiable in a finite clause. The verbs need to be tested for expressions of tense, modality or mood.
   - *seeing*: there is no tense expressed with this verb and it is therefore not limited by time reference. No verbal modality can be added and there is no expression of mood.
   - *was having*: *was* is the past tense of the verb *be*, and consequently *was having* must be finite and there is no need to consider finiteness any further. However, we could also test for modality to see if a modal verb is possible: *seeing their mother and father in such pain may have been having a bad effect on the little girls*.
   - Result: 'seeing' is non-finite; 'was having' is finite.
2. Auxiliary morphology. Two of the verbs occur in the progressive form but only one of them, *having*, has a progressive auxiliary preceding it. Based on the verbal morphology, *having* is accounted for by the presence of a preceding finite auxiliary and *seeing* is not. Therefore, we conclude that *seeing* is non-finite and *having* is finite.
3. Pronoun replacement: The test presumes that there is an embedded clause. In this example, the embedded clause has *see* as its process: <u>*seeing their mother and father in such pain*</u> *was having a bad effect on the little girls*; where the nominal group *their mother and father* is expressing the participant of Phenomenon. If this is functioning as a unit within the clause (i.e. in this case as Subject), a pronoun should be able to replace the entire embedded clause: <u>*It*</u> *was having a bad effect on the little girls*.

We could also apply the Subject test at this point to verify the embedded clause as expressing the Subject:

Was <u>seeing their mother and father in such pain</u> having a bad effect on the little girls?

The result of these tests is that the clause given in example (22) includes a non-finite embedded clause (with *see* as the process), which expresses the function of Subject. This means that the process of the main clause is expressed by *have*. At this point, we would be able to carry out the rest of the analysis.

The important distinction then between finite and non-finite clauses is the identifiability of a Finite element in the clause. Non-finite clauses, once probed, will not display any evidence of finiteness. Furthermore, they maintain observable structural characteristics that make them relatively easy to identify. Finally, as with other units of the clause, they will serve to express a particular function within the clause.

5.5 MODALITY

In this chapter, the concept of modality has so far been introduced in terms of the auxiliary verbs and their contribution to mood. In this section, modality as a meaning is considered and this is presented by looking at the types of modality that can generally be expressed by modal verbs and modal adjuncts. As Halliday and Matthiessen (1999: 526) explain, 'modality is a rich resource for speakers to intrude their own views into the discourse: their assessments of what is likely or typical, their judgments of the rights and wrongs of the situation and of where other people stand in this regard'.

Modality can be a difficult meaning to capture since it is not easily divided into relatively discrete categories. It covers a range of meanings that reflect the speaker's judgement of what he or she is saying. For example, this range extends from subtle expressions of doubt (e.g. *he <u>might</u> arrive today* or *<u>perhaps</u> I'll go*) to explicit indicators of certainty (e.g. *he <u>will</u>*

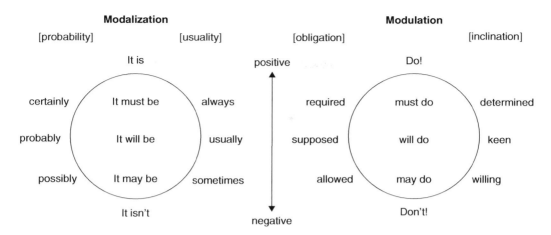

Figure 5.1 Relation of modality to polarity and mood (Halliday and Matthiessen, 2004: 619)

arrive today or *I will <u>certainly</u> go*). Consequently modality is often discussed in terms of degrees (high, median, low), where modality is seen as a continuum.

It is also generally accepted that modality can be expressed on two main axes, or as two main types: epistemic and deontic modality.

Epistemic modality, called modalization in SFL terms, is a kind of connotative meaning relating to the degree of certainty the speaker wants to express about what he or she is saying or the estimation of probability associated to what is being said (e.g. *He <u>could</u> take my car* or *He is <u>probably</u> taking my car*).

Deontic modality, called modulation in SFL terms, is also a kind of connotative meaning but, in contrast to epistemic modality, it relates to obligation or permission, including willingness and ability (e.g. *He <u>can</u> take my car* or *He is <u>absolutely</u> taking my car*).

As the examples above show, modality is expressed by modal auxiliary verbs (e.g. *can, should, must*) and by various lexical items (usually adverbs such as *probably*) or groups which function as modal adjuncts (e.g. *by all means*).

Modal verbs are easy to identify as there are nine of them:

> *can, could, shall, should, will, would, may, might, must*

Modal adjuncts are a much more open class. Although the most frequent lexical representation is using certain adverbs, it also includes fused (or fossilized) forms such as historical verb compounds (e.g. *maybe*) or formulaic expressions such as *by all means*. Figure 5.1 illustrates the relationships amongst the main types of modality (modalization and modulation), and polarity and mood. It also includes a view of modality as continuum or range between positive and negative. As this diagram shows, it can be difficult to associate specific lexical items (especially modal verbs) with a particular type of modality since there is considerable overlap in use. The surrounding context becomes very important in determining the intended meaning of the speaker.

5.6 POLARITY

Polarity refers to the positive or negative value assigned to the clause by the speaker. It is often presented along with the Finite element but, since it is a kind of meaning that can be expressed in both finite and non-finite clauses, it properly deserves a section of its own. It relates most directly to the interpersonal metafunction because of the influence of the speaker in using polarity to interact with others. This section will briefly present polarity and the role it has in finite and non-finite clauses and how it relates to modality.

Polarity captures a dichotomy of the clause in terms of positive and negative polarity. All clauses can be identified as having positive or negative polarity. Positive polarity is the unmarked polarity as there is no marker of positive polarity in English. Negative polarity is always marked and it is expressed by the morpheme *not* (whether by the free morpheme *not* or the bound variation of this morpheme, '-n't', as in *he didn't go* or *he did not go*).

This seems rather straightforward and it frequently is. In finite clauses, there is a gravity between the Finite element of the clause and the polarity marker which results in a fusion or conflation of the negator element and the Finite element (e.g. *can't, didn't, haven't, isn't*). In non-finite clauses, the absence of a Finite element means that only the stressed form of *not* can be used since there is no finite item with which to conflate the negative marker: *Maybe not seeing their mother and father in such pain was having a bad effect on the little girls.*

However, negative polarity can be complex in certain cases. For example, polarity is sometimes transferred to the main clause from an embedded or subordinate clause (e.g. *he doesn't think she is coming* vs. *he thinks she isn't coming*). It can also be difficult to analyse polarity in cases where the negation is aligned with a non-verbal item in the clause. For example, if we compare the following pair of clauses, *She doesn't have a brother/any brothers* vs. *She has no brothers*, the negation in the first instance uses a polarity marker but in the second instance the negation occurs within the nominal group as a determiner. Finally sometimes the negation is expressed through modality rather than polarity, as shown in the following two examples: *he doesn't come here* vs. *he never comes here*. In the second instance, negation is expressed by a modal adjunct and technically the clause expresses positive polarity.

5.7 AN INTERPERSONAL VIEW OF THE CLAUSE

So far, this chapter has concentrated on specific concepts that contribute to interpersonal meaning. This section presents the view of the interpersonal metafunction from the perspective of the clause. Two elements are seen as primary or central to interpersonal meaning. These are the Subject and Finite elements. This is not to say that the other elements described above are not important but rather that these two elements combine to determine the mood of the clause, which will be discussed in more detail in section 5.8. In this section, a functional–structural description of the clause with respect to the interpersonal metafunction will be given, as was done for the experiential metafunction in Chapter 4.

We have already seen how the Subject and Finite elements interact to negotiate meaning in terms of asking questions or making statements. Because of this special relationship in English between the Subject and the Finite element, they are seen as constituting the Mood element of the clause. This is the element that determines the mood choice of the clause (e.g. declarative, interrogative or imperative). The remainder of the clause is referred to as the Residue element of the clause but it does not directly contribute, as an element, to the expression of interpersonal meaning in the same way as the Mood element does. In addition to Subject and Finite, there are other interpersonal elements in the clause: Predicator, Complement and various types of adjunct. Each of these will be explained in the next section, where we will consider how interpersonal meaning maps onto experiential meaning.

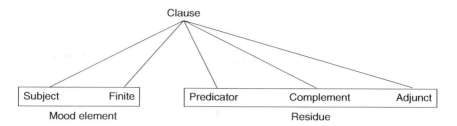

Figure 5.2 Single-strand view of the interpersonal clause

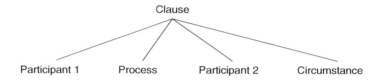

Figure 5.3 Basic generalized view of the experiential clause

5.7.1 Experiential and interpersonal structure

The view of the clause from the interpersonal metafunction is considerably different from what we saw in our presentation of the experiential metafunction. With experiential meaning, the clause is seen as representing experience through processes, participants and circumstances. With the exception of Subject and Finite, interpersonal meaning is less concentrated on particular units than is the case in experiential meaning, and we find interpersonal meaning spread throughout the clause in various ways. This can be, for example, in the use of modal adjuncts, modal finites, or certain lexical items which indicate the speaker's evaluation (e.g. *man* vs. *idiot*). The main distinction made is between mood and modality. As in the experiential metafunction, the functional elements must be expressed in some form but the challenge is that the relationship between function and structure is not as direct as in experiential meaning.

A single-strand view of the clause for interpersonal meaning could be presented as shown in Figure 5.2, where Subject and Finite, as the two most significant elements of the clause interpersonally, are given on the same level. This is not a convenient representation for analysing the clause because the Finite is never a free morpheme; in other words, it is bound to some verbal item. Consequently, it could become quite cumbersome to isolate the Finite element from the rest of the verb group and there would be no analytical advantage to this.

If we take a multifunctional approach, like the position taken in this book, the representation of the multiple functions should, ideally, map onto each other where the same unit expresses more than one function. As a reminder of the basic configuration of the clause in the experiential metafunction, Figure 5.3 illustrates the generic functional elements that express experiential meaning. If we compare this with Figure 5.2 and Figure 5.4, it should be easier to see how the two strands of meaning could map onto each other both function-ally and structurally if the representation in Figure 5.4 is adopted. This is certainly not the only way in which these meanings can be represented and we will refine this representa-tion after the next section, where the verb group will be presented in detail.

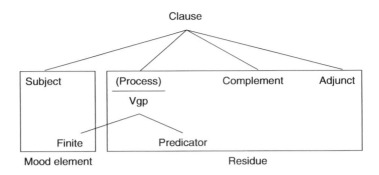

Figure 5.4 Basic view of the interpersonal clause

Based on Figures 5.3 and 5.4, it may already be clear that there is the potential for a direct mapping of experiential and interpersonal meaning for most of the functional elements of the clause as seen so far. For example, Subject will often map onto the first participant (although not always, as in the case of certain process types). The Complement element is the functional label for what are known as objects (direct and indirect objects) in traditional grammar. Any participants which are not functioning as Subject will be conflated with Complement. Circumstance elements conflate with an adjunct element. As there are several types of adjunct, those with a circumstance function are often referred to as a circumstantial adjunct to distinguish them from modal adjuncts. There will be some adjuncts (such as modal adjuncts) which do not have any experiential meaning and therefore they do not express more than one function.

The real challenge is how to reconcile the expression of the process and the Finite. This problem will be considered in the next section, where the verb group is presented. This is the last major structural unit that needs to be covered in order to complete our structural presentation of the clause.

5.7.2 The verb group

The verb group works differently from the other groups described so far. Like other groups, it is centred on a verb but the group itself does not seem to lend itself so easily to the modification of this item as is the case for other groups. Each verb group must have a lexical verb but, given that there are finite and non-finite clauses, it is not a requirement for each verb group to have a Finite element. Most other groups have one pivotal element (e.g. a noun or an adjective) and the other members of the group tend to be expressed by different structural units. The verb group is almost exclusively composed of verbs. This is a feature of how certain types of meaning (e.g. modality, tense) are expressed in English: combinations of auxiliary verbs together with a lexical verb. For every verb group, there will be one pivotal verbal element and the potential for supporting verbal elements.

When considered from a solely structural perspective, the verb group is not really problematic, although of course there are points of debate. The difficulty arises when a multifunctional perspective is taken since it forces us to try to reconcile how each kind of meaning is expressed. If we consider the experiential metafunction, it may simply be that the entire verb group expresses the process, but as we have seen when applying the process test in earlier chapters it is the pivotal verbal element (i.e. the main lexical verb) which primarily determines the meaning of the process. This is not to say that the remaining verbal elements do not contribute to experiential meaning but rather that one element is

Figure 5.5 Span of meaning in the verb group

identifiably more significant than any others from this view, and this element is found towards the right-most end of the verb group, as we shall see in a moment. However, when the verb group is considered in terms of its expression of interpersonal meaning, the main lexical verb is far less significant and, as explained above, it is the Finite element that plays the most important role. In many cases these two functional elements are expressed by a single word (e.g. *he ate*$_{Finite/process}$ *the whole pie*). When this is not the case (e.g. *he didn't*$_{Finite}$ *eat*$_{process}$ *the whole pie*), the Finite is necessarily separated from the main lexical verb and the interpersonal focus of attention moves to the left-most element of the verb group. The result is a span across the verb group where interpersonal meaning peaks on the left-most item and experiential meaning peaks on the right-most item, as shown in Figure 5.5. This isn't very different from the view taken in Chapter 3, where the nominal group was presented as the major grammatical resource for expressing participant functions and, as is being shown in this chapter, also Subject and Complement functions. The verb group is a grammatical resource which expresses complex and multiple functions simultaneously. The difficulty for us is trying to capture this with our limited diagrams.

Children pick up on the complexities of what verbs can do from a very early age. When my youngest son was two years and one month old, he wanted to tell me that his father had gone to get his ball. What he actually said is given in example (27).

(27) Daddy's go getting my ball

We can tell from this that he has some awareness of putting words together to express an action. Clearly we can't be certain about what precisely he is processing but it does seem reasonable to assume that this utterance shows he has grasped the use of some kind of progressive auxiliary and the '-ing' morphology. There isn't necessarily evidence that he hasn't done this right, although we would expect adult speakers to produce either *Daddy is getting my ball* or *Daddy is going to get my ball*. This very young speaker may well have a verb in his lexicon that is *go get*; perhaps due to hearing a high frequency of utterances such as *go get your ball*, *go get your book*, and so forth. With this view then, he has perfectly mastered what seems to be a complex verbal expression of the process. The point here is not to discuss child language acquisition but rather to bring to our attention the complexities of expressing the Finite element (interpersonal meaning) and the process element (experiential meaning).

5.7.2.1 The structure of the verb group

The structure of the verb group is complex for a variety of reasons: the way in which the Finite element works in English; the way verbs combine to express complex (secondary) tenses; and the way words combine to form complex verbal lexical items (e.g. *to make up*). For the reasons discussed above, the Finite and main verbal elements are seen to combine, sometimes with other verbal elements intervening, in the form of a structural unit called the verb group. We can also use a replacement test similar to the pronoun replacement test to show this by replacing even very complex verb groups by a single verb. In all cases, this will be a simple form of the main verb: *he might have been drinking tea* ↔ *he drank tea*).

The question of headedness or the pivotal element of the verb group could be seen as depending on the perspective taken: if considered within the interpersonal metafunction,

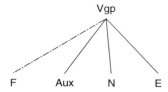

Figure 5.6 A basic view of the verb group

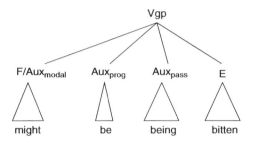

Figure 5.7 Sample verb group for *might be being bitten*

it would have to be the Finite element (F) and if considered within the experiential meta-function it would be the event element (E), which is expressed by the main lexical verb in the verb group (see below). For all finite clauses, the verb group must have both elements, and as already stated both functions can be expressed by a single verb. This may lead to questions as to whether this unit is a group or a phrase but, since not all clauses are finite, not all verb groups require a Finite element. However, all verb groups do require the expression of an event element; in other words, a lexical verb. Therefore, it is simpler to consider that the verb group has one pivotal element (i.e. the event element, E) where the remainder of the verb group serves to expand on this.

The basic structure of the verb group is given in Figure 5.6. In this illustration, the Finite element, F, is indicated by a dashed line since it is an element which cannot be expressed in isolation from other elements; in other words, it must be conflated with at least one other functional element. It always conflates with the first verbal item but this could be one of the various types of auxiliary elements, Aux, or the event element, E. The only remaining element in Figure 5.6 is the negator element, N, which is the element that expresses negative polarity. Halliday refers to this element as the polarity element, but since positive polarity is not marked and only negative polarity is an option this element will be referred to here as negator, a term adopted from Fawcett (2000c).

Although the Auxiliary element, Aux, is optional, there may be more than one type expressed: for example, a modal auxiliary + progressive auxiliary + passive auxiliary, as in *he might be being bitten by a mosquito*. The verb group in this example would be represented as shown in Figure 5.7. Identifying the meaning type is not necessary in all cases; it depends on whether or not the analysis calls for this type of detail. What is important is that the function of the auxiliary element is identifiable.

One final comment should be made concerning the representation of the functional elements of interpersonal meaning in diagrams. As discussed above, mapping the various functions onto the same unit of structure is challenging to show in a diagram. When representing the clause with a tree diagram, the verb group is a convenient way to clearly identify the Finite element and the remaining elements of the verb group. However, the remaining elements of the verb group constitute the Predicator but it would be quite difficult to label all remaining elements additionally as Predicator. The solution proposed here is that tree diagrams should include all elements of the verb group but that box diagrams only need identify the Finite element, and the remainder of the verb group can then be labelled Predicator. Here is an example of this; in fact this is the most common method of labelling the verb group within systemic functional linguistics:

might	*be*	*being*	*bitten*
Finite	Predicator		

5.7.3 Interpersonal analysis of the clause

At this point, the description of the clause from the perspective of the interpersonal metafunction is nearly complete. Mood, as a property of the clause, will be discussed in the next section. However, the functional–structural description of the interpersonal clause has been completed, and in this section some worked examples will be presented in order to show how the interpersonal meanings map onto our description of the clause so far. First, selected examples from Chapter 3 will be reconsidered here by adding the interpersonal functions to the existing description. In addition to this, clauses [1] and [2] taken from Text 5.1 above will be analysed for both experiential and interpersonal meaning in order to show how the analysis is done from the beginning.

In analysing each of these clauses, the steps in the guidelines which were developed in the previous chapter will be expanded to include the content that has been covered in this chapter. New steps have been added related to identifying the Finite and Subject elements and all other interpersonal elements of the clause (mood, modality and polarity). With the additional steps for the elements of interpersonal meaning, there are now nine steps in the guidelines for analysing the clause. These are listed below. The guidelines will be revised again in Chapter 6 after the presentation of textual meaning.

5.7.3.1 Guidelines for analysing experiential and interpersonal meaning

Step 1: Identify the process

> This step involves identifying the main verb (event) of the clause as it will also express the process (see Chapter 4) and in order to do this you will have to identify the Finite element as well, using the criteria given above. It may also be necessary at this point to identify any embedded clauses if there are any but this might be deferred until step 3 in some cases.

Step 2: Use the process test to show how many participants are expected by the process (see Chapters 2 and 4)

Step 3: Use the tests developed in Chapters 3 and 4 to identify the internal boundaries of the clause (different elements of the clause)

> This step relates to the analogy of finding the walls and rooms in the house, as was discussed in Chapter 2. Here the intermediate structural units of the clause are verified (e.g. nominal groups, prepositional phrases).

Step 4: Determine the process type and participant roles

This step involves working with the probes and tests developed in Chapter 4 in order to determine the type of process expressed and the particular participant roles.

Step 5: Identify any circumstance roles

This step considers any potential circumstances in the clause. The questions associated to each type, which were listed in Chapter 4, should be used as probes in identifying the function of the circumstance.

Step 6: Identify the Finite type

The Finite element will have been identified in step 1 above. In this step, the type of Finite is determined (e.g. temporal, modal).

Step 7: Use the Subject test to identify the Subject

In this step you will apply the Subject test as given above in order to verify the structural unit which is expressing the Subject of the clause.

Step 8: Identify all modal elements including markers of negative polarity

In this step, modal adjuncts, modal verbs and/or negator are identified.

Step 9: Draw the tree diagram

The following clauses have been selected from this chapter and Chapter 4 to illustrate the guidelines for analysing both experiential and interpersonal meaning. The first two were analysed in Chapter 4, which means that they are already familiar and it will be easier to see how interpersonal meaning maps on to experiential meaning.

[1] In a high altitude emergency, an oxygen mask will drop in front of you from the panel above

[2] Place the mask over your mouth and nose

[3] Can you believe that?

[4] Women don't know the offside rule

Clause [1] (from Chapter 4 section 4.4.2)

In a high altitude emergency, an oxygen mask will drop in front of you from the panel above

In Chapter 4, this clause was analysed as a material process with one participant, which had the function of Actor. Three circumstances were identified as given in Figure 5.8, which is reproduced here for ease of reference. As is shown by this diagram, the material process is expressed by the verb group *will drop*. The only candidate for Subject is *an oxygen mask*, but this will be tested as the steps are followed below. Since steps 1 to 5 inclusive were completed in Chapter 4, the analysis here will begin with step 6.

Step 6: Identify the Finite type

There are only two verbs in this clause: the first is *will*, which is a modal auxiliary verb, and the other is *drop*, which is a lexical verb. Whenever a modal verb is present in a clause it will always conflate with the Finite element and therefore *will* expresses the Finite element in this clause.

Step 7: Use the Subject test to identify the Subject

Following the Subject test, the clause is re-expressed in the interrogative form: *In a high altitude emergency, will an oxygen mask drop in front of you from the panel above?* Therefore this shows that *an oxygen mask* expresses the Subject in this clause.

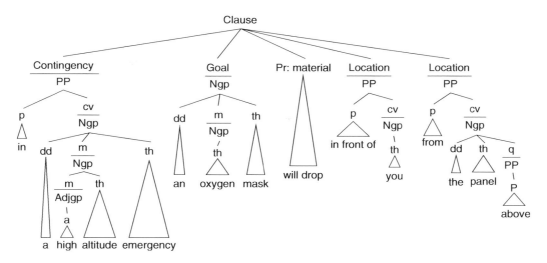

Figure 5.8 Experiential analysis of the clause *In a high altitude emergency, an oxygen mask will drop in front of you from the panel above*

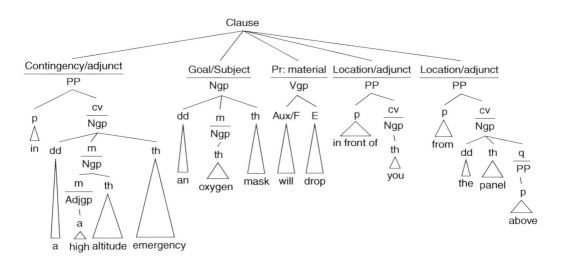

Figure 5.9 Experiential and interpersonal analysis of the clause *In a high altitude emergency, an oxygen mask will drop in front of you from the panel above.*

Step 8: Identify all modal elements including markers of negative polarity

This clause has one modal verb, *will*, but no other markers of modality or polarity.

Step 9: Draw the tree diagram

The interpersonal functions are added to the existing tree diagram, as shown in Figure 5.9.

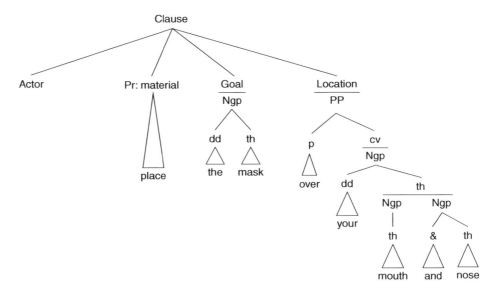

Figure 5.10 Experiential analysis for the clause *Place the mask over your mouth and nose*

Clause [2] (from chapter 4 section 4.4.2)

Place the mask over your mouth and nose

Like the previous example, this clause has already been analysed up to step 6. The analysis is given here in Figure 5.10, where the clause expresses a material process with Actor (unexpressed) and Goal and one circumstance of Location.

Step 6: Identify the Finite type

This clause is particularly challenging in terms of recognizing the Finite element. At a glance there is only one verb, *place*. The problem is that the Finite is not immediately identifiable. There are no auxiliary verbs but we can test for the potential to include an auxiliary verb and we can use the information presented earlier in this chapter to resolve this problem. First, if we refer to Figure 5.1 above, it should be clear that the clause is expressing modulation (obligation) based on the examples given and that therefore the clause is finite. We can also exclude the possibility that the clause is non-finite because it does not match any of the three non-finite clause types for English. If the polarity is reversed, the Finite element will either reveal itself or we will have to reconsider that the clause is non-finite. To do this, we will re-express the clause with negative polarity to see if the negator can conflate with the Finite element: *Don't place the mask over your mouth and nose*. Therefore we can conclude that the clause is finite but that the Finite element is not expressed in this instance.

Step 7: Use the Subject test to identify the Subject

In order to use the Subject test, the clause must be re-expressed with all participants fully expressed. In this case, the Actor was left unspecified but we know from the context that the Actor in this case is the airplane passenger being addressed, i.e. *you*. This gives: *You place the mask over your mouth and nose*.

The Subject test requires an auxiliary verb: *You can place the mask over your mouth and nose*.

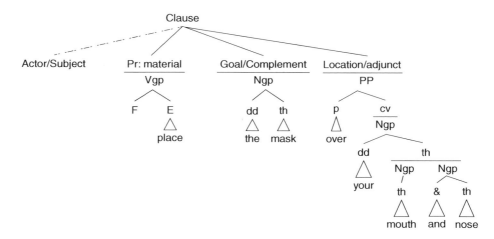

Figure 5.11 Experiential and interpersonal analysis for the clause *Place the mask over your mouth and nose*

Applying the Subject test gives: *Can you place the mask over your mouth and nose?* Therefore this shows that *you* functions as the Subject in this clause, even though it has not been expressed lexically.

Step 8: Identify all modal elements including markers of negative polarity
This clause expresses modality of obligation.

Step 9: Draw the tree diagram
The tree diagram showing experiential and interpersonal meaning is given in Figure 5.11.

Clause [3] (from Text 5.1)

Can you believe that?

Step 1: Identify the process
There are only two verbs in this clause: *can* and *believe*. The first, *can*, is immediately recognized as a modal auxiliary verb. Consequently, the presence of a lexical verb is expected, and *believe* satisfies this. Therefore *believe*, as the lexical verb, is seen as expressing the process.

Step 2: Use the process test to show how many participants are expected by the process
Process test: In a process of believing, we expect someone to be believing someone/something. Therefore two participants are expected by this process.

Step 3: Use the replacement test and/or the movement test to identify the internal boundaries of the clause (different elements of the clause)
Given that the remaining units of the clause are expressed by pronouns, this step is not necessary (i.e. *you* and *that*).

Step 4: Determine the process type and participant roles
Given that the process test determined that two participants were involved, single-participant processes such as behavioural and existential can be eliminated. Verbal processes can be eliminated as well because the meaning of *believe* in this sense does

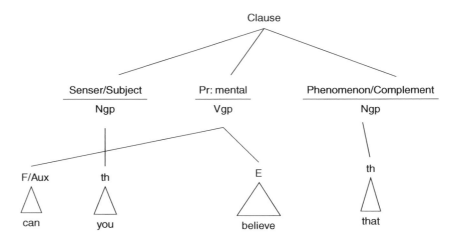

Figure 5.12 Experiential and interpersonal analysis of the clause *Can you believe that?*

not involve any meaning related to saying. The clause is also not expressing a relational process since the two participants cannot be related by the verb *be*. This leaves only material and mental to choose from. As explained in Chapter 4, there is one grammatical way to distinguish between these two process types and this means we can use the present progressive to test for material versus mental processes, since material processes tend to prefer the progressive present. To apply this test, we need to re-express the clause without the modal verb *can* and compare the clause in the simple present to the present progressive: *you believe that* vs. **you are believing that*.

What we find is that the simple present (i.e. *you believe that*) is the preferred version and therefore the process is mental. Consequently, the respective Participant roles are Senser (*you*) and Phenomenon (*that*).

Step 5: Identify any circumstance roles

There are no remaining elements of the clause and therefore no circumstances.

Step 6: Identify the Finite type

The Finite element was identified in step 1 as a modal verb.

Step 7: Use the Subject test to identify the Subject

Given that this clause begins with an auxiliary verb, we can apply the Subject test in reverse: *Can you believe that?* → *You can believe that.*

This indicates that *you* is expressing the Subject.

Step 8: Identify all modal elements including markers of negative polarity

Other than the modal verb already identified for this clause, there are no other markers of modality or polarity.

Step 9: Draw the tree diagram

The tree diagram is given in Figure 5.12.

Clause [4] from Text 5.1

Women don't know the offside rule

Step 1: Identify the process

There are only two verbs in this clause: *don't* and *know*. The first, *don't*, is immediately recognized as a support auxiliary verb (i.e. *do*) with negative polarity ('-n't'). Consequently, the presence of a lexical verb is expected and *know* satisfies this. Therefore *know*, as the lexical verb, is seen as expressing the process.

Step 2: Use the process test to show how many participants are expected by the process

Process test: In a process of knowing, we expect someone to be knowing someone/something. Therefore two participants are expected by this process.

Step 3: Use the replacement test and/or the movement test to identify the internal boundaries of the clause (different elements of the clause)

We can use the pronoun replacement test to verify the unit boundaries: <u>they</u> *don't know* <u>it</u>. This shows that *women* and *the offside rule* each constitute single structural units; both are nominal groups.

Step 4: Determine the process type and participant roles

Given that the process test determined that two participants were involved, single-participant processes such as behavioural and existential can be eliminated. Verbal processes can be eliminated as well because the meaning of *know* in this sense does not involve any meaning related to saying. The analysis for this clause is the same as for the previous clause, and in order to determine the process type the clauses will be compared in the simple present and the present progressive: *women know the offside rule* as compared to **women are knowing the offside rule*.

What we find is that the simple present (i.e. *women know the offside rule*) is the preferred version and therefore the process is mental. Consequently, the respective participant roles are Senser (*women*) and Phenomenon (*the offside rule*).

Step 5: Identify any circumstance roles

There are no remaining elements of the clause and therefore no circumstances.

Step 6: Identify the Finite type

The Finite element was identified in step 1 as a support auxiliary verb (*do*).

Step 7: Use the Subject test to identify the Subject

This clause already has an auxiliary verb so we can apply the Subject test directly: *Women* <u>don't</u> *know the offside rule* → <u>Don't</u> *women* <u>know</u> *the offside rule?*
This indicates that *women* is expressing the Subject.

Step 8: Identify all modal elements including markers of negative polarity

There are no markers of modality, but the clause expresses negative polarity through the negator, '-n't', which is conflated with the Finite element (i.e. *don't*).

Step 9: Draw the tree diagram

The tree diagram is given in Figure 5.13.

These examples show how the main interpersonal meanings conflate with experiential meaning. Although the experiential meaning in the four clauses analysed is quite similar, the interpersonal meaning has differed in terms of the Subject and Finite elements. These differences are attributed to differences in mood, which is explained in the next section.

Before moving to the discussion of mood, one further aspect of interpersonal meaning should be briefly mentioned. The speaker's attitude can also be expressed through the selection of lexical items which have an 'interpersonal element as an inherent part of their meaning, especially those referring to human beings, for example, *idiot, fool, devil, dear*'

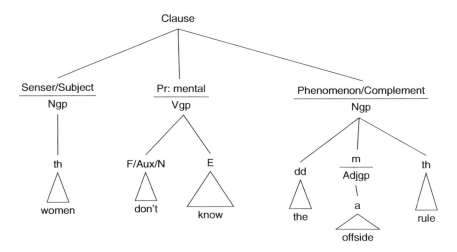

Figure 5.13 Experiential and interpersonal analysis for the clause *Women don't know the offside rule*

(Halliday and Hasan, 1976: 276). Lexical items can express the speaker's attitude across a wide range of interpersonal meanings such as familiarity, distance, contempt, sympathy (Halliday and Hasan, 1976). Thompson (2004: 75) refers to this as appraisal, which he defines as 'the indication of whether the speaker thinks that something (a person, thing, action, event, situation, idea, etc.) is good or bad'. Suggestions for further reading on this topic are given in section 5.11.

5.8 MOOD

This chapter has primarily focused on the identification and expression of specific inter-personal functions within the clause. In this section, we take a look at one of the motivating systems for why the clause functions as it does within the interpersonal strand of meaning. Within the experiential strand of meaning, the speaker can be thought of as a kind of raconteur, someone who recounts experience. Within the interpersonal strand of meaning, the speaker takes on a social role in the speech situation, and in doing so assigns a role to the addressee. According to Halliday (2002: 189), 'language itself defines the roles which people may take in situations in which they are communicating with one another; and every language incorporates options whereby the speaker can vary his (or her) own communication role, making assertions, asking questions, giving orders, expressing doubts and so on'. Speech functions such as question and order are expressed by the mood system (see Figure 5.14). The differences among the different types of mood choice (e.g. interrogative, declarative or imperative) relate to 'differences in the communication role adopted by the speaker in his interaction with a listener' (Halliday, 2002: 189).

The mood system shown in Figure 5.14 (taken from Thompson, 2004: 58) illustrates the range of options potentially available to speakers in terms of the function of the Subject in relation to the Finite, since these two elements combine to define the mood structure of the clause. In other words, the distinction amongst the various mood options is based on the interaction of the Subject and Finite. Interrogative mood and declarative mood are expressed in English by inverting the Subject and Finite (e.g. *can you believe that?* vs. *you*

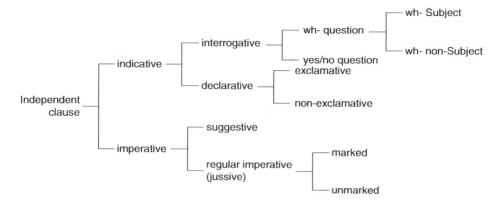

Figure 5.14 The mood system (Thompson, 2004: 58)

can believe that). The non-exclamative declarative clause is what we might call the regular declarative (e.g. *he is a nice man*) and this is in contrast to exclamative clauses such as *what a nice man he is*. With exclamative clauses, the verbal morphology is very clearly indicative and the mood structure remains Subject followed by Finite although the Complement (i.e. *what a nice man*) precedes the Subject. In many cases the Subject and Finite are ellipsed, as in *what a nice man*.

Within the interrogative system, there are two options. One is what is called wh-interrogative and the other is called polar interrogative. These are sometimes referred to respectively as content interrogatives and yes/no interrogatives. Wh- interrogatives include an interrogative pronoun (see Chapter 2) as in, for example, *who ate the cake? what did you eat? where will you go? how can you afford to travel?* The use of an interrogative pronoun often indicates content that the speaker expects the addressee to provide. In this sense, the pronoun is used to seek that content. When the 'sought' element is the Subject, as in *who ate the cake?*, then the Subject and Finite do not appear inverted. In these cases, an auxiliary verb is not needed to form the interrogative (so **what ate he?* but *what did he eat?*).

The distinction between indicative and imperative mood is based historically on verbal inflectional morphology. The two mood types were originally distinguished on verbal inflection alone where the imperative mood in the second person singular (*you*) was expressed by absence of an affix (i.e. null morpheme or null affix), much like Modern English indicative mood (e.g. *you walk* but *he walks*) and in the plural, it was expressed by the '-(e)th' (originally '-eþ') affix. This kind of inflectional marker of mood is maintained in many European languages such as German and Welsh. The extensive loss of verbal inflections in Modern English has meant that there is no overt marking on verbs to indicate mood. Consequently, it has to be determined by deduction.

The third person singular (i.e. *he, she* or *it*) in the indicative mood is the only remaining source of mood indicators. This information can be used to help determine indicative mood if the clause can be expressed in the third person singular. In the example discussed above, *Women don't know the offside rule*, the indicative mood of this clause can be verified by re-expressing the clause in the third person singular without any auxiliary verbs: *women know the offside rule → she knows the offside rule*. The inflection on the verb is proof of the indicative mood.

Recognizing the imperative mood is somewhat more challenging because we have lost the inflectional markers of this mood. Most frequently, neither the Subject nor the Finite is expressed. However, as argued above, imperative clauses are finite and therefore there must be a Finite element which can be recovered. Some would argue that the imperative is marked by a null affix. As concerns the Subject, Halliday (2002: 190) explains that 'it is present in all clauses of all moods, but its significance can perhaps be seen most clearly in the imperative (because) the speaker is requiring some action on the part of the person addressed'. Clearly, then, imperative clauses have both a Finite and Subject element even though they may not be immediately obvious. This information must be used in order to deduce their presence.

To illustrate how imperative clauses can be identified, the imperative clause analysed above, *Place the mask over your mouth and nose*, will be used as an example. The basis for the criteria for imperative clauses is simply to check the effects of adding an overt Subject and Finite element and comparing this with the resultant structures in both positive and negative polarity. What we will find is that the effect of negative polarity contrasts imperative mood with indicative mood in English.

Test for recognizing imperative mood:

    Example: *Place the mask over your mouth and nose*

1. Re-express the clause in negative polarity:

    Don't place the mask over your mouth and nose

2. Add an overt expression of the Subject:

    (positive) You place the mask over your mouth and nose

    (negative) Don't you place the mask over your mouth and nose

3. Compare with indicative mood equivalents:

    (declarative, positive) *You place the mask over your mouth and nose*

    (declarative, negative) *You don't place the mask over your mouth and nose*

    (interrogative, positive) *Do you place the mask over your mouth and nose?*

    (interrogative, negative) *Don't you place the mask over your mouth and nose?*

    Result: the imperative mood inverts Subject and Finite to express negative polarity, whereas indicative mood does not and only inverts Subject and Finite to mark declarative and interrogative mood.

There is one further type of mood that has almost completely disappeared from Modern English and this is the subjunctive mood. It is not included in the main mood selections since its use has become fossilized and occurs relatively rarely. For example, the use of *were* in *if I were you, I would quit*, expresses past subjunctive mood rather than indicative mood, and future subjunctive in *if I were to go, I wouldn't know what to say*. These forms are not so problematic and generally they are considered in analysis to belong to indicative mood. The present subjunctive mood, however, can pose some challenges in analysis since the finite nature of these clauses is difficult to see, as in, for example, the use of *be* in the following examples: *they demanded that he be present* and *so be it* (a highly fossilized form).

The significance of understanding the mood of the clause will be made clear in Chapter 6 when the clause is viewed from the textual metafunction. However, recognizing mood makes it easier to analyse the clause because each mood has set patterns of verb behaviour. As has been shown, verbs 'behave' differently in different moods, whether it is in terms of the order and expression of the Finite verbal element with respect to the rest of the clause or in terms of the ways in which verbs can combine.

5.9 SUMMARY

This chapter has covered the main elements of interpersonal meaning as they are expressed within the clause. It has only scratched the surface, as the interpersonal meta-function extends beyond the clause to the social realm, where language is situated within its social context. Section 5.11 includes suggested reading for exploring speech functions and interaction in relation to the mood system. The goal of this chapter was to demonstrate how the main functional elements of interpersonal meaning can be identified in analysing English grammar. The focus on both function and structural expression has provided a solid basis from which to analyse the interpersonal meanings found within the clause.

This chapter has also presented criteria for recognizing the more challenging areas of the grammar such as Subject, Finite and imperative mood. In doing so, the guidelines for analysing the clause have been further developed, such that a full analysis of both experiential and interpersonal meaning can now be done consistently.

5.10 EXERCISES

Exercise 5.1

For each clause listed below, identify the Subject, Finite and Mood of the clause. You should also identify any modality expressed including the type of modality. These clauses were taken from the Air Canada report on cabin safety briefings (Barkow and Rutenberg, 2002). The verb groups have been underlined.

1. In the event of an emergency over water, you must put on your life jacket
2. The life jacket is located in a bag under your seat
3. You will find a belt at your side
4. On the chest, there are two pull-tabs
5. These lights will guide you to the exits during an emergency
6. The location of the nearest emergency exit should be known
7. Do you know the location of the nearest emergency exit?

Exercise 5.2

For each clause listed below, identify the Subject, Finite and Mood of the clause. You should also identify any modality expressed, including the type of modality. These clauses were taken from a speech by Ronald Reagan during his televised campaign address 'A Vital Economy: Jobs, Growth, and Progress for Americans', on 24 October 1980 (www.reagan. utexas.edu/archives/reference/10.24.80.html).

1. The President says my proposed reduction of tax rates would be inflationary
2. Well, let me ask him a simple question in economics
3. Why is it inflationary
4. if you keep more of your earnings
5. and spend them the way you want to
6. but it isn't inflationary
7. if he takes them
8. and spends them the way he wants to?
9. The fact is this program will give us a balanced budget by 1983, and possibly by 1982
10. We also need faster, less complex depreciation schedules for business

11. Outdated depreciation schedules now prevent many industries from modernizing their plants

12. Faster depreciation would allow these companies to generate more capital internally, permitting them to make the investment necessary to create new jobs, to help workers become more productive, and to become more competitive in world markets

13. Another vital part of this strategy concerns government regulations which work against rather than for the interests of the people

14. No one argues with the intent of regulations dealing with health, safety, and clean air and water

15. But we must carefully re-examine our regulatory structure to assess to what degree regulations have cost jobs and economic growth

16. There should and will be a thorough and systematic review of the thousands of federal regulations that affect the economy

5.11 FURTHER READING

On time reference:

Bache, C. 1995. *The Study of Aspect, Tense and Action: Toward a Theory of the Semantics of Grammatical Categories*. New York: Peter Lang.

Halliday, M. A. K. 1973. *Explorations in the Functions of Language*. London: Edward Arnold.

Halliday, M. A. K. and C. Matthiessen. 2004. *An Introduction to Functional Grammar*. 3rd edn. London: Hodder Arnold.

On grammatical metaphor and metaphors of modality:

Eggins, S. 2004. *An Introduction to Systemic Functional Linguistics*. 2nd edn. London: Continuum.

Halliday, M. A. K. and C. Matthiessen. 2004. *An Introduction to Functional Grammar*. 3rd edn. London: Hodder Arnold.

Simon-Vandenbergen, A.-M., M. Taverniers and L. Ravelli, eds. 2003. *Grammatical Metaphor: Views from Systemic Functional Linguistics*. Amsterdam: John Benjamins.

On the verb group and verbal elements of the clause:

Fawcett, R. 2000a. 'In place of Halliday's "verbal group", part 1: evidence from the problems of Halliday's representations and the relative simplicity of the proposed alternative', *Word* 51.2: 157–203.

Fawcett, R. 2000b. 'In place of Halliday's "verbal group", Part 2: Evidence from generation, semantics and interruptability', *Word* 51.3: 327–75.

Morley, D. G. 2004. *Explorations in Functional Syntax: A New Framework for Lexicogrammatical Analysis*. London: Equinox.

On mood as exchange (speech functions of the clause):

Eggins, S. 2004. *An Introduction to Systemic Functional Linguistics*. 2nd edn. London: Continuum.

Halliday, M. A. K. and C. Matthiessen. 2004. *An Introduction to Functional Grammar*. 3rd edn. London: Hodder Arnold.

On appraisal:

Hunston, S. and G. Thompson, eds. 1999. *Evaluation in Text: Authorial Stance and the Construction of Discourse*. Oxford University Press.

Thompson, G. 2004. *Introducing Functional Grammar*. 2nd edn. London: Arnold.

Chapter 6: Organizing language

6.1 INTRODUCTION

There is no more basic role for the clause than that of creating text. Every clause is either constitutive of a text or part of a larger text. Focusing on the clause in isolation, as has been the case for the previous two chapters, has its advantages since it allows the analyst to focus on the meanings that this unit is able to express. The textual metafunction is different, in many respects, from the other two metafunctions in that its meaning spans across clause boundaries and is fundamental in the creation of text. Whereas the experiential metafunction allows the speaker to represent his or her experience and the interpersonal metafunction enables interaction, as Halliday (1994: xiii) explains, the textual metafunction 'breathes relevance into the other two'. In focusing on textual meaning, this chapter marks a shift towards text but it does so nevertheless from the perspective of the clause.

6.1.1 Goals and outline of the chapter

This chapter introduces the textual metafunction and the main elements of the clause that express textual meaning. Within the clause, the main resource for creating text is referred to as Theme, as will be discussed below. Therefore, the goal here is to show how to recognize Theme in a variety of different clauses and to understand how it contributes to the creation of text. Theme will be discussed in terms of its function and its relation to the other two main strands of meaning.

In addition to Theme, other textual resources relating Theme and text will be presented such as thematic progression, cohesive reference and ellipsis. Throughout the chapter, various texts and examples will be used to illustrate the textual metafunction as viewed from the clause.

This chapter is limited to an introductory presentation of textual meaning and, as such, there is insufficient space to explore the sometimes thorny issues that surround Theme and what it means for an element of the clause to be Theme. Suggested readings around this topic are given in the section on further reading, which will offer a useful starting point for those wanting more detail.

6.2 A TEXTUAL VIEW OF THE CLAUSE

The textual metafunction is the strand of meaning which is most inherently associated to the concept of text. Textual meaning considers the clause as message, and its main function is that of creating text (Halliday, 1978: 48). But what is text? How can we recognize it? It is tempting to say simply that you will know one when you see one, but that's not very satisfying. Text is very difficult to define because it does not have identifiable boundaries, in contrast to a word or a morpheme, or even a larger structural unit such as the nominal group. Texts vary in length and in structure. For example, an email can be thought of as a text but so can a university lecture or a conversation or a book.

The etymology of 'text'[1] offers a helpful metaphor for understanding the meaning of text as it will be used in this chapter. The word came into the English language from the Old French 'texte', which was derived from the Latin nominal form 'textus', which meant literally 'that which is woven'. 'Textus' itself originated from the Latin verb stem 'texere', meaning 'to weave'. With this metaphor, speakers are language weavers and, as part of the language system, they have available to them a variety of resources for weaving their texts. This chapter will focus on some of the main resources available to speakers for creating text.

In their seminal work on cohesion in English, Halliday and Hasan (1976: 2) use the notion of texture to define text: 'a text has texture, and this is what distinguishes it from something that is not a text. It derives this texture from the fact that it functions as a unity with respect to its environment.' In this view, there should be identifiable metaphorical threads that hold the text together; these are cohesive devices in Halliday and Hasan's terms.

6.2.1 On Theme

Irrespective of the experience represented in the clause or the interactive intentions it expresses, the speaker ultimately has to order what he or she is going to say; something has to be said first and whatever is left to be said has to follow in a particular order. This was seen in the invented examples given in Chapter 1, which are repeated below in (1) to (3) for ease of reference.

(1) Kev gave me the new Jamie Oliver recipe book for my birthday
(2) I was given the new Jamie book for my birthday
(3) For my birthday, Kev gave me the new Jamie book

The content and mood in each case is very similar; they express approximately the same experience and with a similar amount of modality. What is most significantly different in each case is how each clause begins. In (1), the Actor/Subject element is first, whereas in (2) it is the Beneficiary/Subject. In clause (3), a circumstance/adjunct begins the clause. These examples have no context since they were invented simply to illustrate a point. However, we would expect to find that in a naturally occurring text the thematic elements of the clause would be motivated by the speaker's method of weaving the text and the relevance that he or she intends to convey. In other words, close examination of the text and context should normally reveal the role Theme has in creating text for the speaker.

In English, the initial position of the clause is significant for a variety of reasons. For example, it often introduces the topic about which something is being said, it may indicate the relevance of the clause to the surrounding text, it may orient the message in a particular way, or it may mark a transition in the text. This is not to say that the thematic elements of the clause are more important than the rest of the clause but rather that they contribute directly and in a pivotal sense to the creation of text.

Within the textual metafunction, the clause is considered to have two main functional elements: Theme and Rheme. Theme is defined by Halliday and Matthiessen (2004: 64) as 'the point of departure of the message ... that which locates and orients the clause within its context'. Within the clause, Theme indicates the clausal element that the speaker has selected as the starting point; a metaphoric peg on which to hang the message. The Rheme of the clause (all that is not Theme) constitutes the message. The relevance of Theme becomes significant when it is viewed within the larger context of the text and not only from the perspective of the clause, which is the view presented in section 6.6.

In comparison with the other two metafunctions, we have seen that the clause most frequently begins with a participant in experiential meaning and with Subject in interpersonal meaning. Therefore Theme will most often conflate with the participant/Subject element of the clause, as illustrated in examples (1) and (2) above. When this is the case, there is a core concentration of meaning in the clause when the functions of participant, Subject and Theme align on the same structural unit. This is not always the case, as will be discussed in the next section.

6.2.2 Thematic status

It is generally accepted that Theme is selected from the speaker's perspective (i.e. what is relevant to the speaker). As stated above, the Theme element is most commonly conflated with the Subject of the clause and is expressed by a unit that will also have a participant role in the experiential strand of meaning. When this happens, the Theme is said to be unmarked because this is the expected or default case. Theme is said to be marked when it is not the Subject of the clause (i.e. a circumstance), as is the case in example (3) above. There are differences in what constitutes an unmarked Theme selection amongst the different mood types, as will be shown in section 6.3.

In order to illustrate the various ways in which Theme can be expressed, two texts from earlier in the book will be compared in terms of Theme. The first text, from Chapter 1, is a short personal email and the second, from Chapter 4, is an excerpt from the Air Canada safety report. The main significant difference between the two texts is that in the first text the Theme in each clause is conflated with the Subject of the clause and in the second text this only happens in one clause.

Text 6.1 Personal email
We'll be going to Scotland from March 30 to April 2nd. We'll go to London April 14th. It's a nice day here too. John has taken Tom to the dentist for a check-up, we'll see if he agrees to open his mouth!!

Text 6.2 Audio and caption script for high altitude emergencies for the general public
In a high altitude emergency, an oxygen mask will drop in front of you from the panel above. Place the mask over your mouth and nose, straighten out the strap, and pull the strap to be sure it is tight on your face. After you are wearing it securely, a tug on the hose will start the oxygen flow. It makes sense to put your own mask on first, before helping others.

The Themes in Text 6.1, given in Table 6.1, are expressed by personal pronouns except in clause (7) where it is expressed by a personal name. In each of these clauses the Theme is conflated with the Subject of the clause, as shown in Table 6.1. In contrast, the Themes in Text 6.2 vary considerably in terms of the unit which serves to express this meaning. Unlike Text 6.1, the Themes are not conflated with Subject except for clause (14) as shown in Table 6.2.

In clauses (9) and (13) the Subject of each clause is expressed but it is not the initial element of the clause since there is a circumstantial adjunct before the

Table 6.1: List of Themes for Text 6.1

	Theme	Rheme
(4)	We	'll be going to Scotland from March 30 to April 2nd.
(5)	We	'll go to London April 14th.
(6)	It	's a nice day here too.
(7)	John	has taken Tom to the dentist for a check-up,
(8)	we	'll see if he agrees to open his mouth!!

Table 6.2: List of Themes for Text 6.2

	Theme	Rheme
(9)	In a high altitude emergency,	an oxygen mask will drop in front of you from the panel above.
(10)	Place	the mask over your mouth and nose,
(11)	straighten out	the strap,
(12)	and pull	the strap to be sure it is tight on your face.
(13)	After you are wearing it securely,	a tug on the hose will start the oxygen flow.
(14)	It	makes sense to put your own mask on first, before helping others.

Subject. In these clauses, the Theme is marked. The Themes for clauses (10), (11), and (12) will be discussed in section 6.3, which considers the relationship between Theme and Mood.

The brief analysis of Theme in these two texts illustrates that texts may differ considerably in terms of the ways in which Theme is expressed. More detail about Theme will be given in section 6.4, where the three types of Theme will be explained. Following this, section 6.5 introduces several special thematic constructions which affect the textual meaning of the clause.

6.3 THEME AND MOOD

Theme is identified by default as the first functional element of the clause (e.g. Subject) and any other items which may occur before it. However, as shown in Chapter 5, the organization of the clause is different for different mood types. The nature of how mood is expressed in English relies not only on the presence of Subject and Finite elements but in how they are organized. Consequently, what can normally appear first in a clause is determined by the mood structure of the clause. This is illustrated in the invented examples (15) to (17), where the same clause is re-expressed in each mood type.

(15) **Kev** gave me the new Jamie Oliver recipe book for my birthday

(16) Did **Kev** give me the new Jamie book for my birthday?

(17) (you) **Give** me the new Jamie book!

Table 6.3: Clause listing for Text 6.3

Clause	Mood
(18) I sent Steven a little note and some pages from the Christmas catalogue,	Declarative
(19) but don't tell him	Imperative
(20) as he'll be looking for it every day	Declarative
(21) and I don't know how long it will take.	Declarative
(22) It's just a letter.	Declarative
(23) By the way did you ever pay that dollar to the post office?	Interrogative
(24) Do you want me to send that Insurance letter to you?	Interrogative
(25) Have you heard from Suzanne?	Interrogative
(26) Roger and Joce are gone to Marathon.	Declarative

As these three clauses show, the expected onset of the clause is largely determined by mood due to the relationship between Subject and Finite. However, this has implications for the thematic structure of the clause.

In order to consider Theme in each of the three main mood types, a short text will be examined. Text 6.3 is an excerpt from a personal email and it includes all three mood types. The clause list from this text is given in Table 6.3.

Text 6.3 Excerpt from a personal email (1999)
I sent Steven a little note and some pages from the Christmas catalogue, but don't tell him as he'll be looking for it every day and I don't know how long it will take. It's just a letter. By the way did you ever pay that dollar to the post office? Do you want me to send that Insurance letter to you? Have you heard from Suzanne? Roger and Joce are gone to Marathon.

As Table 6.3 shows, most of the clauses in Text 6.3 are expressed in declarative mood but there are also several interrogative clauses and one imperative clause. The analysis of textual meaning, as it is presented here, is based on an understanding of both experiential and interpersonal meaning. This means that, from the analyst's perspective, knowing the mood and the transitivity analysis is key to understanding textual meaning. The clauses from this text will be grouped by mood type and then discussed in terms of Theme in the next three sections.

In this section, the analyses of the clauses will be presented using box diagrams (see Chapter 1) rather than tree diagrams. This is for two reasons. The first is that the box diagrams tend to show the alignment of the various strands of meaning quite clearly. The second is that they are much easier to present since tree diagrams can take up time and space. However, the box diagrams are less informative than the tree diagrams in many respects and specifically the ease of readability is at the cost of detail in the analysis. Ideally

(18)	**I**	sent	Steven	a little note and some pages from the Christmas catalogue
Experiential	**Actor**	Pr: material	Beneficiary	Goal
Interpersonal	**Subject**	Finite/Predicator	Complement	Complement
Textual	**Theme**	Rheme		

(20)	**as**	**he**	'll	be looking	for it	every day
Experiential		**Actor**	Pr: material		Goal	Extent
Interpersonal		**Subject**	Finite	Predicator	Complement	Adjunct
Textual		**Theme**	Rheme			

(21)	**and**	**I**	don't	know	how long it will take
Experiential		**Senser**	Pr: mental		Phenomenon
Interpersonal		**Subject**	Finite	Predicator	Complement
Textual		**Theme**	Rheme		

Figure 6.1 Three-strand analysis of the declarative clauses from Text 6.3

the analysis would be presented using both tree diagrams and box diagrams, as will be shown in section 6.6 below.

6.3.1 Declarative mood

Declarative mood is perhaps the most common mood structure. As shown in Figure 6.1, these clauses often begin with the Subject but in some cases an adjunct of one type or another will begin the clause. Although there are some adjuncts in this text, they do not occur at the onset of the clause. However, it is clear from the tables of analysis given below that there are some thematic items which occur before the Subject and these will be explained in section 6.4. For now, they will simply be labelled as Theme along with the Subject.

6.3.2 Interrogative mood

The interrogative mood is primarily recognized by the inverted organization of the Subject and Finite elements, as was shown in Chapter 5. Consequently, the Finite

(22)	**It**	's	just	a letter
Experiential	**Carrier**	Pr: relational		Attribute
Interpersonal	**Subject**	Finite/Predicator	Adjunct (modal)	Complement
Textual	**Theme**	Rheme		

(26)	**Roger and Joce**	are	gone	to Marathon
Experiential	**Actor**	Pr: material		Location
Interpersonal	**Subject**	Finite	Predicator	Adjunct
Textual	**Theme**	Rheme		

Figure 6.1 (cont.)

element will always precede the Subject in clauses expressing interrogative mood. This means that the Finite element will have thematic value in these clauses and be considered part of Theme. Examples of Theme in interrogative mood are given in examples (23) to (25) (see Figure 6.2). In these cases Theme includes everything from the beginning of the clause up to and including the Subject. The Theme is unmarked in each of these examples since there is no preceding experiential element. More detail about the various elements within Theme and the different types of Theme will be given in section 6.4.

Not all interrogatives begin with a Finite element. The interrogative mood system, as shown in Chapter 5, has two main options: wh- interrogative and yes/no interrogative. Within the textual metafunction, there is a significant difference between these two in terms of what appears in Theme position. As shown above, the Finite element is always thematized in unmarked Theme. However, since it does not express any experiential function, it is not considered to have the full meaning of Theme in the sense of textual relevance. It is in initial position because it has to be, as it is governed by the interrogative mood of the clause. In contrast, wh- interrogatives do express an experiential function and consequently it is generally the interrogative pronoun (or wh-word), and not the Finite element, which is Theme in the unmarked case for these clauses.

In order to see how Theme works in wh- interrogative clauses, the invented examples in Figure 6.3 have been analysed for all three metafunctions. This allows us to see precisely why the wh- interrogative pronoun expresses the function of Theme and the Finite element in these cases is part of the Rheme.

(23)	**By the way**	**did**	**you**	ever	pay	that dollar	to the post office?
Experiential			**Actor**		Pr: material	Goal	Beneficiary
Interpersonal	**Adjunct**	**Finite**	**Subject**	Adjunct (modal)	Predicator	Complement	Complement
Textual	**Theme**				Rheme		

(24)	**Do**	**you**	want	me to send that Insurance letter to you?
Experiential		**Sensor**	Pr: mental	Phenomenon
Interpersonal	**Finite**	**Subject**	Predicator	Complement
Textual	**Theme**		Rheme	

(25)	**Have**	**you**	heard	from Suzanne?
Experiential		**Receiver**	Pr: verbal	Sayer
Interpersonal	**Finite**	**Subject**	Predicator	Complement
Textual	**Theme**		Rheme	

Figure 6.2 Three-strand analysis of the interrogative clauses from Text 6.3

It is important to note that if the wh- word is part of a particular structural unit then the entire unit becomes Theme. For example, in *how well do you know her?*, the entire unit *how well* would express Theme and not simply *how*.

6.3.3 Imperative mood

In Chapter 5, imperative clauses were discussed in detail and the status of the Finite and Subject were explained as being significant elements of these clauses even though they are rarely expressed. It was noted that the Finite is always made explicit when the clause also expresses negative polarity, as is the case for clause (19), in Figure 6.4. The most common and unmarked structure for the imperative clause is for the Subject and Finite to be covert or unexpressed (although always recoverable) and for the clause to begin with the process (or event in interpersonal terms). This

(27)	**What**	did	you	eat
Experiential	**Goal**		Actor	Pr: material
Interpersonal	**Complement**	Finite	Subject	Predicator
Textual	**Theme**	Rheme		

(28)	**Who**	is	happy
Experiential	**Carrier**	Sensor	Attribute
Interpersonal	**Subject**	Finite/Predicator	Complement
Textual	**Theme**	Rheme	

(29)	**How**	can	you	eat	that cake
Experiential	**Circ: Manner**		Actor	Pr: material	Goal
Interpersonal	**Adjunct**	Finite	Subject	Predicator	Complement
Textual	**Theme**	Rheme			

Figure 6.3 Three-strand analysis of invented interrogative examples

means that as these types of clauses are analysed it is important to remember that the Subject and Finite are understood as being present. If tree diagrams were being used to illustrate the analysis of the clause, then these elements would be included (see Chapter 5). With the box diagrams used here, it can cause some clutter to the tables if items which are not expressed are represented, but this is up to each individual's preferences.

In Text 6.2 above, several of the clauses are in imperative mood, where the Theme is expressed by a verb (examples (10) to (12), which are repeated in Figure 6.5). Since Subject is rarely expressed in imperative clauses, it does not provide a regular option for beginning the clause. These clauses typically begin with the event unless the Finite element is overtly expressed (e.g. to express negative polarity). Note that for all finite clauses, including imperative clauses, the Finite should always be labelled in the analysis even if it is not explicitly expressed since it has such a significant role in determining mood.

6.4 TYPES OF THEME

It may have been noted that in several of the clauses presented above, Theme included some parts of the clause before the Subject. These are thematic elements in the sense

(19)	but	don't	tell	him
Experiential			**Pr: verbal**	Receiver
Interpersonal		**Finite**	**Predicator**	Complement
Textual	**Theme**			Rheme

Figure 6.4 Three-strand analysis for imperative clause from Text 6.3

(10)	(you)		**place**	the mask	over your mouth and nose
Experiential	(Actor)		**Pr: material**	Goal	Location
Interpersonal	(Subject)	(Finite)	**Predicator**	Complement	Adjunct
Textual	**Theme**			Rheme	

(11)	(you)		**straighten out**	the strap
Experiential	(Actor)		**Pr: material**	Goal
Interpersonal	(Subject)	(Finite)	**Predicator**	Complement
Textual	**Theme**			Rheme

(12)	and	(you)		**pull**	the strap	to be sure it is tight on your face
Experiential		(Actor)		**Pr: material**	Goal	Cause
Interpersonal		(Subject)	(Finite)	**Predicator**	Complement	Adjunct
Textual		**Theme**			Rheme	

Figure 6.5 Three-strand analysis for clauses (10) to (12)

that they are the way in which the clause begins and they have a textual function. Just as the clause has three types of meaning, there are three types of Theme. The main Theme element is referred to as the experiential Theme since it is generally the Theme carrying the initial experiential content and will often conflate with the Subject of the clause. In addition to this core thematic element, there are two extra and optional types of Theme: interpersonal Theme and textual Theme. Each of these three types is explained in the following sections.

A sample of the analysis of textual meaning within the clause will be given in section 6.6, where examples of these three types of Theme will be illustrated.

6.4.1 Experiential Theme

Experiential Theme, also referred to as topical Theme by some authors, is considered the core element of the textual metafunction in the sense that it is the only required element. It is referred to as experiential Theme because Theme generally corresponds to the first clausal element expressing experiential meaning. In the vast majority of cases, this will correspond to the first participant in the clause. As was discussed in section 6.3.3, when a clause expresses imperative mood, the first experiential element is most likely to be the process rather than a participant. Finally, some clauses begin with a circumstance, as shown in Table 6.2 above. In these cases then the experiential Theme conflates with a circumstance and is considered marked.

Some textbooks will refer to the core Theme element as topical Theme (see for example, Halliday and Matthiessen, 2004 and Bloor and Bloor, 2004). As Thompson (2004:159) argues, this terminology can introduce some problems because of the use of the term 'topic' in other types of analyses. Furthermore, it seems that 'topic' may inadvertently introduce meanings that are not intended by the meaning of Theme.

Identifying what is the Theme in a clause can become difficult when certain constructions are used. This will be discussed in section 6.5, where certain special constructions are considered in terms of Theme analysis.

The textual metafunction is in some ways more complex than the other strands of meaning because it extends beyond the clause. As a consequence, the view of Theme has to take multiple perspectives at once (for example, textual meaning within the clause and textual meaning within the text). Suggested readings on Theme and textual meaning will be given in section 6.10 for readers who are interested in more than an introductory discussion of the textual strand of meaning, as is presented here.

6.4.2 Textual Theme

Textual Themes are elements of the clause which do not have any other function than to express textual meaning. They do not express any experiential or interpersonal functions. They tend to have an explicit relevance function and serve to indicate the relevance of the clause to neighbouring clauses within the text. In traditional terms, textual Themes are expressed by conjunctions (e.g. *but*, *and*, *or*) or continuatives (e.g. *well*, *so*).

As an illustration of the importance of these themes, the text given in Figure 6.6 will be analysed in terms of the textual metafunction. The original writing has been reproduced in Text 6.4 for ease of reading. This text is a homework sample from a ten-year-old boy. The goal of the worksheet was to have students use connectives to 'improve' their writing. The 'connectives' referred to in this assignment are functionally textual Themes.

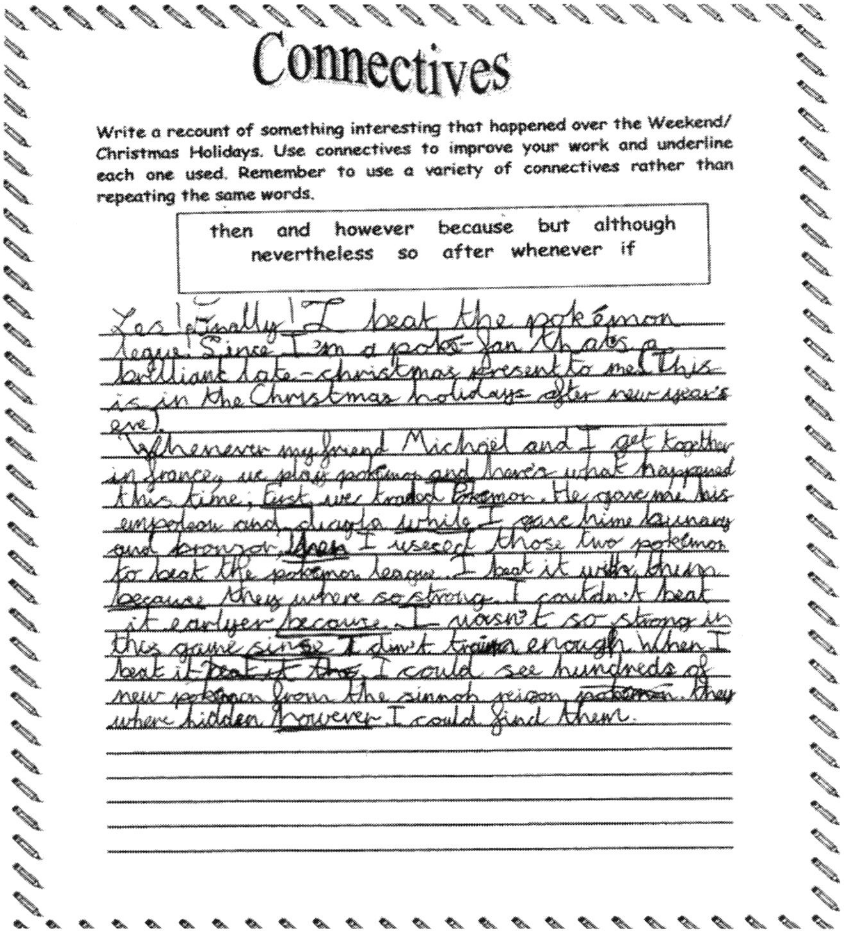

Figure 6.6 Written class work on connectives, ten-year-old boy, January 2008

Text 6.4 Written text on 'connectives' from Figure 6.6

Yes! Finally! I beat the pokémon league! Since I'm a poké-fan that's a brilliant late-Christmas present to me. (This is in the Christmas holidays after New Year's Eve.) Whenever my friend Michaël and I get together in France, we play Pokémon and here's what happened this time. First we traded Pokémon. He gave me his Empoleon and Diagla while I gave him Bunary and Bronzor. Then I used those two Pokémon to beat the Pokémon league. I beat it with them because they were so strong. I couldn't beat it earlier because I wasn't so strong in this game since I didn't train enough. When I beat it, I could see hundreds of new Pokémon from the Sinnoh region. They were hidden however I could find them.

Table 6.4: Theme analysis for Text 6.4 on 'connectives'

| | Theme | | |
	Textual Theme	Experiential Theme	Rheme
(30)		I	beat the pokémon league!
(31)	*Since*	I	'm a poké-fan
(32)		that	's a brilliant late-Christmas present to me.
(33)		(This	is in the Christmas holidays after New Year's Eve.)
(34)	*Whenever*	my friend Michaël and I	get together in France,
(35)		we	play Pokémon
(36)	*and*	here	's what happened this time.
(37)	*First*	we	traded Pokémon.
(38)		He	gave me his Empoleon and Diagla
(39)	*while*	I	gave him Bunary and Bronzor.
(40)	*Then*	I	used those two Pokémon to beat the Pokémon league.
(41)		I	beat it with them
(42)	*because*	they	were so strong.
(43)		I	couldn't beat it earlier
(44)	*because*	I	wasn't so strong in this game
(45)	*since*	I	didn't train enough.
(46)		**When I beat it**,	I could see hundreds of new Pokémon from the Sinnoh region.
(47)		They	were hidden
(48)	*however*	I	could find them.

The analysis for Text 6.4 is given in Table 6.4, where the text is listed clause by clause. The textual Themes are given in italics and any marked Themes (e.g. a circumstance in initial position) are indicated in bold. The analysis shows that the student has used a variety of textual Themes and although some may seem slightly awkward (e.g. clause (48) use of *however*), they are used to orient the organization of the clauses within the text and to show relevance with neighbouring clauses. In some cases, as for example in clauses (32) and (36), the experiential Theme is also expressing the meaning of a textual Theme (*that* and *here*). This is because these items are deictic and inherently serve a pronoun function simultaneously with a relevance function.

Before moving on to consider interpersonal Themes, there is one issue concerning the distinction between experiential Themes and textual Themes that should be addressed. If we compare clauses (40) and (46), it may not be immediately clear why clause (46) is considered to have a marked Theme but clause (40) is not. This reflects the difficulty at times in determining whether an element has an experiential circumstance role or whether it is functioning only textually to indicate organization and/or relevance.

Table 6.5: Textual analysis for Text 6.5

	Theme			
	Textual Theme	Interpersonal Theme	Experiential Theme	Rheme
(49)			He	might be someone she could do something with once in awhile,
(50)	of course	maybe	she	wouldn't want to.
(51)		Is	he	still working at that plant?
(52)			Jack	took your address
(53)	so		he	'll likely be emailing you,
(54)			I	tried to send it to him
(55)	but		there	's still something wrong.
(56)	Well	guess	I	'll go
(57)	and		(I)	(will) put my washing on the line.

In Text 6.4, the use of *then* in clause (40) has the function of orienting the clause with respect to the neighbouring clause (e.g. *first, while, then*) rather than functioning as a Location circumstance which indicates when in time the process took place. In this example, *then* could have been replaced with *next*, which indicates its sequencing function (and therefore a textual Theme). However, in clause (46), *When I beat it* is indicating a point in time, a location at which point the process took place. This could be replaced by a specific date and time when the 'seeing' took place; e.g. *On Saturday 29 December 2007, I could see hundreds of new Pokémon from the Sinnoh region*. In terms of experiential meaning, *when I beat it* has the function of a Location circumstance and therefore is a marked experiential Theme.

6.4.3 Interpersonal Theme

The third type of Theme considered here is the interpersonal Theme. This includes any element of the clause that has an interpersonal function and is in a thematic role. These elements will generally be expressed by various modal adjuncts (e.g. *maybe, certainly*), auxiliary verbs (e.g. *can, do*), interrogative pronouns (e.g. *who, how*, see Chapter 2) or vocatives (e.g. *Lise, Tom*). As was noted in section 6.3.2, interrogative clauses thematize the Finite element. However, all interpersonal elements occurring before the experiential Theme will have the function of interpersonal Theme.

In order to illustrate how interpersonal Themes can work in a text, the excerpt given in Text 6.5 is examined in terms of textual meaning. The context for this is an email from a mother to her adult daughter, which approximates casual conversation. The analysis of textual meaning is given in Table 6.5.

Text 6.5 Excerpt from a personal email, in original orthography (1999)
He might be someone she could do something with once in awhile, of course maybe she wouldn't want to. Is he still working at that plant? Jack took your address so he'll likely be emailing you, I tried to send it to him but there's still something wrong. Well guess I'll go and put my washing on the line.

As the analysis above shows, many of the clauses include textual Themes, which were discussed in the previous section. The interpersonal Themes, as in clauses (50), (51) and (56) in Table 6.5, express interpersonal meaning (i.e. modality and mood). The full analysis of these clauses would show that *maybe* in clause (50) expresses simultaneously a modal adjunct and an interpersonal Theme. In clause (51), *is* expresses the Finite element and interpersonal Theme. Clause (56) is different in terms of the structural unit expressing the modal adjunct and interpersonal Theme since it is a reduction of *I guess* and serves a similar meaning to *maybe* or *perhaps* in this clause.

The identification of interpersonal Theme is based on an understanding of the interpersonal metafunction. Any interpersonal element of the clause which appears before the Subject will also have a thematic function and, therefore, in the analysis of the clause these elements will have a textual role as interpersonal Theme. Consequently, interpersonal Themes will always have two simultaneous functions in each of interpersonal meaning and textual meaning, whereas textual Themes have only a textual function. As stated earlier, experiential Themes will often express meaning from all three strands of meaning at the same time.

One final observation to be made from Table 6.5 is the unexpressed or covert experiential Theme in clause (57). In this clause, the Theme has been ellipsed and is recoverable from the preceding clause. Ellipsis will be discussed in more detail in section 6.7.2.2 below.

Having now considered the three types of Theme, the next section takes a look at some particular grammatical structures which challenge our understanding of Theme. Following this brief presentation, section 6.6 provides step-by-step guidelines for a full three-strand analysis of the clause since this chapter completes the view of the three main metafunctions.

6.5 THEMATIC CONSTRUCTIONS

This section considers certain grammatical constructions which can cause some difficulty when analysing Theme. The criteria for identifying experiential Theme developed here state that the experiential Theme will be the first experiential element of the clause up to and including the Subject. Therefore, if there are no other experiential elements before the Subject, then the participant/Subject will also express the Theme. In cases where a circumstance occurs before the Subject of the clause, Theme is conflated with the circumstance rather than the participant and Theme is said to be marked. However, we have already seen one exception to this and this concerns clauses in the imperative mood. These clauses typically begin with the process, which is seen as experiential Theme since it is the first expressed experiential element of the clause.

The constructions that will be discussed in this section are being referred to as thematic constructions because they enhance Theme in some way. It should be noted that there are varied views about what should be considered Theme in these cases but the keen reader will find references to more detailed discussions of this topic in section 6.10. The examples cited in this section have all been taken from L. Frank Baum's *The Wonderful Wizard of Oz*.[2]

6.5.1 Existential Theme

The difficulty with existential clauses is that the Subject, *there*, has no experiential function. Consequently the first experiential element of the clause is the existential process, *be*, but it could not possibly be considered as experiential Theme as it does not fit with the

153

function of Theme. It does not begin the clause nor does it have any relevance function. If Theme is taken to be the first core element of the clause, where core is intended to mean obligatory element, then it becomes easier to see that the Subject of existential clauses may also express Theme when it is the first core functional element of the clause, as is most commonly the case.

The potential for beginning a clause with a circumstantial element is present for all clause types and, as already explained, in these cases Theme is considered marked. This distinction is shown in examples (58) and (59), where the experiential Theme is underlined. In example (58), Theme is unmarked as it conflates with Subject but note that it has no experiential meaning. Theme in example (59) is marked since it conflates with a fronted circumstance.

(58) <u>There</u> is no place like home
(59) <u>At the East</u>, not far from here, there is a great desert

6.5.2 Extraposed participant

The structures being grouped under this heading include those known traditionally as cleft-constructions, predicated theme constructions and other structures where a participant is postponed later in the clause. There are differences among the various types but they all have *it* as Subject. The *it* Subject is coreferential with a participant which has been displaced or extraposed to the Rheme of the clause. Examples of this type of construction are given in (60) and (61), where the extraposed participant is underlined. The *it* in these cases is said to be anticipatory because its referent anticipates the extraposed participant.

(60) It was a bit of good luck <u>to have their new comrade join the party</u>
(61) It was a great mistake <u>my ever letting you into the Throne Room</u>

The Theme in these cases is considered to be the anticipatory *it*, which parallels the treatment of Theme in existential clauses. Unlike existential clauses, however, one could argue that *it* is not empty of experiential meaning as is *there*, but rather that it shares the same experiential function as its coreferential participant. That is to say that, for example, in clause (60), the *it* shares the role of Carrier with *to have their new comrade join the party*. In this way the *it* Subject/Theme causes some anticipation of the extraposed participant, which also has a thematic function because of the *it* Subject.

6.5.3 Preposed Theme

This construction is almost the inverse of the extraposed participant construction. It is a way of highlighting the Theme by announcing it before the clause. It also allows the speaker to direct the addressee's focus. The grammatical pattern is most frequently two adjacent nominal groups (or nominal-like units such as a prepositional phrase), where the first is fully lexical and the second is a personal pronoun. The important feature is that the pair of expressions is coreferential. Examples of this construction are given in (62) and (63), where the preposed Theme is underlined. It is important to note that these forms are not expressing a circumstance, and this can be shown by the fact that they cannot be displaced elsewhere in the clause. Furthermore, due to the coreferential nature of these expressions, they share the same experiential function as its pronominal counterpart.

(62) <u>As for the Lion</u>, he wiped his eyes so often with the tip of his tail that it became quite wet
(63) <u>As for the little old woman</u>, she took off her cap

There is one other similar construction which is referred to in Thompson (2004) and this is what he calls preposed attributives. They are similar to preposed Theme in the sense that a participant occurring later in the clause is preposed to have prominence, but the difference is that the preposed element itself is an attributive of the Subject. This is illustrated in example (64), which is taken from Thompson (2004: 163).

> (64) <u>Priced from under £200 to around £20,000</u>, our choice of rings is seemingly endless

6.6 ANALYSING THEME

So far in this chapter, we have not considered structure explicitly. This is largely because experiential Theme is conflated with an existing element of the clause and, consequently, the relevant structures have been covered in previous chapters (especially Chapters 4 and 5). As already stated earlier in this chapter, the clause has only two elements when viewed from the textual metafunction: Theme and Rheme. A basic view of this structure is given in Figure 6.7.

Since the view given in Figure 6.7 considers only one strand of meaning, it is not particularly useful when the goal is a multifunctional analysis of the clause, which must incorporate the functions from three strands of meaning. As discussed above, Theme will often conflate with the first participant/Subject in the clause; this is shown in Figure 6.8. However, Rheme does not conflate with any other single element of the clause; it is simply the rest of the clause that is not Theme. It can become quite difficult to label Rheme on a tree diagram and so this element is generally omitted from tree diagrams, as illustrated in Figure 6.9, which attempts to show how the various strands of meaning can be integrated in a tree diagram. Although this diagram uses a material clause for illustrative purposes, the same schema would work for any type of clause. However, different mood types have different configurations, and the diagram shown in Figure 6.9 is only representative of declarative clauses with unmarked

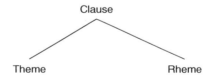

Figure 6.7 Basic clause structure for the textual metafunction

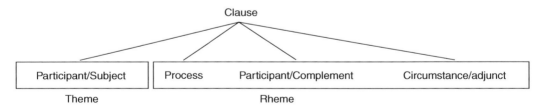

Figure 6.8 Three-strand representation of the clause

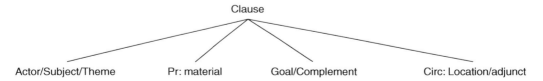

Figure 6.9 Integrated three-strand view of the clause

Theme. Examples of other configurations including different mood types and marked Theme are given below in the analysis of clauses from Text 6.6.

The remainder of this section will present the analysis of Theme by drawing on a text excerpt that was previously analysed in Chapters 4 and 5 (see Text 6.6 below, which was first presented in Chapter 4). First the guidelines for analysing the clause will be reviewed (compare this with Chapter 5) and then the new steps relevant to analysing Theme will be added. Finally the analysis of the text will be presented, which offers a full three-strand analysis of the clause in detail.

6.6.1 Towards a full three-strand multifunctional analysis

The guidelines presented here follow on from those listed in Chapter 5 with two additional steps added which relate to analysing textual meaning. Once these new steps are included, the guidelines will be nearly complete and they will be presented in full in Chapter 8. There is a very important precursor to these guidelines, which involves the guidelines for recognizing clause boundaries within a text, which will be detailed in Chapter 7. For now, as in previous chapters, the guidelines presented here assume that the clause boundaries have been correctly identified.

6.6.1.1 Guidelines for analysing experiential, interpersonal and textual meaning

Step 1: Identify the process and use the process test to show how many participants are expected by the process

> This step relies on the process test to identify the number of participants which are expected by the process.

Step 2: Use the replacement test and/or the movement test to identify the internal boundaries of the clause (different elements of the clause)

> This step relates to the analogy of finding the walls and rooms in the house, as was discussed in Chapter 2. Here the intermediate structural units of the clause are verified. See Chapter 3 for detail about nominal group boundaries.

Step 3: Determine the process type and participant roles

> This step involves working with the criteria and tests developed in Chapter 4 in order to determine the type of process and the particular participant expressed.

Step 4: Identify any circumstance roles

> This step considers any potential circumstances in the clause. The strategies given in Chapter 4 should help in working out the function of any circumstances. The questions associated to each type (see Table 2 in Chapter 4) should be used as probes in identifying the function of the circumstance.

Step 5: Identify the Finite type

> In this step, the type of Finite is determined. If the Finite is conflated with an auxiliary verb, it would be useful at this point to check for any other auxiliary verbs (see Chapter 5).

Step 6: Use the Subject test to identify the Subject

> In this step you will apply the Subject test as given in Chapter 5 in order to verify the boundaries of the structural unit which is expressing the Subject of the clause.

Step 7: Determine the mood of the clause

> The mood is determined by the order of the Subject and Finite (see Chapter 5). If a non-finite clause is being analysed, this step would be skipped, as non-finite clauses do not express a mood choice.

Step 8: Identify all modal elements including markers of negative polarity

> In this step, any modal adjuncts, modal verbs and/or negator are identified (see Chapter 5).

Step 9: Locate the experiential Theme of the clause and indicate whether it is marked or not

> For most clauses, the experiential Theme will correspond to the first experiential element of the clause. This is most likely to be the first participant in declarative and interrogative clauses or the process in imperative clauses. Certain grammatical constructions provide alternative Theme specification (see section 6.5 on thematic constructions). For all clause types, when a circumstance occurs first in a clause it is labelled the experiential Theme and is considered to be marked.

Step 10: Check for any other thematic elements (i.e. textual and/or interpersonal Themes)

> This step could easily be integrated with step 9, but is kept separate in order to make it easier to recognize the different thematic functions expressed in the clause.

Step 11: Draw the tree diagram

6.6.2 A sample three-strand analysis of the clause

Now that the steps in the guidelines for analysing the clause have been reviewed, the analysis can be done. The approach taken here is to build up the three-strand analysis by beginning first with the experiential strand of meaning, then mapping the interpersonal functions onto the clause and then finally completing the analysis with textual meaning. Selecting a text that has already been analysed will make this task much easier. In this way, the focus can be exclusively on the textual meaning of the clause without struggling to work out the functions within the other two strands of meaning.

The text being analysed here was fully analysed for experiential meaning in Chapter 4. Parts of it were analysed interpersonally in Chapter 5. As a consequence most of the steps in the guidelines listed above have already been completed. The list of clauses is given below. Following this, each clause will be analysed completely and represented both as a tree diagram and as a box diagram.

Text 6.6 Excerpt from the Air Canada report

In a high altitude emergency, an oxygen mask will drop in front of you from the panel above. Place the mask over your mouth and nose, straighten out the strap, and pull the strap to be sure it is tight on your face. After you are wearing it securely, a tug on the hose will start the oxygen flow. It makes sense to put your own mask on first, before helping others.

Clause list for Text 6.6

[1] In a high altitude emergency, an oxygen mask will drop in front of you from the panel above

[2] Place the mask over your mouth and nose

[3] straighten out the strap

[4] and pull the strap to be sure it is tight on your face

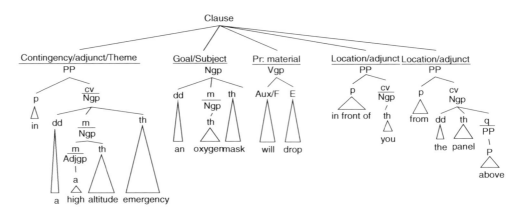

Exp.	Cir: Contingency		Actor	Pr: material		Location	Location
Int.	Adjunct		Subject	Finite	Predicator	Adjunct	Adjunct
			Declarative mood				
Text.	marked Theme		Rheme				

Figure 6.10 Full three-strand analysis for clause [1]

[5] After you are wearing it securely a tug on the hose will start the oxygen flow

[6] It makes sense to put your own mask on first, before helping others

Clause [1]

In a high altitude emergency, an oxygen mask will drop in front of you from the panel above.

This clause was analysed in Chapters 4 and 5 so therefore all steps related to experiential meaning and interpersonal meaning have been completed, with the exception of step 6, which involves determining the mood of the clause. This means that the analysis here can begin with step 9.

Step 9: Locate the experiential Theme of the clause and indicate whether it is marked or not

This clause is not in the form of any special thematic construction. The first experiential element of the clause is the circumstance, *in a high altitude emergency*. Therefore this element also expresses experiential Theme and it is marked.

Step 10: Check for any other thematic elements (i.e. textual and/or interpersonal Themes)

As there is nothing before the experiential Theme, there is no textual or interpersonal Theme.

Step 11: Draw the tree diagram

The tree and box diagrams are given in Figure 6.10. As was discussed in Chapter 5, tree diagrams do not indicate Predicator since this label refers to the remainder of

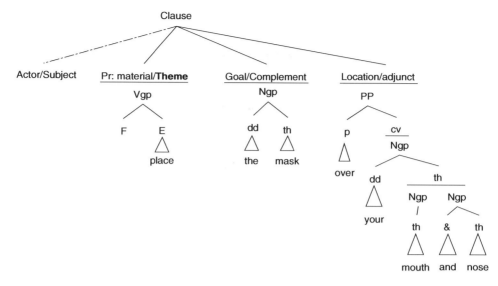

Figure 6.11 Full three-strand analysis for clause [2]

the verb group after the Finite element has been identified. When using box diagrams, however, Predicator is included.

Clause [2]

Place the mask over your mouth and nose
As with the previous clause, this one was also analysed in Chapters 4 and 5. The analysis given here will begin with step 9.

Step 9: Locate the experiential Theme of the clause and indicate whether it is marked or not
This clause is not in the form of any special thematic construction. The first experiential element of the clause is the process, *place*. Therefore this element also expresses experiential Theme and since it is the expected first experiential element, given the imperative mood of the clause, it is an unmarked Theme.

Step 10: Check for any other thematic elements (i.e. textual and/or interpersonal Themes)
As there is nothing before the experiential Theme, there is no textual or interpersonal Theme.

Step 11: Draw the tree diagram
The tree and box diagrams are given in Figure 6.11.

Clause [3]

Straighten out the strap

Although this clause was analysed in Chapter 4, it was not analysed in Chapter 5. Consequently all steps up to and including step 4 have been completed. The analysis here will resume with step 5.

Step 5: Identify the Finite type

There does not appear to be a Finite element in this clause. This would suggest that the clause is either imperative or non-finite. In order to be certain that it is a finite imperative clause, the polarity can be reversed and, as a result, the Finite element will either reveal itself or we will have to reconsider that the clause is non-finite. Re-expressing the clause with negative polarity shows that the negator conflates with the Finite element: *Don't straighten out the strap*. Therefore we can conclude that the clause is finite but that the Finite element is not expressed in this instance.

Step 6: Use the Subject test to identify the Subject

In order to use the Subject test, the clause must be re-expressed with all participants fully expressed and an auxiliary verb must be added. This gives: *you can straighten out the strap*. The Subject test re-expresses the declarative clause as an interrogative, which forces the Finite element to precede the Subject element. The result of this test is: *Can you straighten out the strap?*

This shows that *you* functions as the Subject in this clause, even though it has not been expressed lexically.

Step 7: Determine the mood of the clause

This clause looks as though it has no Subject or Finite and it begins with a verb. It can be tested for imperative mood by negating the clause: *don't straighten out the strap*. Furthermore the Subject can be explicitly expressed: *you straighten out the strap* and *don't you straighten out the strap*. This shows that the clause is expressed in imperative mood.

Step 8: Identify all modal elements including markers of negative polarity

This clause expresses modality of obligation through imperative mood. There are no other expressions of modality or polarity.

Step 9: Locate the experiential Theme of the clause and indicate whether it is marked or not

This clause is not in the form of any special thematic construction. The first experiential element of the clause is the process, *place*. Therefore this element also expresses experiential Theme and since it is the expected first experiential element, given the imperative mood of the clause, it is an unmarked Theme.

Step 10: Check for any other thematic elements (i.e. textual and/or interpersonal Themes)

As there is nothing before the experiential Theme, there is no textual or interpersonal Theme.

Step 11: Draw the tree diagram

The tree and box diagrams are given in Figure 6.12.

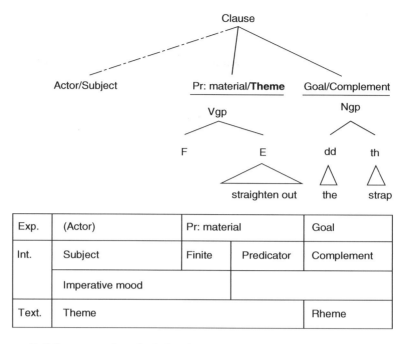

Exp.	(Actor)		Pr: material		Goal
Int.	Subject		Finite	Predicator	Complement
	Imperative mood				
Text.	Theme				Rheme

Figure 6.12 Full three-strand analysis for clause [3]

Clause [4]

And pull the strap to be sure it is tight on your face

This clause also was analysed in Chapter 4 but not Chapter 5. The analysis here will begin here with step 5.

Step 5: Identify the Finite type

As with the previous imperative clauses, the question here is where the Finite element is. Re-expressing the clause with negative polarity shows that the negator conflates with the Finite element: *and don't pull the strap to be sure it is tight on your face.* Therefore we can conclude that the clause is finite but that the Finite element is not expressed in this instance. The clause is imperative.

Step 6: Use the Subject test to identify the Subject

In order to use the Subject test, the clause must be re-expressed with all participants fully expressed and an auxiliary verb must be added. This gives: *and you should pull the strap to be sure it is tight on your face.* The Subject test re-expresses the declarative clause as an interrogative, which forces the Finite element to precede the Subject element. The result of this test is: *and should you pull the strap to be sure it is tight on your face?*

This shows that *you* functions as the Subject in this clause, even though it has not been expressed lexically.

Step 7: Determine the mood of the clause

This clause looks as though it has no Subject or Finite and it begins with a verb. It can be tested for imperative mood by negating the clause: *don't pull the*

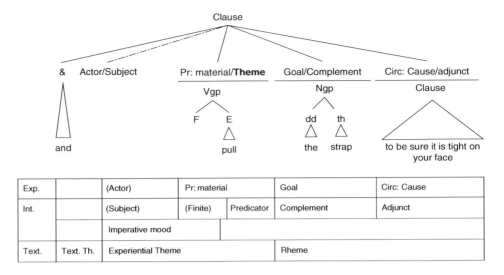

Figure 6.13 Full three-strand analysis for clause [4]

strap... Furthermore the Subject can be explicitly expressed: *you pull the strap...* and *don't you pull the strap...* This shows that the clause is expressed in imperative mood.

Step 8: Identify all modal elements including markers of negative polarity

This clause expresses modality of obligation through imperative mood. There are no other expressions of modality or polarity.

Step 9: Locate the experiential Theme of the clause and indicate whether it is marked or not

This clause is not in the form of any special thematic construction. The first experiential element of the clause is the process, *pull*. Therefore this element also expresses experiential Theme and since it is the expected first experiential element, given the imperative mood of the clause, it is an unmarked Theme.

Step 10: Check for any other thematic elements (i.e. textual and/or interpersonal Themes)

The only element preceding the experiential Theme is the conjunction *and*. As this has no other function in the other strands of meaning we can be confident that it expresses a textual Theme; however, it should be clear that it functions to link the clause with the preceding clause.

Step 11: Draw the tree diagram

The tree and box diagrams are given in Figure 6.13.

Clause [5]

After you are wearing it securely a tug on the hose will start the oxygen flow.

This clause also was analysed in Chapter 4 but not Chapter 5. The analysis here will begin here with step 5.

Step 5: Identify the Finite type

Identifying the Finite in this clause is dependent on earlier steps that would have determined the internal unit boundaries. This was done in Chapter 4 with the following result:

After you are wearing it securely	a tug on the hose	will start	the oxygen flow
Location	Actor	Pr: material	Goal

The circumstance of Location includes an embedded finite clause (see Chapter 7), which could cause some challenges for identifying the Finite type here since the embedded clause, *you are wearing it securely*, also includes a Finite element (i.e. *are*). However, in the analysis of the main clause (i.e. a process of starting) there are only two verbs involved: *will* and *start*.

Since *will* is a modal auxiliary verb and *start* is a lexical verb, there is no doubt that the Finite element is expressed by the modal auxiliary verb, *will*.

Step 6: Use the Subject test to identify the Subject

In order to use the Subject test, the clause must be in the declarative mood and it needs to have an auxiliary verb. It meets both criteria. Applying the Subject test gives the following result: *After you are wearing it securely will a tug on the hose start the oxygen flow?*

This shows that *a tug on the hose* functions as the Subject in this clause.

Step 7: Determine the mood of the clause

The Subject precedes the Finite, which indicates declarative mood.

Step 8: Identify all modal elements including markers of negative polarity

This clause includes a modal verb and in this clause it is expressing modalization of probability. There are no other markers of modality or polarity.

Step 9: Locate the experiential Theme of the clause and indicate whether it is marked or not

This clause is not in the form of any special thematic construction. The first experiential element of the clause is the Location circumstance, *After you are wearing it securely*. Therefore this element also expresses experiential Theme but since it is not the expected first experiential element, it is a marked Theme.

Step 10: Check for any other thematic elements (i.e. textual and/or interpersonal Themes)

There is no other element preceding the experiential Theme.

Step 11: Draw the tree diagram

The tree and box diagrams are given in Figure 6.14.

Clause [6]

It makes sense to put your own mask on first before helping others

This last clause, like the preceding ones, was analysed for experiential meaning in Chapter 4 only. The analysis here will begin here with step 5.

Step 5: Identify the Finite type

Identifying the Finite in this clause is dependent on earlier steps that would have determined the internal unit boundaries (see Chapter 7). The analysis done in Chapter 4 gave the following result:

163

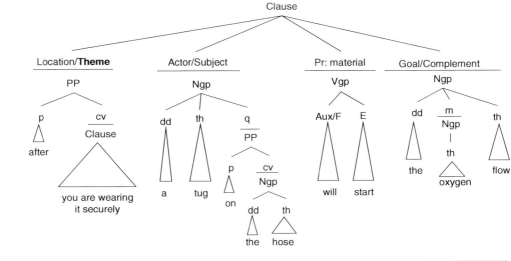

Figure 6.14 Full three-strand analysis for clause [5]

it	makes	sense	to put on your own mask first	before helping others
(Carrier)	Pr: relational	Attribute	Carrier	Location

There are two verbs in this clause: *makes* and *helping*. However, they are not part of the same verb group. The use of *helping* in this case is non-finite because there is no progressive auxiliary (*be*) supporting it. If the clause containing *helping* were finite, there would have to be a progressive auxiliary and indeed we would continue to look left in the verb group to see if a Finite element could be identified. In any case, given that *before helping others* is expressing a circumstance, it cannot be considered to include the Finite element of the main clause where the process is *makes*.

We can test that *makes* is expressing the Finite element by changing the tense to past. The Finite element will inflect the past tense. The result of doing so is as follows: *it made sense to put your own mask on first before helping others*.

This shows that there is only one Finite element in this clause and it is expressed by *makes*.

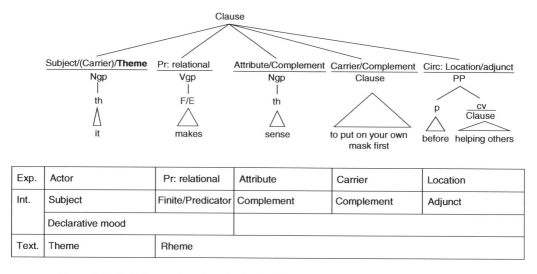

Exp.	Actor	Pr: relational	Attribute	Carrier	Location
Int.	Subject	Finite/Predicator	Complement	Complement	Adjunct
	Declarative mood				
Text.	Theme	Rheme			

Figure 6.15 Full three-strand analysis for clause [6]

Step 6: Use the Subject test to identify the Subject

In order to use the Subject test, the clause must be in the declarative mood and it needs to have an auxiliary verb. This clause is in declarative mood but an appropriate auxiliary verb must be added. In this case, the auxiliary verb *do* will be added as follows: *it does make sense to put your own mask on first before helping others.* Applying the Subject test gives the following result: *does it make sense to put your own mask on first before helping others?*
This shows that *it* functions as the Subject in this clause.

Step 7: Determine the mood of the clause

The Subject precedes the Finite, which indicates declarative mood.

Step 8: Identify all modal elements including markers of negative polarity

There are no markers of modality or polarity.

Step 9: Locate the experiential Theme of the clause and indicate whether it is marked or not

This clause is in the form of a special thematic construction: Extraposed participant. The *it* Subject in this case is coreferential with *to put on your own mask first*, which expresses a Carrier role. This structure allows the Carrier to be in a position after the Attribute. As explained in section 6.5.2, the Theme in these cases is the Subject, *it*.

Step 10: Check for any other thematic elements (i.e. textual and/or interpersonal Themes)

There is no other element preceding the experiential Theme.

Step 11: Draw the tree diagram

The tree and box diagrams are given in Figure 6.15.

This section completes the multifunctional view of the clause since all three main metafunctions have been examined for their treatment of the clause. However, there are some remaining issues concerning the identification of clause boundaries. So far, the clause boundaries have been presented as given. In Chapter 7 the ways in which clauses combine will be explained, which will offer some detail as to how clauses can be identified within text. Chapter 8 summarizes everything concerning analysing the clause and works through the full functional–structural approach which was developed throughout this book. Before moving on to these chapters, there are still some aspects of textual meaning that need to be explained. This concerns how textual meaning within the clause contributes to the creation of text.

6.7 TEXTURE

At the start of this chapter, texture was identified as that which distinguishes a text from something that is not a text. In other words, all texts have texture according to Halliday and Hasan (1976). In the metaphor of a text being something woven, texture is then the threads that hold the text together. Theme, by its very nature, provides one kind of texture in the sense that it inherently connects the clause to the text as a reference point, indicating relevance.

In this section, the discussion of textual meaning extends beyond the clause to show some of the ways in which Theme contributes to the text. A selection of key textual devices which contribute to a text's texture will be discussed. These include thematic progression, cohesive reference and ellipsis. This presentation is necessarily selective as it is meant to provide an introductory overview of texture and its relation to Theme.

6.7.1 Thematic progression

It has already been established that one of the main functions of Theme is to indicate relevance. This view of Theme suggests that the Theme of a given clause will be the main link between the clause and the text. The idea that Theme is a relevance indicator implies that ideally there should always be an attributable source for the Theme. In other words, in theory, Theme is always motivated by something. However, in practice, speakers are not necessarily going to adhere to this principle and there may be reasons why what seems to be the relevance of the clause is not found in the Theme. In these cases, Theme would not be motivated by relevance. Consequently, precision about the definition and function of Theme is very important.

An approach which attempts to capture, at least in abstract terms, the source of a given Theme was developed by Daneš (1974), which he called thematic progression. His idea was that every Theme will have progressed from one of three possible sources:

- Constant Theme progression, where the Theme of a given clause is derived from the Theme of a preceding clause;
- Linear Theme progression, where the Theme is derived from the Rheme of a preceding clause;
- Derived Theme progression, where the Theme is derived from what Daneš referred to as a Hypertheme, a general overriding topic of a larger stretch of text such as a paragraph.

These three types of thematic progression are illustrated (adapted from Daneš, 1974) in Figures 6.16 to 6.18, inclusive.

In order to explore thematic progression in text, an explanatory text will be used. The extract given here as Text 6.7 is taken from a website[3] that is dedicated to explaining weather-related phenomena. The topic of this text is snowflakes and how they are formed. The text is addressing school-age children.

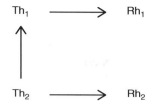

Figure 6.16 Constant Theme progression

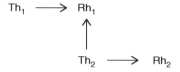

Figure 6.17 Linear Theme progression

Figure 6.18 Derived Theme progression

Text 6.7 What Are Snowflakes?

Snowflakes are made of ice crystals. Each snowflake is made of as many as 200 ice crystals. Some snow crystals are symmetrical, like the type that you cut from paper. They form a hexagonal shape because that is how water molecules organize themselves as they freeze. Others are small and irregularly shaped. If they spin like tops as they fall to the ground, they may be perfectly symmetrical when they hit the Earth. But if they fall sideways, they will end up lopsided.

The clauses have been listed and analysed for Theme and Rheme as shown in Table 6.6. The final column is used to indicate the co-textual source for each Theme, wherever this is possible.

Although this is a relatively simple text, the analysis shows that in this text Theme is very often relevant to a preceding clause. The most common Theme is *snow crystals* although this also refers indirectly to *snowflakes*, since snowflakes are made from snow crystals. Constant Theme progression was frequent here, which reinforces the topic of this stretch of text. The change from constant to linear progression in clauses [8] to [9] indicate a shift in the text from a focus on the snowflake to the snow crystal. It is also relevant to note that the Theme in clause [12] is derived from the Theme in clause [9] through a contrast (i.e. *some snow crystals ← others*). Although the connection between these two Themes is not adjacent, the relevance of the Theme in clause [12] can be attributed to the one in clause [9].

Most research on thematic progression in text shows that, generally speaking, the source of Theme can be seen to be derived from a preceding clause (i.e. constant or linear progression) in the majority of instances. Different authors and different texts will combine the resources for the use of Theme in making explicit the relevance of a particular clause to the text.

Table 6.6: Thematic progression for Text 6.7, 'What Are Snowflakes?'

	Theme		Rheme	Thematic progression
	Textual Theme	Experiential Theme		
[7]		Snowflakes	are made of ice crystals.	Derived (from title)
[8]		Each snowflake	is made of as many as 200 ice crystals.	Constant
[9]		Some snow crystals	are symmetrical, like the type that you cut from paper.	Linear
[10]		They	form a hexagonal shape	Constant
[11]	because	that	is how water molecules organize themselves as they freeze.	Linear
[12]		Others	are small and irregularly shaped.	Constant
[13]	If	they	spin like tops as they fall to the ground,	Constant
[14]		they	may be perfectly symmetrical when they hit the Earth.	Constant
[15]	But if	they	fall sideways,	Constant
[16]		they	will end up lopsided.	Constant

Table 6.7: Modified selection from the 'Snowflake' text

	Experiential Theme	Rheme	Thematic progression
[7]	Snowflakes	are made of ice crystals.	Derived (from title)
[9]	Some snow crystals	are symmetrical, like the type that you cut from paper.	Linear
[10]	They	form a hexagonal shape	Constant
[17]	Meteorologists	know how snowflakes are formed	Ruptured Theme

If the source of a Theme cannot be attributed, it is considered to be a ruptured Theme. This may be for rhetorical effect or because the speaker has misjudged the addressee's needs in receiving the text. If, for example, the text above included a Theme which seemed to be unmotivated or ruptured from the text, it would likely signal a problem area. A modification of Text 6.7 is given in Table 6.7, where some clauses have been omitted and an invented one has been added. The progression of Theme in each clause is illustrated in Figure 6.19.

A ruptured Theme can indicate a weak point in the text. This is something that I encountered frequently when working as language editor for the MIT journal *Evolutionary Computation*. International authors writing in English often had difficulties in negotiating Theme use. Many studies have shown the merits of teaching students of writing how thematic progression can help to improve the flow of a text.

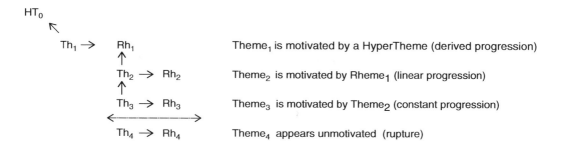

HT_0

$Th_1 \rightarrow Rh_1$ Theme$_1$ is motivated by a HyperTheme (derived progression)

$Th_2 \rightarrow Rh_2$ Theme$_2$ is motivated by Rheme$_1$ (linear progression)

$Th_3 \rightarrow Rh_3$ Theme$_3$ is motivated by Theme$_2$ (constant progression)

$Th_4 \rightarrow Rh_4$ Theme$_4$ appears unmotivated (rupture)

Figure 6.19 Illustration of thematic progression from the modified 'Snowflake' text given in Table 6.7

6.7.2 Textual cohesion

The concept of cohesion is semantic rather than structural in the sense that it functions around the clause rather than within it. According to Halliday and Hasan (1976: 4) cohesion is recognized when 'the interpretation of some element in the discourse is dependent on that of another'. The use of personal pronouns is a very common example of this since they have no complete interpretation of their own so they must be understood by reference to something else. Cohesion contributes to texture by creating a tie or thread between a point in the text and another point either within the text or within the context. In other words, texture is traceable through cohesion.

Three types of textual cohesion will be discussed in this section: reference, ellipsis and conjunction. Each of these will be described briefly below by looking at examples of them in Text 6.8, an excerpt from *The Wonderful Wizard of Oz*.[4]

Text 6.8 An excerpt from The Wonderful Wizard of Oz

Line no.	Speaker	Text
1.	Oz	*Don't speak so loud, or you will be overheard and*
2.		*I should be ruined. I'm supposed to be a Great Wizard.*
3.	Dorothy	*And aren't you?*
4.	Oz	*Not a bit of it, my dear, I'm just a common man.*
5.	Scarecrow	*You're more than that. You're a humbug.*
6.	Oz	*Exactly so! I am a humbug.*
7.	Tin Woodman	*But this is terrible. How shall I ever get my heart?*
		. . .
8.	Scarecrow	*Can't you give me brains?*
9.	Oz	*You don't need them. You are learning something*
10.		*every day.*

6.7.2.1 Cohesive reference

Halliday and Hasan (1976: 31) define reference as 'a type of cohesive relation in which a linguistic item, having no semantic interpretation of its own, refers to a thing or place. These linguistic items make REFERENCE to something else for their interpretation.' This refers to expressions which take their meaning from elsewhere. There are two types of cohesive reference: endophoric reference, where the item takes its interpretation from within the text and exophoric reference, where the interpretation is found in the situational context, external to the text.

In the *Wizard of Oz* extract in Text 6.8, every instance of a personal pronoun is an example of reference. For example, the uses of *you* and *I* throughout the extract are examples of exophoric reference, creating a cohesive link between the text and the situation. There is no way to know who *you* refers to unless you know who is being addressed and, similarly, there is no meaning to *I* without knowing who is speaking. There is only one instance of endophoric reference, or text-internal reference, and this occurs on line 9 with the use of *them*, when Oz says, *You don't need them*. This pronoun has no meaning of its own other than grammatical meaning such as plural, for example. It can only be interpreted meaningfully by reference to *brains* in the preceding clause on line 8.

6.7.2.2 Ellipsis

Ellipsis is an interesting phenomenon because it is identifiable by nothingness or absence within a bounded context, usually a clause. For example, if a person asks a friend, *would you like another cup of coffee?*, the response might be *yes I would like another cup of coffee* but it is more likely to be simply *yes I would*. This response is based on a particular understanding and this is that the speaker is confident that the addressee will be able to interpret the presupposition being made. We can use the null symbol, Ø, to indicate that something structural has been omitted. In the current example, we could write: *yes I would Ø*, where Ø represents the absence of *like another cup of coffee*. As Halliday and Hasan (1976: 144) explain, 'ellipsis occurs when something that is structurally necessary is left unsaid'.

Ellipsis creates texture because it forces a connection – or a tie, in Halliday and Hasan's terms – between the point of ellipsis and another part of the text (endophoric ellipsis). In this extract from Text 6.8, there are two instances of ellipsis. These are shown in Figure 6.20 on lines 1 and 3, where the ellipsed structure is indicated by Ø.

Line no.	Speaker	Text
1.	Oz	*Ø Don't speak so loud, or you will be overheard and*
2.		*I should be ruined. I'm supposed to be a Great Wizard.*
3.	Dorothy	*And aren't you Ø?*

Figure 6.20 Examples of ellipsis in Text 6.8

Ellipsis is a kind of structural 'place-holding device' (Halliday, 1994: 317) that requires the addressee to recover or retrieve meaning from elsewhere in the text. The ellipsis found in line 1 does meet this description of ellipsis even though, with imperative clauses such as this one, the Subject (i.e. the pronoun *you*) is expected to be left implicit. In line 3, the Complement of the clause is ellipsed and what must be retrieved is *a Great Wizard*, as in *Aren't you a Great Wizard?*

For the grammar analyst, ellipsis is perhaps more important than any other type of cohesion because it is signified by an understanding based on the absence of some

Line no.	Speaker	Text
1	Oz	*Don't speak so loud, <u>or</u> you will be overheard <u>and</u>*
2		*I should be ruined. I'm supposed to be a Great Wizard.*
3	Dorothy	*<u>And</u> aren't you?*
		...
7	Tin Woodman	*<u>But</u> this is terrible. How shall I ever get my heart?*

Figure 6.21 Examples of cohesive conjunction in Text 6.8

structure. In terms of the multifunctional analysis of the clause, the meaning obtained in the clause by ellipsis still expresses the same function as if it were expressed. For example, in line 3, the presupposed *a Great Wizard* expresses, by its null place-holder, the functions of Complement and Attribute. If this empty space is not acknowledged at some point in the analysis of the clause, then the meaning it expresses can easily be ignored or lost. Therefore, an important step must be added to the guidelines to analysing the clause so that the ellipsed items are recognized and included in the analysis. This will be discussed in Chapter 7 as it can be relevant to the process of identifying the clause boundaries.

6.7.2.3 Conjunctions

According to Halliday and Hasan (1976: 226), conjunctions 'express certain meanings which presuppose the presence of other components in the discourse'. Examples of conjunctions include *but, or, and, consequently, because* and many others. When conjunctions are used at the beginning of a clause, they function as textual Theme in the textual meaning of the clause and serve to relate the clause to a neighbouring clause. In this sense, they 'constitute a cohesive bond between the two clauses' (Halliday, 1994: 324) and are explicit markers of relevance.

In the *Oz* text, very few instances of conjunctions are found; however, this is only a short extract. There are four uses of conjunctions in thematic roles in total. These are found on lines 1, 3 and 7, as shown in Figure 6.21.

6.8 SUMMARY

This chapter has provided an overview of the textual metafunction from the perspective of the clause and a view of its role in creating text. The focus has been on how to recognize Theme in a variety of different clauses and texts. Theme has been discussed in relation to the three main mood structures (declarative, interrogative and imperative), showing how the configurations of each clause contribute textual meaning. Certain thematic constructions were briefly introduced since they often prove challenging to analyse due to their unexpected thematic structure. Finally the contributions of Theme and other related cohesive devices were introduced in order to understand how they contribute to the creation of text.

This chapter completes the third and final metafunction. As with the two previous chapters, the analysis of this metafunction requires a particular analytical approach. Two steps were added to the guidelines which have been developed so far. The first of these is to locate the experiential Theme of the clause by considering all experiential elements up to and including the Subject. In this step, consideration must also be given to the particular structure of the clause since mood structure determines the expected experiential Theme and certain thematic constructions have a textually motivated Theme, which may deviate from standard declarative clauses. The second step involves checking for any other thematic elements such as textual Themes and/or interpersonal Themes.

The analysis of the textual metafunction can seem misleadingly straightforward. There are some very challenging issues that analysts face when considering this metafunction both from within the clause and from its perspective on the text. Section 6.10 highlights some suggestions for further reading. These should provide an excellent starting point for a deeper understanding of the concepts introduced in this chapter.

6.9 EXERCISES

Exercise 6.1

Use the guidelines developed so far (see section 6.6.1) to analyse each clause in the text below. You should now be able to analyse all three main strands of meaning: experiential, interpersonal and textual. The clause boundaries have already been identified and the main lexical verb (indicating the process) for each clause has been underlined. You will also need to consider whether any items have been ellipsed (see section 6.7.2.2) before you begin the first step.

'Bill the Bloodhound', by P. G. Wodehouse

From P. G. Wodehouse (1917) *The Man with Two Left Feet and Other Stories.*[5]
1. There's a divinity that shapes our ends
2. Consider the case of Henry Pifield Rice, detective
3. I must explain Henry early, to avoid disappointment
4. If I simply said he was a detective
5. and let it go at that
6. I should be obtaining the reader's interest under false pretences
7. He was really only a sort of detective, a species of sleuth
8. At Stafford's International Investigation Bureau in the Strand where he was employed, they did not require him to solve mysteries which had baffled the police
9. He had never measured a footprint in his life
10. and what he did not know about bloodstains would have filled a library
11. The sort of job they gave Henry was to stand outside a restaurant in the rain and note what time someone inside left it

6.10 FURTHER READING

On cohesion and text:
Halliday, M. A. K. and R. Hasan. 1976. *Cohesion in English*. London: Longman.
Martin, J. 1992. *English Text: System and Structure*. Amsterdam: John Benjamins.

On cohesion and text:

Berry, M. 1996. 'What is Theme? – A(nother) personal view', in M. Berry, C, Butler, R. Fawcett and G. Huang, eds., *Meaning and Form: Systemic Functional Interpretations. Meaning and Choice in Language: Studies for Michael Halliday.* Norwood, NJ: Ablex: 1–64.

Fawcett, R. 2007b. *The Many Types of 'Theme' in English: Their Semantic Systems and their Functional Syntax.* Research Papers in the Humanities. www.cardiff.ac.uk/chri/researchpapers/humanities/papers1-10/Fawcett4.html.

Fries, P. 1995. 'Themes, methods of development, and texts', in R. Hasan and P. Fries, eds., *Subject and Theme: A Discourse Functional Perspective.* Amsterdam: John Benjamins: 317–59.

Halliday, M. A. K. and C. Matthiessen. 2004. *An Introduction to Functional Grammar.* 3rd edn. London: Hodder Arnold.

Thompson, G. 2007. 'Unfolding theme: the development of clausal and textual perspectives on Theme', in R. Hasan, C. Matthiessen and J. Webster, *Continuing Discourse on Language: A Functional Perspective*, Vol. **2**. London: Equinox: 669–94.

On information structure:

Davies, M. 1994. '"I'm sorry, I'll read that again": information structure in writing', in S. Čmejrková and F. Sticha, eds., *The Syntax of Sentence and Text.* Amsterdam: John Benjamins: 75–88.

Chapter 7: From text to clause

7.1 INTRODUCTION

Having now completed the internal view of the clause, this relatively short chapter looks at how to recognize the boundaries of the clause within text. It may seem odd that what will be the first step in analysing text is presented after the analysis of the clause but this is because, in order to identify the boundaries of the clause, it is essential to have a firm understanding of the way that the components of the clause work both structurally and functionally. This information has to be relied upon in order to recognize clauses within a text.

This chapter together with Chapter 8 provides the full set of guidelines for text analysis. This chapter, as already stated, explains how clause boundaries can be identified within a text, and Chapter 8 summarizes the guidelines that have been being developed throughout this book. These two chapters combined offer a complete view of analysing text. However, as is explained in Chapter 9, this is only the first stage in understanding language. Grammatical analysis forms the basis on which to build an interpretation of text. Chapter 9 describes how to manage the results of grammatical analysis so that the patterns of meaning in text can be understood.

7.1.1 Goals and limitations

This chapter summarizes the key details from all previous chapters which are relevant to recognizing clause boundaries. While this chapter, and indeed this book, will provide a very good basis from which to analyse the grammar of English, it has been an introduction to grammatical analysis and couldn't possibly offer the degree of detail necessary to equip someone with everything necessary to be able to analyse any clause encountered. There is no single volume which could manage a comprehensive view of English grammar. Halliday (1994: xiii) describes his introduction to functional grammar as a 'short introduction because, despite any illusion of length, it is no more than a mere fragment of an account of English grammar. Anything approaching a complete grammar would be hundreds of times this length.'

The goal of this book has not been explicitly to introduce the grammar but instead an approach to how to analyse the grammar within a functional framework. However, grammar isn't something we find when we want to analyse and understand text. Language is presented to us as text, as an output of the language system. It is generally agreed that this output is organized and structured in units. Exactly what these units are may be debatable. This book is based on the premise that the main organizing unit is the clause. The challenge for the analyst interested in understanding language in use is recognizing this unit. This chapter builds on the knowledge and understanding gained so far about the clause and provides a foundation for moving from text to clause. However, it is in many ways only a starting point. Language always throws curve balls; it is dynamic not static, and furthermore it is creative and inventive. Those who find it fascinating will certainly rise to the challenges it presents. In this view, this chapter is a springboard for a continuing journey into understanding language.

7.2 TEXTUAL THEMES AND CLAUSE BOUNDARIES

The previous chapter considered the relationship between the clause and text by focusing on Theme within the textual metafunction. The function of textual Theme was described as having an explicit relevance function since it serves to indicate the relevance of the clause to neighbouring clauses within the text. By their very nature, when they occur they will be located at the start of the clause as the first element of the clause.

Understanding Theme and specifically textual Theme is useful in identifying clause boundaries since a clause which expresses a textual Theme will be explicitly marking its initial boundary. Of course, this doesn't provide any information about how the clause ends. The final boundary of the clause is more challenging.

Another feature of Theme is that if there are no textual or interpersonal Themes the clause will begin with either the Subject element or an adjunct element with the exception of imperative clauses, which, as seen in Chapter 6, omit the Subject and whose first element is often the Event.

One of the particular functions of textual Theme is to link one independent clause to another (for example, from Chapter 6, *I tried to send it to him but there's still something wrong*). A very common way to do this is with the use of a conjunction. In Chapter 5, the ampersand symbol, '&', was used to indicate the co-ordination of any two units within the clause. However, at the clause level, a conjunction will serve to express the function of textual Theme. It may be useful to consider this use of textual Theme as a linking or co-ordinating textual Theme since it explicitly expresses the co-ordination of two clauses.

In addition to linking independent clauses, textual Themes can also show mutual relevance between clauses when one clause is functioning dependently on the other clause (e.g. *I tried to send it to him since there's still something wrong*). The textual Theme in these dependent clauses links the clause so strongly that it is seen as binding it to the other clause. This use of textual Theme subordinates one clause in relation to the other, effectively binding it.

7.3 COMBINING CLAUSES

All clauses have the potential to be simple or complex. The complexity of the clause is usually determined by the degree of complexity of the structural units which express it. It is generally agreed that a simple clause has one lexical verb (and perhaps one auxiliary verb) and a simple nominal group expressing the participant elements. More complex clauses will have more than one lexical verb and, consequently, this means that more than one clausal unit is involved. When analysing a text, knowing where one clause ends and another begins can be the greatest challenge. Understanding how clauses can combine is one more step towards unlocking this problem.

Perhaps it would be useful at this point to explain what is meant by the use of 'combine'. There is an assumption being made with regard to written text at least that clause combining is something made explicit by the speaker. This is done through the sentence, which is an orthographic written unit that marks the speaker's deliberate combination of clauses (or not in the case of a simple sentence). This is very similar to the use of indentation or white space around a section of text to indicate a paragraph. However, in one sense, it could be argued that the only true sense of clause combining is embedding, where one clause is literally combined within another. Most other ways of combining clauses, as will be shown below, are more a question of juxtaposition with explicit textual markers.

In the previous three chapters, the clause has been considered from three functional perspectives, each with its own configuration of elements. Now that a full functional–structural description of the clause has been presented, we will look at the three main types of clause in English. The clause types are distinguished in terms of how they can potentially combine with other clauses. The three types are independent, dependent and embedded clauses. In this section each one will be described in turn with a focus on how each one can combine with other clauses. The goal of this chapter is to develop guidelines for identifying clause boundaries, so the discussion of these clause types will concentrate on what these types tell us about recognizing clauses in text.

7.3.1 Co-ordinating clauses

The examples presented so far in this book have most often been what are traditionally called independent clauses (e.g. *This is the house that Jack built*; *In a high altitude emergency, an oxygen mask will drop in front of you from the panel above*; *By the way did you ever pay that dollar to the post office?*). In most grammar classes in school, these clauses were most often referred to as stand-alone sentences. In other words, they are fully complete in the sense that they satisfy the requirements for acceptable grammatical status.

This is a vague description but it is quite challenging to explain what makes a clause a clause and how we can tell when it is complete or not. In experiential terms, the clause would be seen as complete if all participants required by the process were expressed. From the interpersonal perspective, the clause would be seen as complete if it includes a Subject and Finite element along with an Event and any required Complements. Of course, it is possible for some of these elements to be left out and still have a complete clause – for example, passive clause structure and ellipsis permit certain elements to be left covert but recoverable, so in a sense it is not the case that they are not at all present. Furthermore, a clause may include more elements than those expected as in the case of adjuncts and certain types of Theme. The independent status of a given clause depends therefore on the specific clause in question. The determining factor is whether or not it satisfies the expectations of both speaker and addressee.

Recognizing an independent clause is simplified when the clause has only one lexical verb and expresses one process. When this is not the case, then it can be assumed that the clause combines with another clause. As this section intends to show, there are three main ways of combining clauses. When two independent clauses combine, they are said to be co-ordinated. Clause co-ordination is usually recognized by the presence of a co-ordinating conjunction such as *and* or *but*. In written language, this is sometimes indicated by a semi-colon.

In SFL, the two co-ordinated clauses are seen to be of equal status and they are referred to as being in a relationship of parataxis. Although any clause type can be co-ordinated (including finite or non-finite clauses), independent clauses combined this way are finite. However, finiteness is not a determining factor for recognizing an independent clause since subordinate clauses are also finite and some embedded clauses are finite. Identifying two co-ordinated independent clauses will be based on punctuation in written texts and the presence of potential textual Themes which explicitly indicate co-ordination. Recognizing independent clauses is based on the discussion above in terms of recognizing the core elements of the clause with respect to both experiential and interpersonal meaning.

7.3.2 Subordinating clauses

Another way in which clauses can be combined is through a relationship of subordination, or hypotaxis as it is called in SFL. When clauses are combined in this way, one clause is an independent clause and the other is a dependent clause. All dependent clauses are combined with an independent clause since they are inherently dependent on another clause, hence their label. Subordinate clauses are very similar in terms of structure and function to independent clauses but they are marked textually as being bound to another clause by a textual Theme.

In addition to being textually marked, these clauses do not meet the completeness criterion for independent clauses since, if stranded on their own, they maintain a sense of expectation. For example, if someone were to say, *if I win the lottery*, the addressee would be expecting more to come; they would expect a clause on which this one is dependent, such as *if I win the lottery I will buy a house in Canada*. The combination of subordinated clauses can be reversed: *I will buy a house in Canada if I win the lottery*.

Dependent clauses can be as complex as any other type of clause (e.g. *if this is the dog that chased the cat that ate the rat that lived in Jack's house then it must be the same dog that ran through my garden*). Therefore, the problem of recognizing them is just as challenging as for independent clauses. However, they are somewhat more easily recognized by the textual Theme, which orients and relates the subordinate clause to the clause on which it is dependent.

7.3.3 Embedding clauses

As was pointed out in Chapter 2, it is possible to find one clause within another. When clauses combine in this way, it is referred to as embedding. The example used to illustrate embedding was the 'House that Jack Built' example, where the humour in the story is the result of the very lengthy series of embedded clauses. In these cases, the embedded clause is not of the same status as the clause it combines with, nor is it subordinated. It is used as a resource for expressing a function within an independent or dependent clause. In fact, it can even be embedded within an embedded clause. Embedded clauses can express a variety of functions within the clause. This is what makes them a fundamentally different clause. However, this is precisely what makes embedded clauses so challenging in grammatical analysis.

A further complication in recognizing clause boundaries involves the finite status of the clause. As was explained in Chapter 5, all clauses are either finite or non-finite. All independent and dependent clauses are finite. In contrast, embedded clauses can be either finite or non-finite. In a sense, non-finite clauses, once understood, are relatively straightforward since there are only three types (e.g. *to eat an apple a day can be very healthy*; *eating an apple a day can be very healthy*; *eaten once a day, apples can be very healthy*). This feature makes them much easier to recognize in a clause than their finite counterpart.

If non-finite clauses can be recognized by their structure and the absence of any identifiable or recoverable Finite element, then finite embedded clauses are the problem ones. As stated above and in Chapter 5, all embedded clauses serve to express a function within a clause. Some of the most common functions that embedded clauses express are participating entities, circumstances, qualifier in the nominal group (e.g. relative clause), completive in the prepositional phrase and finisher in the adjective group. Examples of each will be discussed below. Understanding how these clauses function and what indicators they may have should help in recognizing them in a text.

Garden-path sentences are often quite useful for talking about the challenges of recognizing embedded clauses. Examples of garden-path sentences are given in (1) to (3).

(1) The horse raced past the barn fell

(2) Mary gave the child the dog bit a bandaid

(3) I convinced her children are noisy

Garden-path sentences are misleading because they trick you in some way, often because adjacent words in certain contexts trigger a particular interpretation but then this interpretation is proved false by what follows. In this sense, these sentences lead you down the garden path. Often, when trying to understand such sentences, readers will construct a scenario where the sentence can make sense. For example, students will often interpret example (1) as referring to a thing that is called a 'barn fell'. They assume that there must be such a thing on a farm and that a horse is able to run past it. Or, they assume that the word 'and' is missing, which would give: *The horse raced past the barn and fell*.

Each sentence in examples (1) to (3) is an independent clause which includes an embedded clause. However, there is no marker of the embedded clause as there is sometimes with relative clauses, for example. These sentences would suddenly not be problematic if a relative pronoun such as *that* had been used. See if you can resolve the interpretation by adding *that* to each sentence and then check your results below.

The sentences in (1) to (3) have been rewritten as examples (1′) to (3′) where the embedded clause is now clearly introduced by *that* and the embedded clause is underlined.

(1′) The horse <u>that raced past the barn</u> fell

(1″) The horse raced past the barn <u>that fell</u>

(2′) Mary gave the child <u>that the dog bit</u> a bandaid

(3′) I convinced her <u>that children are noisy</u>

There is an alternative to (1′), which is given in (1″), but it is less likely since it sounds awkward and unnatural. What these examples show is that embedded clauses can be finite and that the relative pronoun which introduces some embedded clauses can be ellipsed.

Each embedded clause serves to express a particular function. In (1), the embedded clause, *that raced past the barn*, expresses the qualifier in the nominal group which is expressing the participant function (*the horse that raced past the barn*). The embedded clause in example (2) works in the same way as in example (1), as qualifier (*the child that the dog bit*). In (3), the embedded clause expresses a participant in the clause (or Complement in interpersonal meaning).

Embedded clauses make the analysis of English grammar challenging. Standard written punctuation may help to identify clause boundaries for co-ordinated and subordinated clauses since in these cases the clauses are in some sense separate clauses that are simply more closely textually connected than other clauses in the text. In contrast, embedded clauses are integrated as part of a clause and occur within the boundaries of an independent or dependent clause.

There have been several examples of clauses with embedded clauses throughout this book. It is actually quite difficult to find any text that only includes simple independent clauses. One example of embedding was given in Chapter 6, although the focus there was on Theme. The tree diagram for this clause (*After you are wearing it securely, a tug on the hose will start the oxygen flow*) is given in Figure 7.1. The embedded clause is expressing the completive element within a prepositional phrase. The entire prepositional phrase is expressing the circumstance/adjunct/Theme elements in the clause.

This example is debatable because one could argue that this example is rather similar to the following: *if you are wearing it securely, a tug on the hose will start the oxygen flow*, where

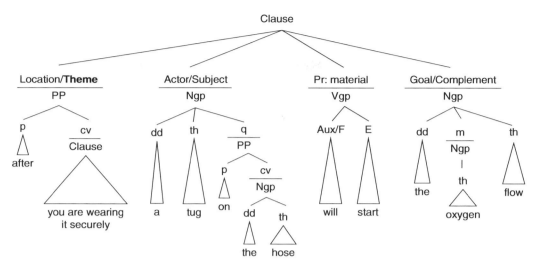

Figure 7.1 Embedded clause as completive in a prepositional phrase

it is referring to *oxygen mask*. If viewed this way, one might want to suggest that *after you are wearing it securely* is a subordinated clause. There are reasons why I would argue against such a view, although I would like to stress that there is room for different interpretations in the application of the grammar.

It is easy when taking a retrospective view of language, as is the case in analysing grammar, to make inferences based on our understanding of patterns and how we think things work. However, the core of the functional approach to language within SFL is based on the notion of choice and, in the two possible interpretations being discussed here, the speaker either did or did not intend to include a circumstance in the situation in order to modify the process.

The question is really whether there is sufficient evidence to suggest the speaker selected a circumstance or not. The answer can be found in whether in this case *after* is a textual Theme introducing a subordinate clause and binding it to the independent clause, and therefore it is an element of the clause *after you are wearing it securely*, or whether it is a preposition element in a prepositional phrase which is expressing a circumstance function. If the completive in the prepositional phrase were a nominal group rather than a clause, there would be no need for this discussion because in that case it could not be considered as a clause at all. One test to determine the status of the clause in question is to see whether the completive could be re-expressed as a nominal group without losing the sense of the entire clause. Consider for example, *after this stage, a tug on the hose will start the oxygen flow*. This kind of re-expression supports the view that the unit is expressing a circumstance which functions to indicate a point in time and also simultaneously a marked experiential Theme.

Furthermore, if the clause had been non-finite, there would be no need to consider the clause as subordinated since all subordinate clauses are finite. Therefore, re-expressing the clause as a non-finite clause would also suggest that it should not be seen as a subordinated clause. Consider for example, *after wearing it securely, a tug on the hose will start the oxygen flow*. This suggests that the analysis given in Figure 7.1 is preferred.

Of course, we could always suggest that the clause is badly written and *after* is not the best expression for the meaning intended by the speaker and that *once* would have been more appropriate. There would be no ambiguity with *once*. Consider, for example, *once you are wearing it securely, a tug on the hose will start the oxygen flow*. In this case there is no doubt that *once you are wearing it securely* is a subordinated clause. However, this is not what the speaker said and we would be distracted if we started to evaluate the clause.

The next section focuses, in very practical terms, on how to identify clause boundaries in a text. It draws on the contents of previous chapters to present a set of guidelines for segmenting the text into clauses so that the analysis can be done.

7.4 IDENTIFYING CLAUSE BOUNDARIES

When first beginning to analyse text, it is a good idea to select relatively short texts. It is also a good idea to work initially with texts having a relatively straightforward or simple structural representation; in other words, the fewer the number of embedded clauses, the easier it will be to identify the clause boundaries within the text. This does not mean that such a text will be any less interesting to analyse from a functional perspective. Examples of relatively simple texts include recipes written for children, some health and safety rules, and basic instructions. However, it is often the case that texts that may appear simple to the untrained eye are in fact quite complex from the analytic perspective. Once some experience has been gained from working on these types of texts, more and more challenging texts can and should be attempted. This advice is similar to learning to do puzzles, where it is often a good idea to start off with simpler versions of the puzzle before progressing to increasingly challenging ones.

The text being analysed here is a short email from a mother to her adult daughter (see Text 7.1). It is not a particularly easy text but it is not overly challenging so it should be at the right level for our purposes here. The goal is to segment the text into clause units. In the next chapter, the full set of guidelines will be presented which will serve as a walkthrough of the approach to analysing the clause. The remainder of this section is organized in terms of the steps involved in recognizing clause boundaries.

> **Text 7.1 Personal email text extract: email message from November 1999, a mother emailing her daughter**
>
> It's about 6 am and I couldn't sleep. I have to work at 8 as I went to Timmins yesterday for my mammogram so didn't get to work. John drove me. I said if the roads were good I would drive myself but he said he would so it was nice. Went to the fishbowl for lunch and then did some shopping. I got Robert the Thomas with the case. I was going to get him clothes as I saw some cute things but the Thomas thing is cute.

7.4.1 Identifying possible clauses

When working with punctuated text (print, electronic, etc.), the main guidance for identifying clauses comes from the punctuation marks which the speaker has included. These are the explicit signals which the speaker has used to mark up his or her text. But not all texts use punctuation regularly or in a traditional way. For example, in many types of electronic texts, punctuation is often absent or irregular. Any reliance on punctuation must be carefully considered. The first step in approaching the text is to use punctuation to help

Table 7.1: List of possible clauses

[1] It's about 6 am and I couldn't sleep.
[2] I have to work at 8 as I went to Timmins yesterday for my mammogram so didn't get to work.
[3] John drove me.
[4] I said if the roads were good I would drive myself but he said he would so it was nice.
[5] Went to the fishbowl for lunch and then did some shopping.
[6] I got Robert the Thomas with the case.
[7] I was going to get him clothes as I saw some cute things but the Thomas thing is cute.

identify sentences. Each sentence becomes a possible clause; a unit that is expected to include at least one clause. The list of possible clauses based on Text 7.1 is given in Table 7.1.

At this point each clause given in Table 7.1 is only potentially a single clause, as explained above. The next step is to test whether or not each possible clause is in fact a single clause or whether further distinctions are required.

The way in which this is done is by considering whether or not there are any other clauses present within the boundaries of what has been identified as a possible clause. There are only three possibilities for each; it may represent:

- one single independent clause, which may (or not) have embedded clauses within it;
- more than one clause, in which case it will have to be divided further into individual single clauses and it will be necessary to decide whether the clauses are related through
  - co-ordination,
  - subordination, or
  - a combination of both (in the case of more than two clauses); or
- not a complete clause.

If it is not a complete clause, a potential problem arises where we need to see how it relates to the surrounding text or, in other words, we need to figure out what it is doing in the text. If the text is published writing, then it is unlikely that the text being analysed will include any incomplete clauses unless you are analysing poetry, speeches, lyrics, and so on. Typically, such a clause will not have a clear Subject or Finite verb. Rather than being a clause, the expression may simply be a nominal group (for example, a minor clause such as *Good morning*). It may also be an exclamative clause such as *What a great day!*, although some might consider this to have ellipsed *it is*, as in *What a great day it is!*

It may be the case that this clause is in fact an embedded clause and, if so, it will have a role (or function) in another clause.

Another possibility is that it simply appears not to be an incomplete clause but in fact some elements have been ellipsed and it only 'looks' incomplete. To be certain of this, it is important to check whether anything has been ellipsed (see ellipsis in Chapter 6). Recall that ellipsed elements are retrievable. If this is a case of ellipsis, we need to retrieve the missing bits.

Once the list of possible clauses has been identified, the actual clause boundaries should be confirmed. This involves determining which of the three possibilities given above apply. The steps for achieving this are explained below. These include: restoring any ellipsed items, identifying all verbs, verifying the word class for all verbs, identifying the verb group(s), identifying the Finite element, and identifying any textual indicators of clause combining.

Table 7.2: Possible clauses with ellipsed items retrieved

[1] It's about 6 (hours) am and I couldn't sleep.
[2] I have to work at 8 (hours) as I went to Timmins yesterday for my mammogram so (I) didn't get towork.
[3] John drove me.
[4] I said if the roads were good I would drive myself but he said he would (drive) so it was nice.
[5] (we) went to the fishbowl for lunch and then (we) did some shopping.
[6] I got Robert the Thomas (train) with the case.
[7] I was going to get him clothes as I saw some cute things but the Thomas thing is cute.

7.4.2 Restoring ellipsed items

The first thing we want to do is check for any ellipsed elements (refer to Chapter 6 and the section on ellipsis). If anything has been left out but can be put back, then the analysis will be much easier if we restore the ellipsed items before beginning the analysis. This way we won't be led astray by their absence. This step involves retrieving any ellipsed elements and putting them back in the text using parenthesis or some other visual means to mark their place for your analysis later on. It is important to mark the fact that they were ellipsed by the speaker so that this distinction is kept clear.

In Text 7.1, there are a few cases of ellipsis. They are shown in Table 7.2 using parentheses to indicate what is believed to have been ellipsed. The reference to time in these clauses requires some comment. In possible clauses [1] and [2] listed in Table 7.2, there is an ellipsed element (thing) in the nominal groups expressing clock time. This way of referring to clock time is so frequent that it is almost unanalysable. However, the numeral is referring to an amount of something. In clause [1] the *am* means 'in the morning' and, even if it isn't a prepositional phrase, it is still functioning as a qualifier. In clause [2], this specification isn't expressed (i.e. *at 8*) but this isn't considered to be ellipsed since the qualifier is not a required element whereas the thing element is. The structure of the nominal group in clause [1] is: qd th q (i.e. quantifying determiner, thing, qualifier) and even if we would probably never express 'hours', it is understood. The fact that *6* is a quantifying determiner rather than thing is shown by the presence of *about*. This is also true for *at 8* since there is the potential for this kind of modification (e.g. *at about 8*).

7.4.3 Identifying all verbs

In this step, all the verbs are identified for each possible clause. This is because every clause has one and only one main verb (see Chapter 2), and if a possible clause has more than one verb it may mean that there is more than one clause. In Chapter 2, some guidelines were given for identifying verbs. The list of possible clauses is repeated in Table 7.3 with the verbs underlined and any items that might be verbs indicated in italics.

7.4.3.1 Verify word class of verbs

This is a sub-step to identifying the verbs in the clause. Here, we simply want to make sure each word identified as a verb is really functioning as a verb and not something else like a noun or an adjective or anything else that might initially look like a verb. There are two

Table 7.3: Possible clauses with verbs underlined

[1] It's about 6 (hours) am and I <u>couldn't sleep</u>.
[2] I <u>have to work</u> at 8 (hours) as I <u>went</u> to Timmins yesterday for my mammogram so (I) <u>didn't get</u> to *work*.
[3] John <u>drove</u> me.
[4] I <u>said</u> if the roads <u>were</u> good I <u>would drive</u> myself but he <u>said</u> he <u>would</u> (drive) so it <u>was</u> nice.
[5] (we) <u>went</u> to the fishbowl for lunch and then (we) <u>did</u> some *shopping*.
[6] I <u>got</u> Robert the Thomas (train) with the case.
[7] I <u>was going to get</u> him clothes as I <u>saw</u> some cute things but the Thomas thing <u>is</u> cute.

instances where this step applies in the text we are analysing. The first is the use of *work* in clause [2] and the second is the use of *shopping* in clause [5].

Clause [2], *I didn't get to work*, is ambiguous at first glance because it could be possible that the speaker is saying that she couldn't work, as in *I didn't manage to work* (cf. *I didn't get to see him*). If this were the case, *work* would clearly be a verb, expressing the process of working. The context of the clause indicates that the speaker was not able to go to her place of employment (i.e. *I didn't get to my office*). Therefore, *work* in this context refers to an entity. Consequently, *work* is in this instance a noun and not a verb.

The second item we need to test is *shopping*. It occurs in the following context: *I did some shopping*. The '-ing' suffix would normally indicate a verb. In this instance, though, *shopping* is being used to refer to a thing and consequently it is seen as a noun. We can be confident about this since it is preceded by a determiner, *some*. We could test it further by seeing whether it can be modified since this is another determining principle of nouns (see Chapter 3). Since it is possible to say *I did some great shopping the other day*, we can feel very confident that this instance of *shopping* is functioning within a nominal group as a noun rather than as part of a verb group.

7.4.4 Identify verb groups

An essential part of identifying a clause is understanding how verbs work together as a group. As explained in Chapters 2 and 5, each clause has only one main verb. If any of the possible clauses have only one verb then it is usually easy to sort out the clause because it means that there can only be one clause represented. However, if we find more than one, it can be quite tricky because we need to figure out how the verbs relate to each other, and specifically whether they are working together as a group (i.e. in a single clause) or whether they are in fact part of separate verb groups (i.e. involved in different clauses). In order to resolve this, we need to identify any verb groupings.

In Chapter 5, we saw how the English verb system works and generally there are some rather regular rules for how verbs combine with auxiliary verbs. For example, any verb following the auxiliary *have* will occur in the past participle form, as in *John has eaten the pie*. We use this knowledge to recognize verb groupings.

There are verb groupings that are less straightforward of course (see Chapter 4 for complex expressions of the process). These involve the ways in which we can extend the verb group. There are generally two types. The first are instances of phrasal verbs, where a preposition or particle attaches to the main verb and alters its main lexical meaning.

Table 7.4: Possible clauses with verb groups underlined

[1] It's about 6 (hours) am and I <u>couldn't sleep</u>.
[2] I <u>have to work</u> at 8 (hours) as I <u>went</u> to Timmins yesterday for my mammogram so (I) <u>didn't get</u> to work.
[3] John <u>drove</u> me.
[4] I <u>said</u> if the roads <u>were</u> good I <u>would drive</u> myself but he <u>said</u> he <u>would (drive</u> me) so it <u>was</u> nice.
[5] (we) <u>went</u> to the fishbowl for lunch and then (we) <u>did</u> some shopping.
[6] I <u>got</u> Robert the Thomas (train) with the case.
[7] I <u>was going to get</u> him clothes as I <u>saw</u> some cute things but the Thomas thing <u>is</u> cute.

An example of this type is *John ran up a huge telephone bill*. In this case, *ran up* constitute a single lexical item; in other words, there are two words working together to express the sense of 'incurred'. In an example such as *John ran up a huge tree*, the meaning is quite different and *up* in this case does not work with the verb *ran* but rather with *a huge tree* to indicate the location where John ran. The second example shows instances of a complex of verbs and these involve more than one lexical verb. These cases can be debatable since we are trying to infer which lexical verb represents the process for the speaker. An example of this is *John tried to phone her*. In this case, we need to determine whether the process is *try* or *phone*. If it is *try* then *to phone her* would be seen as working as an embedded clause which expresses the Complement of *try*. However, if it is *phone* then *try to phone* is seen as a complex verb group which expresses the process of the clause. These problem cases will generally appear in the form verb + to + verb. In some cases, it will not be obvious which approach to take in the analysis. It is a question of the complexity of the lexical item expressing the process (experientially) and the Event (interpersonally). The relevant chapters for this are Chapters 2, 4 and 5. The key to a good analysis is to use the tools available and to be as consistent and systematic as possible.

The verb groups for each possible clause are listed in Table 7.4. Since each verb group represents a clause, we can quickly see how many clauses each possible clause has. From a glance at our revised possible clause list in Table 7.4, it is easy to see that only possible clauses [3] and [6] are single clauses. The clause boundaries for the remaining five clauses still have to be determined. To do this, we need to consider the relationships amongst the various clauses. This involves determining the finite status of each clause, which is the subject of the next step.

7.4.5 Finding the Finite element

The key to understanding the finiteness of the clause, as was seen in Chapter 5, is the Finite element of the clause. In order for a clause to be finite, it must have an identifiable (or recoverable) Finite element. Any clause without such an element is either a non-finite clause, or a minor clause or some other unit of structure. If the clause is non-finite (see Chapters 5 and 7), it will be embedded in another clause; in other words a non-finite clause cannot function as a main or independent clause.

As explained in Chapter 5, the Finite element is always expressed by the first element of the verb group. If a modal verb (e.g. *may*, *can*, *shall*, *will*) occurs in a clause, it expresses the Finite element. If there is no modal verb, then the Finite element will be expressed by a primary auxiliary verb (e.g. *be*, *have*, *do*) or the Event (e.g. *eat*, *drink*, *sleep*).

Table 7.5: Possible clauses with Finite identified by subscript, F

[1] It's$_F$ about 6 am and I could$_F$n't sleep.
[2] I have$_F$ to work at 8 as I went$_F$ to Timmins yesterday for my mammogram so (I) did$_F$n't get to work.
[3] John drove$_F$ me.
[4] I said$_F$ if the roads were$_F$ good I would$_F$ drive myself but he said$_F$ he would$_F$ (drive me) so it was$_F$ nice.
[5] (we) went$_F$ to the fishbowl for lunch and then (we) did$_F$ some shopping.
[6] I got$_F$ Robert the Thomas (train) with the case.
[7] I was$_F$ going to get him clothes as I saw$_F$ some cute things but the Thomas thing is$_F$ cute.

It is important to remember that it can be challenging to recognize the Finite in the imperative mood since it is often ellipsed. As explained in Chapter 5, it is expressed by an empty verbal element but it is easily recovered by negating the clause (e.g. *eat your food* → *don't eat your food*).

The revised list of possible clauses given in Table 7.5 now includes a subscript F to indicate which item is expressing the Finite element in each verb group.

7.4.6 Verifying clause boundaries

We now have all the information needed in order to verify the boundaries of the possible clauses. As stated above, there are three outcomes for each possible clause. Recall that we initially identified these clauses using the speaker's original punctuation. What we see from the clause list above is that most cases (all but clauses [3] and [6]) have more than one verb and more than one verb group, which represents more than one clause. Therefore, we have to determine how the multiple clauses relate to each other. There are three ways in which two clauses can be related: co-ordination (one clause relates to the other through parataxis); subordination (second clause relates to the other through hypotaxis); or embedding (one clause relates to the other through embedding). The following aids can be useful for recognizing these types of clauses.

- Co-ordinated clauses can often be identified by linking textual themes such as *and, but, or,* or punctuation such as ';' or ':'.
- Subordinated clauses will usually be introduced by binding textual themes such as *if, as* or *because*.
- Embedded clauses will fill a function of an element of a higher unit (e.g. participant, circumstance, qualifier, completive, finisher) and may be introduced by a relative pronoun (e.g. *that*).

Using the information we have gained from the previous steps and our knowledge of how clauses combine (through co-ordination, subordination or embedding), we can now verify the actual clause boundary for each possible clause, as shown in Table 7.6.

What can be highlighted from this step is that there are no verb groups with non-finite verbs in the text which is being analysed. This means that there are no instances of non-finite embedded clauses. In order to show that this step is needed when the text does include a possible clause with a non-finite verb group, we will look briefly at another clause from a separate email message (also from November 1999). We will return to the problem of verifying all clause boundaries in a moment.

Table 7.6: A comparison of possible clauses and verified clauses, with textual indicators in bold

No.	Possible clauses	No.	Verified clauses
[1]	It's$_F$ about 6 am **and** I could$_F$n't sleep.	[1]	It's$_F$ about 6 (hours) am
		[2]	and I could$_F$n't sleep.
	Note: the co-ordinating Textual Theme *and* joins the two clauses, and therefore the clause can be split into two separate clauses; each one is a finite clause.		
[2]	I have$_F$ to work at 8 **as** I went$_F$ to Timmins yesterday for my mammogram **so** (I) did$_F$n't get to work.	[3]	I have$_F$ to work at 8 (hours)
		[4]	as I went$_F$ to Timmins yesterday for my mammogram
		[5]	so (I) did$_F$n't get to work.
	Note: the subordinating textual Theme *as* marks a clause boundary and so does *so*; therefore the clause is split into three separate finite clauses.		
[3]	John drove$_F$ me.	[6]	John drove$_F$ me.
[4]	I said$_F$ **if** the roads were$_F$ good I would$_F$ drive myself **but** he said$_F$ he would$_F$ (drive me) **so** it was$_F$ nice.	[7]	I said$_F$ [if the roads were$_F$ good I would$_F$ drive myself]
		[7.1]	if the roads were$_F$ good
		[7.2]	I would$_F$ drive myself
		[8]	but he said$_F$ [he would$_F$ (drive me)]
		[8.1]	he would$_F$ (drive me)
		[9]	so it was$_F$ nice.
	Note: both *but* and *so* mark clause boundaries and they therefore split the clause into at least three distinct clauses, as follows: </br> /I said if the roads were good I would drive myself / </br> /but he said he would / </br> /so it was nice / </br> The last clause (*so it was nice*) is straightforward since there is only one verb and it is therefore a single clause. </br> The remaining two are problematic because each has more than one verb group. There are no explicit markers indicating a clause boundary with the exception of *if*. The conditional clause introduced by *if* (*if the roads were good*) is subordinate to the clause which follows it (*I would drive myself*). This tells us how these two clauses are related, but it doesn't help us sort out the relationship they have with *said*. It is possible to insert *that* between *said* and *if*, which would give *I said that if the roads were good I would drive myself*. This introduces an embedded clause (see section 7.3.3). Furthermore we can use the pronoun replacement test (see Chapter 2) to see if any of the clauses are embedded in any other. Since we suspect *if the roads were good I would drive myself* is embedded because of the potential of a *that* binder, it makes sense to try to replace it with a pronoun: for example, *I said it* or *I said so*. This indicates that the two clauses together are filling a single 'slot' in the main clause (*said*) and therefore constitute an embedded clause. However, this embedded clause is a clause complex of two clauses related through subordination as just discussed, and each of these is a single finite clause. Depending on the levels of analysis you are interested in, you might not choose to list embedded clauses. The notation used here (e.g. [7.1] and [8.1]) indicates that the clause analysed is part of another clause. In other words, clause [7.1] is an embedded clause within clause [7].		
[5]	(we) went$_F$ to the fishbowl for lunch **and** then (we) did$_F$ some shopping.	[10]	(we) went$_F$ to the fishbowl for lunch
		[11]	and then (we) did$_F$ some shopping.
	Note: the *and* indicates a clause boundary so the clause is split into two separate finite clauses.		
[6]	I got$_F$ Robert the Thomas (train) with the case.	[12]	I got$_F$ Robert the Thomas (train) with the case.
[7]	I was$_F$ going to get him clothes **as** I saw some cute things **but** the Thomas thing is cute.	[13]	I was$_F$ going to get him clothes
		[14]	as I saw$_F$ some cute things
		[15]	but the Thomas thing is$_F$ cute.
	Note: *as* and *but* indicate clause boundaries so the clause is split into three separate finite clauses.		

Table 7.7: List of verified clause boundaries

[1]	It's about 6 (hours) am
[2]	and I couldn't sleep.
[3]	I have to work at 8 (hours)
[4]	as I went to Timmins yesterday for my mammogram
[5]	so (I) didn't get to work.
[6]	John drove me.
[7]	I said [if the roads were good I would drive myself]
[7.1]	if the roads were good
[7.2]	I would drive myself
[8]	but he said [he would (drive me)]
[8.1]	he would (drive me)
[9]	so it was nice.
[10]	(we) went to the fishbowl for lunch
[11]	and then (we) did some shopping.
[12]	I got Robert the Thomas (train) with the case.
[13]	I was going to get him clothes
[14]	as I saw some cute things
[15]	but the Thomas thing is cute.

(4) It's hardly normal for an 18 year old to sit at home reading and sleeping all the
      time.

In (4) above, in order to verify the clause boundaries, we need to consider whether we find more than one verb group which has a Finite verbal element. In this example, there is only one Finite verbal group (*'s*) and therefore we can conclude that the possible clause here does in fact indicate a single main clause. This verifies that the possible clause boundaries are in fact the actual (or confirmed) clause boundaries. However, we are left with the problem of what to do with the other verbal groups indicated by *to sit, reading* and *sleeping*. We know that these constitute embedded clauses because all non-finite clauses are embedded and have a role in the main clause. Determining the role of the embedded clauses is handled at a later step (as shown in Chapters 4, 5 and 6) when we use the process test (see Chapter 2) and work out the internal boundaries of the clause (see Chapter 3) in order to complete the analysis.

We have now completed the goal of identifying the clause boundaries. The original seven possible clauses have resulted in fifteen main clauses, as shown in Table 7.7.

What has been presented here may well represent the most difficult part of grammatical analysis. The clause itself is almost impossible to define, making it difficult to recognize in text. Its composition and configuration alters with each metafunction, which is why a full understanding of the clause is needed before it can be identified and described in text.

187

7.5 SUMMARY

Now that the clause boundaries have been verified, the analysis of each clause can begin. To illustrate this, Chapter 8 presents the full set of guidelines for grammatical analysis. These guidelines were introduced and developed in Chapters 4, 5 and 6. In a sense, everything that has been covered to this point has been in preparation for the grammatical analysis. Before a text can be functionally analysed, it has to be segmented into clauses, but before it can be segmented into clauses, the components of the clause must be understood so that they can be relied upon in the identification of the clause as a unit.

The relationship between clause and text is similar to the relationship between functional elements and structural units that we have been discussing throughout this book. Just as the meaning of Actor is expressed or realized by a nominal group, the meaning of the text must also have a form in order for its expression to be realized. As explained by Halliday and Hasan (1976: 2), 'a text does not consist of sentences; it is realized by, or encoded in, sentences'. This is why a functional analysis of the clause leads to an understanding of text. The next chapter will offer a summary of the approach to grammatical analysis that has been developed in this book. Then, Chapter 9 will demonstrate an example of how grammatical analysis can be interpreted in terms of the meaning of the text. In this sense, these three chapters – Chapters 7, 8 and 9 – combine to form a full cycle of analysis and interpretation, moving from text to clause to text again.

7.6 EXERCISES

These exercises give you practice in working with text and identifying the clause boundaries. For each text, use the guidelines developed in this chapter to list all the finite clauses.

Exercise 7.1

> I always get to this computer later at night. John is out golfing and Jane is at a sleepover birthday party where they are sleeping outside in tents and Sue has three friends over for a sleep over. They are watching a movie now.

(Excerpt from a personal email written by an adult female to a female friend, June 2005)

Exercise 7.2

> When it first happened, there was a big thunderstorm that shook the house and the rain fell really fast. My brother was startled because he was outside. Now the water is knee-high but we're alright. We went canoeing to a nice park which is really fun! We saw some iguanas today, and we even had a black snake at our house and I saw a snake on a canoe too! Every time I go out we go out in a canoe or our dad carries us because me and my brother don't like going out in the water because of the snakes. We should be going back to school in three weeks. It's a long time off.

(BBC, CBBC Newsround. 2011. *Press Pack Reports: I'm stuck in the Australian floods.* http://news.bbc.co.uk/cbbcnews/hi/newsid_9340000/newsid_9341900/9341995.stm)

Exercise 7.3

> The future must see the broadening of human rights throughout the world. People who have glimpsed freedom will never be content until they have secured it for themselves. In a truest sense, human rights are a fundamental object of law and government in a just society. Human rights exist to the degree that they are respected by people in relations with each other and by governments in relations with their citizens. The world at large is aware of the tragic consequences for human beings ruled by totalitarian systems. If we examine Hitler's rise to power, we see how the chains are forged which keep the individual a slave and we can see many similarities in the way things are accomplished in other countries. Politically men must be free to discuss and to arrive at as many facts as possible and there must be at least a two-party system in a country because when there is only one political party, too many things can be subordinated to the interests of that one party and it becomes a tyrant and not an instrument of democratic government.

(Roosevelt, Eleanor. 1948. *The Struggle for Human Rights.* [speech] Paris, France, 28 September 1948. http://edchange.org/multicultural/speeches/eleanor_roosevelt_rights. html)

7.7 FURTHER READING

Although no book specifically addresses guidelines for recognizing clause boundaries, the following books include sections which discuss how clauses combine.

Bloor, T. and M. Bloor. 2004. *The Functional Analysis of English: A Hallidayan Approach.* 2nd edn. London: Arnold.

Halliday, M.A.K. and C. Matthiessen. 2004. *An Introduction to Functional Grammar.* 3rd edn. London: Hodder Arnold.

Martin, J., C. Matthiessen and C. Painter. 1997. *Working with Functional Grammar.* London: Edward Arnold.

Thompson, G. 2004. *Introducing Functional Grammar.* 2nd edn. London: Arnold.

Chapter 8: Guidelines for grammatical analysis

This chapter is really a summary of all the steps and tools that have been covered in Chapters 1 through 6 and it follows directly from Chapter 7, which explained how to identify clause boundaries. The main goal of this chapter is to integrate all the information covered so far and present it as a proposal for a functional–structural approach to analysing grammar.

The very first step in analysing text is to identify individual clauses, since the clause is the main unit of interest for the systemic functional linguist and it is through the clause that the meanings of the text are realized. However, it would have been impossible to begin this book with an explanation of how to confidently recognize clause boundaries simply because so many factors contribute to this identification and it would be confusing to attempt to deal with all of them at the same time.

Developing an understanding of the clause is best approached in stages. In this book a decision was made to begin the first stage in Chapter 4 by considering the clause as representation and analysing the experiential meaning in the clause. Then building onto this Chapter 5 explored how to analyse the interpersonal meanings of the clause. The third and final stage in analysing the clause was presented in Chapter 6, which focused on the textual metafunction. Having now covered the various concepts in sufficient detail, the structures and meanings related to the clause, all this information can be put together in a single approach to grammatical analysis. The goal of this chapter is to present a set of guidelines for the beginner analyst that will cover all stages of the analysis so that it can be carried out in a systematic and consistent way.

In a sense, there is nothing new in this chapter. It is an organized compilation of the key knowledge and tools needed to analyse the clause. It represents the middle stage in the cycle of text analysis. Text analysis begins with a text and moves from that to a segmented state in the form of its component clauses, as shown in Chapter 7. These clauses, which realize the text, are then analysed individually – this is the focus of the current chapter. The final stage of the analysis, as will be shown in Chapter 9, involves analysing the results of the grammatical analysis so that the meanings in the text can be interpreted.

In this chapter, the full set of guidelines for analysing the clause will be reviewed and then demonstrated by using it to analyse the clauses of a text. The text used here is the same text which was segmented into clauses in Chapter 7. Before working through the demonstration of the guidelines, section 8.1 explains why the guidelines have been developed for analysing written rather than spoken texts. Following this, section 8.2 provides a brief summary of the various tests that are used in the guidelines and where to find them in this book. As with all other chapters, several exercises are provided at the end of the chapter followed by a section indicating a selection of further reading in the area of grammatical analysis.

8.1 A FOCUS ON WRITTEN TEXTS

Analysing language is challenging regardless of the type of text being considered. In order to keep this presentation as simple as possible, we will not use spoken or transcribed language and instead the focus will be on written (or punctuated) language. The main reason for this is that written language tends to identify clausal units of language (through the sentence) by the speaker's use of punctuation. Spoken data presents different challenges for the analyst, including for example interruptions in mid-utterance, which make identifying clauses difficult. Some suggestions for reading in this area are given in section 8.6.

8.2 SUMMARY OF GRAMMATICAL TESTS

Throughout this book various tests, probes and steps have been proposed as tools to assist in grammatical analysis. The guidelines presented in this chapter integrate all of these at various stages of the analysis. This section provides a summary of all the tests covered with a quick reference guide to finding them in the chapter where they were originally presented.

Chapter 2:
- Process test. This test is used to determine the number of expected participants, which identifies the number of core experiential elements of the clause.
- Word category criteria. The characteristics of the various lexical categories indicate features of a given lexical category which can be used to identify members of the category (e.g. recognizing nouns, verbs, adjectives).

Chapter 3:
- Pronoun replacement test. This test is used to identify nominal group boundaries within the clause.
- Movement test. This test includes, for example, the cleft test and passivization. It is used to test whether units are separate or not.

Chapter 4:
- Probes for determining process types.
- Probes for determining participant roles.
- Tests for circumstances. This test uses Halliday's questions for circumstances to help determine the function of the circumstance.

Chapter 5:
- Subject test. This test is used to identify the location and boundary of the Subject in the clause.
- Tag question test. This test can be used to identify the Subject through the anaphoric pronoun reference in the tag.
- Conditions for finite clauses. This is not explicitly a test but these conditions must be met if a clause is finite.
- Three types of non-finite clause. The characteristics of non-finite clauses make them easier to identify.
- Test for recognizing imperative mood. This test is used to determine whether a clause is expressed in the imperative mood or not.

Chapter 6:
- Identifying Theme. Guidelines are presented here for identifying experiential Theme and other thematic functions.

8.2.1 Key to abbreviations

Wherever possible the full spelling for any term has been used but in some diagrams this becomes quite challenging due to space constraints. Table 8.1 lists the abbreviations that may be used when space does not allow the full term.

Table 8.1: List of abbreviations

Strand of meaning	Abbreviation	Term	Abbreviation	Term
Experiential	Exp	Experiential meaning	Att	Attribute
	Pr:	Process	Idr	Identifier
	Circ:	Circumstance	Idd	Identified
	Act	Actor	Rel	Relational
	Gl	Goal	Say	Sayer
	Mat	Material	Verb	Verbiage
	Ben	Beneficiary	Rec	Recipient
	Sc	Scope	Verl	Verbal
	Sen	Senser	Behr	Behaver
	Ph	Phenomenon	Beh	Behavioural
	Men	Mental	Ext	Existent
	Car	Carrier	Exl	Existential
Interpersonal	Int	Interpersonal meaning	P	Predicator
	S	Subject	C	Complement
	F	Finite	A	Adjunct
	Aux	Auxiliary	N	Negator
	E	Event		
Textual	Tex	Textual meaning	ExTh	Experiential Theme
	Th	Theme	InTh	Interpersonal Theme
	Rh	Rheme	TTh	Textual Theme

8.3 THE THREE-STRAND ANALYSIS

The three-strand analysis refers to the analysis of the clause with respect to each main metafunction (strand of meaning). Grammatical analysis, when envisaged in this way, forms the basis of a functional investigation into language use and as such it is a critically important step in any interpretation of the functions of language. The approach to the analysis has been built up over the past chapters, beginning with a very general view of a systemic functional model of language and developing a more specific understanding of the individual functions expressed by the clause.

In this section, the guidelines developed in this book have been refined to ten steps, which offer a consistent and systematic approach to analysing the clause. As already stated, grammatical analysis is applied to the unit of the clause and therefore this analysis cannot begin until the text has been segmented into clauses and the boundaries of the individual clauses have been verified. Therefore, the guidelines for the three-strand analysis are based on having already worked out not only the clause boundaries but also the unit boundaries of the verb group, although these may need to be re-evaluated as the analysis progresses.

The remainder of this section is organized as follows. First, an overview of the steps in the guidelines will be presented. Then the text which will be used in the demonstration of the guidelines is reviewed, as it was the text used in Chapter 7 to illustrate how to segment a text into clauses. Following this the grammatical analysis of the individual clauses is presented in step-by-step fashion, as has been done in previous chapters to show the progression of the analysis.

8.3.1 Overview of the ten steps

The grammatical analysis is applied to individual clauses and as already stated it constitutes the second stage or phase in the analysis, following on from the initial analysis of the text in terms isolating the clauses. As described in Chapter 7 the segmentation stage involves identifying possible clauses, restoring any ellipsed items, identifying all verb groups, locating the Finite element, and verifying clause boundaries based on number of verb groups and the recognition of any embedded clauses. The ten steps in grammatical analysis, as presented below, assume that the initial segmentation stage has been completed.

Step 1: Identify the process and expected participants

Having already identified the main verb (as in Chapter 7) to identify clause boundaries, apply the process test from Chapter 2. It is a useful tool for understanding the importance of the process in determining the nature of the clause and figuring out what is expected in the clause. Recall that idiomatic or formulaic uses of language can obscure this and paraphrasing may help you to consider the meaning of the process.

Step 2: Verify boundaries of internal structures

Use tests given in Chapters 3 and 4 (e.g. pronoun replacement test or movement test) to determine the internal structural units.

Step 3: Determine the process type and participant roles

Use the probes and re-expression tests given in Chapter 4 to determine the process type and the function of the participants.

Step 4: Identify any circumstance roles

In this step you will identify any parts of the clause that are not core experiential elements (i.e. processes and participants). Use the tests given in Chapter 4 to identify circumstance roles. If no circumstance type seems to work, verify the internal boundaries of the clause (step 3). However, if a circumstance role cannot be found, then one of the following options will apply: it may be an interpersonal adjunct (e.g. modal) with no experiential function, or it may be a circumstance but not one that matches one of the nine general categories of circumstances. In this case, either a best fit approach should be taken or additional literature should be consulted for a more detailed or broader account of these functions (see section 8.6).

Step 5: Identify the Finite

Determine the type of Finite element (see Chapter 5).

Step 6: Identify the Subject

In this step you will apply the Subject test (see Chapter 5) in order to confidently identify the Subject.

Step 7: Determine the mood of the clause

The mood is determined by the order of the Subject and Finite (see Chapter 5). If a non-finite clause is being analysed, this step would be skipped as non-finite clauses do not express a mood choice. Similarly, any minor clauses or other units without a Mood element would not be analysed in this step.

Step 8: Identify all markers of modality and polarity

In this step, the type of modality expressed is determined (see Chapter 5) and any markers of negative polarity are noted.

Step 9: Locate the experiential Theme of the clause

The experiential Theme will be the first experiential element of the clause up to and including the Subject. If there is no such element, then it is very likely that the clause is in a special thematic construction. If a circumstance element precedes the Subject then the Theme will be marked (see Chapter 6).

Step 10: Check for any other thematic elements

This involves identifying any other thematic elements (see Chapter 6).

Drawing the tree diagram (or box diagram): this is not actually a formal step in the analysis. As will be explained in Chapter 9, it is possible to use computer software to assist in managing the analysis and, in this case, diagrams would not be drawn for each clause. However, tree diagrams are essential for viewing the clause with all its integrated meanings (see Chapters 3, 4, 5 and 6). Different analysts may have slightly different interpretations but if the tree diagram cannot be satisfactorily drawn, then this may indicate a fundamental problem with the analysis or the theory. It is also a question of personal preference and some may find the tree diagrams very useful while others prefer to use only box diagrams. In practical terms, tree diagrams can be very time consuming when working on a computer. I always have a pencil and note pad handy when I am analysing grammar so that I can draw out the grammar for any clauses that are particularly tricky.

8.3.2 The text and clause list

The text used as an example for the demonstration of the set of steps is the same text that was segmented in Chapter 7. It is repeated here in Text 8.1 below.

Text 8.1 Personal email text extract: email message from November 1999, a mother emailing her daughter

It's about 6 am and I couldn't sleep. I have to work at 8 as I went to Timmins yesterday for my mammogram so didn't get to work. John drove me. I said if the roads were good I would drive myself but he said he would so it was nice. Went to the Fishbowl for lunch and then did some shopping. I got Robert the Thomas with the case. I was going to get him clothes as I saw some cute things but the Thomas thing is cute.

The clause listing for this text is also reproduced here for ease of reference as shown in Table 8.2.

Table 8.2: Clause listing for Text 8.1

[1]	It's about 6 (hours) am
[2]	and I couldn't sleep.
[3]	I have to work at 8 (hours)
[4]	as I went to Timmins yesterday for my mammogram
[5]	so (I) didn't get to work.
[6]	John drove me.
[7]	I said [if the roads were good I would drive myself]
[8]	but he said [he would (drive me)]
[9]	so it was nice.
[10]	(we) went to the Fishbowl for lunch
[11]	and then (we) did some shopping.
[12]	I got Robert the Thomas (train) with the case.
[13]	I was going to get him clothes
[14]	as I saw some cute things
[15]	but the Thomas thing is cute

8.3.3 Analysing the clause, step by step

Each clause in Text 8.1 will now be analysed in full. The analysis of the first ten clauses will be detailed, following the ten steps described above. The remaining five clauses will be presented without discussion. This will give the reader the opportunity to attempt the use of the guidelines and compare with the analysis presented here.

Clause [1]

> *It's about 6 (hours) am*

Step 1: Identify the process and the expected participants

The main verb is *'s* (be). This is a process of being.

Process test: In a process of being, we expect someone/something to be being something.

Therefore this process expects two participants.

Step 2: Verify the boundaries of internal structures

There is only one group following the verb group. This clause cannot easily be rearranged in its current form but if *it* is seen to refer to 'the time', then the second participant can be moved to Subject position, showing that *about 6 am* is a group, as in 'about 6 am is the time'.

it	's	about 6 (hours) am
Ngp	Vgp	Ngp

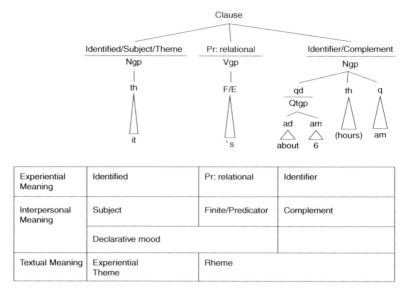

Figure 8.1 Tree and box diagram for *it's about 6 am*

Step 3: Determine the process type and participant roles

When the main verb is *be* the only possible types of process are relational and existential processes. In this case, *it* seems to refer to 'the time' and so is a participant. With two participants identified, the best analysis for this clause is that of a relational process. The two participants can be inverted, provided *it* which is accepted as referring to 'the time': *about 6 am is the time*. Therefore the clause expresses an Identifying relational process, *it*, which is Identified and the second participant, *about 6 am*, is Identifier. There are no other participants.

The transitivity structure is therefore: Identified + relational process + Identifier.

Step 4: Identify any circumstance roles

There are no circumstance roles.

Step 5: Identify the Finite type

The Finite is a temporal Finite (tense) and is expressed by the main verb (Predicator). This is shown by contrasting simple present tense with simple past tense: *It's about 6 am → It was about 6 am*.

Step 6: Identify the Subject

Original clause: *it is about 6am.*
Yes/no question: *is it about 6am?*
Therefore, *it* is the Subject.

Step 7: Determine the mood of the clause

Subject followed by Finite indicates declarative mood structure.

Step 8: Identify any markers of modality and polarity

No modal elements were identified in this clause.

Step 9: Locate the experiential Theme

The experiential Theme is the first experiential element of the clause up to and including Subject; therefore *it* is the experiential Theme.

Step 10: Check for any other thematic elements

There are no other thematic elements.

Clause [2]

and I couldn't sleep

Step 1: Identify the process and the expected participants

The main verb is *sleep*. This is a process of sleeping.

Process test: In a process of sleeping we expect someone to be sleeping.

Therefore we should expect one participant.

Step 2: Verify the boundaries of internal structures

and	I	couldn't sleep
	Ngp	Vgp

There are no internal boundaries to resolve in this clause as there are no groups following the verb group.

Step 3: Determine the process type and participant roles

First, eliminate three processes that clearly do not apply in this case. This clause does not represent a relational process or a verbal process or an existential process. Therefore, it may be a material process, a mental process or a behavioural process. Sleeping is not a mental process since the main participant here is not physically perceiving anything nor is she having a good or bad feeling about anything. Sleeping does not involve cognition. The choice we are left with is between a material process and a behavioural process. The main distinction is whether or not the main participant is being represented as Actor or Behaver. Here the implication is that the participant was actively trying to sleep so the participant role of Actor best fits and the clause will be analysed as representing a material process. There are no other participants.

The transitivity structure is therefore: **Actor + material process**.

Step 4: Identify any circumstance roles

There are no circumstance roles in this clause.

Step 5: Identify the Finite type

The Finite is identified by the modal verb *could*.

Step 6: Identify the Subject

Original clause: *and I couldn't sleep*.

Yes/no question: *and couldn't I sleep?*

The Finite has created a boundary around *I* and therefore *I* is the Subject. It should be noted that certain personal pronouns (e.g. *I, he, she, they, we*) in English show

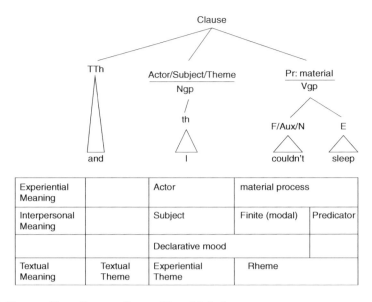

Figure 8.2 Tree and box diagram for *and I couldn't sleep*

Subject case (see Chapter 2) and it may seem unnecessary to use the Subject test in these cases.

Step 7: Determine the mood of the clause

The Subject is followed by the Finite and therefore this clause is in declarative mood.

Step 8: Identify any markers of modality and polarity

Modality is expressed through the modal verb *could*. In this use, it indicates modality of ability. Negative polarity is expressed through the negator *n't*.

Step 9: Locate the experiential Theme

The experiential Theme is *I* (i.e. Actor/Subject/Theme).

Step 10: Check for any other thematic elements

The conjunction *and* has the function of textual Theme.

Clause [3]

I have to work at 8 (hours)

Step 1: Identify the process and the expected participants

The main verb is work. This is a process of working.
Process test: In a process of working, I expect someone to be working.
Therefore I expect one participant.

Step 2: Verify the boundaries of internal structures

I	have to work	at 8 (hours)
Ngp	Vgp	PP

There are no internal boundaries to resolve in this clause as there is only one possible group following the verb group.

Step 3: Determine the process type and participant roles

First, eliminate three processes that clearly do not apply in this case. This clause does not represent a relational process or a verbal process or an existential process. Therefore it may be a material process, a mental process or a behavioural process. This is a straightforward case since 'working' is an action process and the main participant in this clause is being represented as doing something. The test for Actor works: *I have to work → what she has to do is work*. There are no other participants.

The transitivity structure is therefore: **Actor + material process**.

Step 4: Identify any circumstance roles

There is one remaining element in the clause which appears to be a circumstance: *at 8* answers the question 'when?' in relation to the process. Therefore the type of circumstance represented is that of **Location** (time).

Step 5: Identify the Finite type

The Finite is expressed by the auxiliary verb *have* and is a temporal Finite (tense).

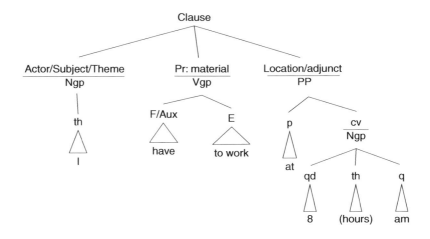

Experiential Meaning	Actor		Material process		Location
Interpersonal Meaning	Subject		Finite (modal)	Predicator	Adjunct
	Declarative mood				
Textual Meaning	Experiential Theme		Rheme		

Figure 8.3 Tree and box diagram for *I have to work at 8 am*

This is shown by contrasting simple present tense with simple past tense: *I have to work at 8 → I had to work at 8.*

Step 6: Identify the Subject

Original clause: *I have to work at 8.*

Yes/no question: *?have I to work at 8?*

Add do-support: *I do have to work at 8.*

Yes/no question: *do I have to work at 8?*

The auxiliary Finite *do* has created a boundary around *I* and therefore *I* is the Subject.

Step 7: Determine the mood of the clause

The Subject is followed by the Finite so the mood represented in this clause is declarative.

Step 8: Identify any markers of modality and polarity

Modality is expressed in this clause through the use of *have (to)*, which indicates modality of obligation (see Chapter 5).

Step 9: Locate the experiential Theme

The experiential Theme is *I* (Actor/Subject/Theme).

Step 10: Check for any other thematic elements

There are no other thematic elements in the clause.

Clause [4]

as I went to Timmins yesterday for my mammogram

Step 1: Identify the process and the expected participants

The main verb is *went*. This is a process of going.

Process test: In a process of going I expect someone to be going.

Therefore, I am expecting one participant.

Note that your application of the process test may produce a different result if you see this process as being one of someone going somewhere, for example, where the somewhere (Location) would be considered a participant rather than a circumstance.

Step 2: Verify the boundaries of internal structures

The movement test will show how many groups are involved in the clause following the main verb. The conjunction (*as*) should be left out of the tests to make it easier.

*To Timmins yesterday I went for my mammogram.

*To Timmins yesterday for my mammogram I went.

Yesterday I went to Timmins for my mammogram.

This indicates that *yesterday* is a separate group from the remainder of the clause. Consequently *to Timmins* and *for my mammogram* must also be separate groups since *yesterday* falls between them. However, we can use the pronoun replacement test to show that *to Timmins* is indeed a separate group from *for my mammogram*:

Yesterday I went there for my mammogram.
Therefore the internal boundaries of the clause are as follows:

as	I	went	to Timmins	yesterday	for my mammogram
Ngp	Vgp	PP	Ngp	PP	PP

Step 3: Determine the process type and participant roles

First eliminate three processes that clearly do not apply in this case. This clause does not represent a relational process or a verbal process or an existential process. Therefore it may be a material process, a mental process or a behavioural process. This is a straightforward case since *going* is an action process and the main participant in this clause is being represented as doing something. The test for Actor works: *I went to Timmins → what she had to do was go to Timmins*. There are no other participants. The core transitivity structure is therefore: **Actor + material process**.

Step 4: Identify any circumstance roles

This clause represents three different circumstances:
to Timmins
yesterday
for my mammogram
    Each answers the following questions respectively: where?, when?, and why?
    Therefore each circumstance has the following functions:
Location: Space *(to Timmins)*
Location: Time *(yesterday)*
Cause: *(for my mammogram)*

Step 5: Identify the Finite type

The Finite in this clause is expressed by the main verb *(went)* and is a temporal verbal element (tense). This is shown by contrasting simple past tense with simple present tense: *I went to Timmins / she went to Timmins → I go to Timmins / she goes to Timmins.*

Step 6: Identify the Subject

Original clause: *I went to Timmins yesterday for my mammogram.*
Add do-support: *I did go to Timmins yesterday for my mammogram.*
Yes/no question: *did I go to Timmins yesterday for my mammogram?*
The auxiliary Finite *did* has created a boundary around *I* and therefore *I* is the Subject.

Step 7: Determine the mood of the clause

The Subject is followed by the Finite. Therefore the mood is declarative.

Step 8: Identify any markers of modality and polarity

There are no expressions of modality and no markers of negative polarity.

Step 9: Locate the experiential Theme

I is the experiential Theme (Actor/Subject/Theme).

Step 10: Check for any other thematic elements

There is a conjunction *as* before the experiential Theme and it has the function of textual Theme.

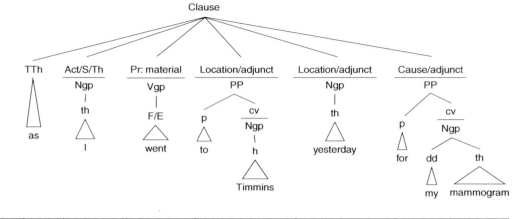

Exp.		Actor	Pr: material	Location	Location	Cause
Int.		S	F/P	A	A	A
		Declarative mood				
Tex.	TTh.	ExTh.	Rheme			

Figure 8.4 Tree and box diagram for *as I went to Timmins yesterday for my mammogram*

Clause [5]

so (I) didn't get to work

Step 1: Identify the process and the expected participants

The main verb is *get*. This is a process of getting.

Process test: in a process of getting we expect someone to be getting someone/somewhere.

Therefore I expect two participants.

Step 2: Verify the boundaries of internal structures

The internal boundaries for this clause are straightforward, so no need for tests to determine group boundaries. There is only one group following the verb group.

So	(I)	didn't get	to work
	Ngp	Vgp	PP

Step 3: Determine the process type and participant roles

This clause is similar to *I didn't go to work* or *I didn't arrive at work*. First eliminate three processes that clearly don't apply in this case. This clause does

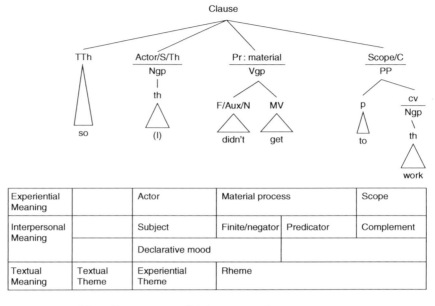

Experiential Meaning		Actor	Material process		Scope
Interpersonal Meaning		Subject	Finite/negator	Predicator	Complement
		Declarative mood			
Textual Meaning	Textual Theme	Experiential Theme	Rheme		

Figure 8.5 Tree and box diagram or *so didn't get to work*

not represent a mental process or a verbal process or an existential process. Therefore it may be a material process, a relational process or a behavioural process. This is a relatively straightforward case since 'getting' in the sense it is used here is an action process (like 'go' or 'arrive') and the main participant in this clause is being represented as doing something (or not doing something as in this case). The test for Actor works (ignore the negative polarity): *I got to work →* *what she had to do was get to work*. The second participant represents the somewhere expected from the process test. This participant could be either Goal or Scope. Since it is not affected by the process, the best interpretation of the function of this participant is Scope. In some approaches, the locational participant is labelled Location just as for the circumstance. This clause differs from the previous one (*go*) since the Location is optional and therefore it is difficult to determine whether the Location in a process of going is a participant or a circumstance (or interpersonally a Complement or an adjunct); however, in this case, *get* requires a Complement.

The transitivity structure is therefore: **Actor + material process + Scope**.

Step 4: Identify any circumstance roles

There are no circumstances in this clause.

Step 5: Identify the Finite type

The Finite in this clause is expressed by the auxiliary verb *do* and is therefore a temporal verbal element (tense). This is shown by contrasting past tense with present tense: *I didn't get to work / she didn't get to work → I don't get to work / she doesn't get to work.*

Step 6: Identify the Subject

Original clause: *so (I) didn't get to work.*
Yes/no question: *so didn't I get to work?*
The auxiliary Finite *did* has created a boundary around *I* and therefore *I* is the Subject.

Step 7: Determine the mood of the clause

The Subject is followed by the Finite so therefore the mood choice is declarative.

Step 8: Identify any markers of modality and polarity

There is no modality expressed in this clause. The polarity is negative (*n't*).

Step 9: Locate the experiential Theme

The experiential Theme is *I* (Actor/Subject/Theme).

Step 10: Check for any other thematic elements

The only element preceding the experiential Theme is the conjunction *so*. It has the function of textual Theme.

Clause [6]

John drove me

Step 1: Identify the process and the expected participants

The main verb is *drove*. This is a process of driving.

Process test: in a process of driving we expect someone to be driving OR we expect someone to be driving something OR we expect someone to be driving someone somewhere.

Therefore I could expect one, two or three participants. In this instance, two participants are represented, even though the clause fits the third possibility (i.e. someone drove someone somewhere).

Step 2: Verify the boundaries of internal structures

There is no need for tests to determine the group boundaries since there is only one possible group following the verb group.

John	drove	me
Ngp	Vgp	Ngp

Step 3: Determine the process type and participant roles

First eliminate three processes that clearly do not apply in this case. This clause does not represent a relational process or a verbal process or an existential process. Therefore it may be a material process, a mental process or a behavioural process. This is a straightforward case since 'driving' is an action process and the main participant in this clause is being represented as doing something. The test for Actor works: *John drove me → what John did was drive me*. The second participant, *me*, is either Goal or Scope. By applying the tests for Goal and Scope, it is clear that Scope is the most appropriate role: **what happened to me was that John drove me* (Goal) vs. *who was it that John drove?* (Scope).

The transitivity structure is therefore: **Actor + material process + Scope**.

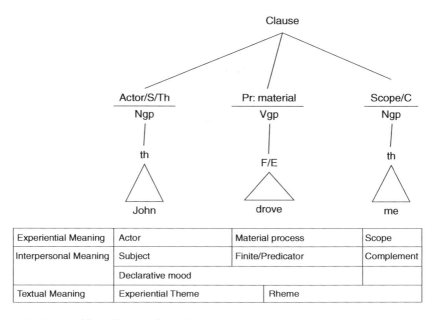

Figure 8.6 Tree and box diagram for *John drove me*

Step 4: Identify any circumstance roles

There are no circumstance roles in this clause.

Step 5: Identify the Finite type

The Finite is expressed by the main verb *drove* and is a temporal verbal element (tense). This is shown by contrasting simple past tense with simple present tense: *John drove me → John drives me.*

Step 6: Identify the Subject

Original clause: *John drove me.*
Add do-support: *John did drive me.*
Yes/no question: *did John drive me?*
The auxiliary Finite *did* has created a boundary around *John* and therefore *John* is the Subject.

Step 7: Determine the mood of the clause

The Subject is followed by the Finite, which indicates that the clause is in the declarative mood.

Step 8: Identify any markers of modality and polarity

There is no modality expressed in this clause. The polarity is positive.

Step 9: Locate the experiential Theme

The experiential Theme is expressed by *John* (Actor/Subject/Theme).

Step 10: Check for any other thematic elements

There are no elements preceding the experiential Theme.

Clause [7]

I said if the roads were good I would drive myself

Step 1: Identify the process and the expected participants

The main verb is *said*. This is a process of saying.

Process test: In a process of saying, I expect someone to be saying something.

Therefore I expect two participants.

Step 2: Verify the boundaries of internal structures

The internal boundaries for this clause were resolved when the clause boundaries were determined due to the embedded clauses. Therefore there is no need to apply any further tests at this point.

I	said	if the roads were good I would drive myself
Ngp	Vgp	Clause

Step 3: Determine the process type and participant roles

Three process types are typically unacceptable for any given clause and can be eliminated immediately. In this case, it is not a relational process, an existential process or a behavioural process. It could be a material process, a mental process or a verbal process. A process of saying is always a verbal process. Therefore the participant roles included are easily identified as Sayer and Verbiage.

The transitivity structure for this clause is: **Sayer + verbal process + Verbiage**.

The embedded clauses will not be analysed here but they certainly could be if this were desirable. Figure 8.8 shows the tree diagram for this clause with the embedded clauses analysed.

Step 4: Identify any circumstance roles

There are no circumstance roles represented in this clause.

Step 5: Identify the Finite type

The Finite is expressed by the main verb, *said*, and is a temporal Finite element (tense). This is shown by contrasting simple past tense with simple present tense: *I said... / she said... → I say... / she says...*

Step 6: Identify the Subject

Original clause: *I said if the roads were good I would drive myself.*

Add do-support: *I did say if the roads were good I would drive myself.*

Yes/no question: *did I say if the roads were good I would drive myself?*

The auxiliary Finite *did* has created a boundary around *I* and therefore *I* is the Subject.

Step 7: Determine the mood of the clause

The Subject is followed by the Finite and therefore the clause is declarative.

Step 8: Identify any markers of modality and polarity

There is no modality expressed in the main elements of the clause; however, there is a modal verb in the embedded clause (*would*) and the use of *were* is in

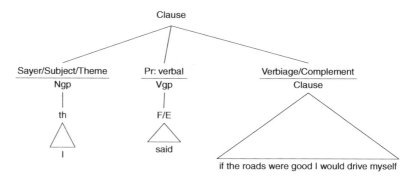

Experiential Meaning	Sayer	Verbal process	Verbiage
Interpersonal Meaning	Subject	Finite/Predicator	Complement
	Declarative mood		
Textual Meaning	Experiential Theme	Rheme	

Figure 8.7 Tree and box diagram for *I said if the roads were good I would drive myself*

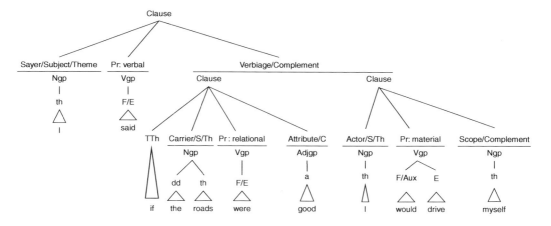

Figure 8.8 Clause 7 including an analysis for the embedded clauses

fact a fossilized verbal form, which is historically the subjunctive mood. However, this distinction is largely lost in Modern English. Nevertheless the embedded clause does express a kind of hypothetical condition which is within the modality of probability.

Step 9: Locate the experiential Theme

The experiential Theme is *I* (Sayer/Subject/Theme).

Step 10: Check for any other thematic elements

There are no other thematic elements.

Clause [8]

but he said he would (drive me)

Step 1: Identify the process and the expected participants

The main verb is *said* ('say'). This is a process of saying.

Process test: In a process of saying, I expect someone to be saying something. Therefore I expect two participants.

Step 2: Verify the boundaries of internal structures

The internal boundaries of the clause were determined when the clause boundaries were analysed. Consequently there is only one element following the verb group and this is the embedded clause.

but	he	said	he would (drive me)
	Ngp	Vgp	Clause

Step 3: Determine the process type and participant roles

We should be able to discount three processes without much difficulty. In this case, it is not a relational process, an existential process or a behavioural process. It could be a material process, a mental process or a verbal process. A process of saying is always a verbal process. Therefore the participant roles included are easily identified as Sayer and Verbiage.

The transitivity structure for this clause is: **Sayer + verbal process + Verbiage**.

As for Clause 7, the embedded clause won't be analysed in detailed steps here. Figure 8.10 shows the tree diagram for this clause with the embedded clauses analysed.

Step 4: Identify any circumstance roles

There are no circumstance roles for this clause.

Step 5: Identify the Finite type

The Finite element is expressed by the main verb, *said*, and is a temporal Finite element (tense).

This is shown by contrasting simple past tense with simple present tense:

He said... → *He says...*

Step 6: Identify the Subject

Original clause: *but he said he would (drive me)*

Add do-support: *but he did say he would (drive me)*

Yes/no question: *but did he say he would (drive me)?*

The auxiliary verb, *did*, has created a boundary around *he* and therefore *he* is the Subject.

Step 7: Determine the mood of the clause

The Subject is followed by the Finite and therefore the mood of this clause is declarative.

Step 8: Identify any markers of modality and polarity

There is no expression of modality in the main clause; however, as with the previous clause, there is a modal verb in the embedded clause (Verbiage). The polarity is unmarked (positive).

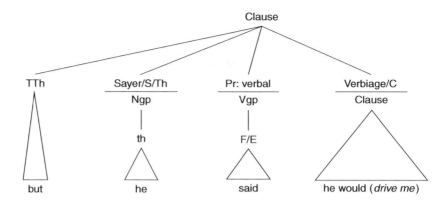

Experiential Meaning		Sayer	Verbal process	Verbiage
Interpersonal Meaning		Subject	Finite/Predicator	Complement
		Declarative mood		
Textual Meaning	Textual Theme	Experiential Theme	Rheme	

Figure 8.9 Tree and box diagram for *but he said he would*

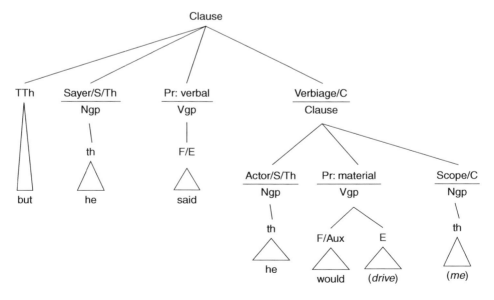

Figure 8.10 Clause 8 with embedded clause analysed

Step 9: Locate the experiential Theme

The experiential Theme is *he* (Sayer/Subject/Theme).

Step 10: Check for any other thematic elements

The conjunction *but* has the function of textual Theme.

Clause [9]

so it was nice

Step 1: Identify the process and the expected participants

The main verb is *was* 'be'. This is a process of being.

Process test: In a process of being, I expect someone/something to be being something. Therefore I expect two participants.

Step 2: Verify the boundaries of internal structures

There is only one group following the verb group (see Chapter 2 for lexical categories and Chapter 3 for group structure).

so	it	was	nice
	Ngp	Vgp	Adjgp

Step 3: Determine the process type and participant roles

When the main verb and process is the verb *be*, then the process type is always relational. In this case it is an attributive type of relational process. As explained in Chapter 4, relational processes can be attributive or identifying. Identifying clauses are reversible and therefore the two participants can swap places, but for this clause it will not work: **nice it was*. Furthermore, although it is not always the case, Attributes are often expressed by an adjective (or adjective group). Since *nice* is an adjective and the clause cannot be Identifying, there are good reasons for determining that the process is attributive.

The transitivity structure is: **Carrier + relational process + Attribute**.

Step 4: Identify any circumstance roles

There are no circumstance roles.

Step 5: Identify the Finite type

The Finite is expressed by the main verb (*be*) and is a temporal Finite element (tense). This is shown by contrasting simple past tense with simple present tense: *it was nice → it is nice*.

Step 6: Identify the Subject

Original clause: *so it was nice*.

Yes/no question: *so was it nice?*

The Finite created a boundary around *it*. Therefore *it* is the Subject.

Step 7: Determine the mood of the clause

The Subject is followed by the Finite, which indicates declarative mood structure.

Step 8: Identify any markers of modality and polarity

There is no modality or negative polarity expressed in this clause.

Step 9: Locate the experiential Theme

The experiential Theme is *it* (Carrier/Subject/Theme).

Step 10: Check for any other thematic elements

The conjunction *so* has the function of textual Theme.

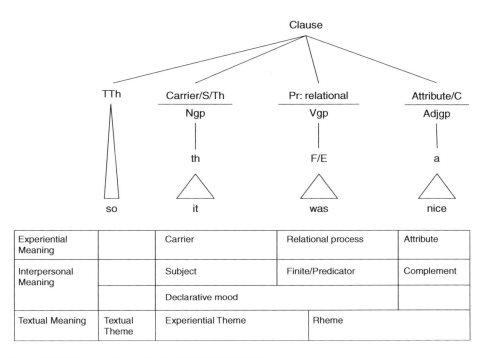

Experiential Meaning		Carrier	Relational process	Attribute
Interpersonal Meaning		Subject	Finite/Predicator	Complement
		Declarative mood		
Textual Meaning	Textual Theme	Experiential Theme	Rheme	

Figure 8.11 Tree and box diagram for *so it was nice*

Clause [10]

(we) went to the Fishbowl for lunch

Step 1: Identify the process and the expected participants

The main verb is *went* ('go'). This is a process of going.

Process test: In a process of going, I expect someone to be going.

Therefore one participant is expected.

Step 2: Verify the boundaries of internal structures

Following the verb group we find a prepositional group (phrase) and another prepositional group. In this step we have to sort out the relationship between the two. They could combine to form a single group where the second one is embedded in the first or they could function as two separate groups with respect to the clause. By applying the movement test we can see whether *for lunch* can successfully be moved and, if so, this would indicate that it is separate from *to the Fishbowl*.

For lunch we went to the Fishbowl.

*to the Fishbowl for lunch we went.

The pronoun replacement test will also support the result from the movement test: *we went there for lunch*

(we)	went	to the Fishbowl	for lunch
(Ngp)	Vgp	PP	PP

Step 3: Determine the process type and participant roles

As in the analyses above, we should be able to immediately eliminate three process types. A process of going is not likely to be relational, mental or existential. The participant tests lead us to analysing this clause as material since the test for Actor works: *we went to the Fishbowl → what we did was go to the Fishbowl.*

There are no other participant roles.

The core transitivity structure is: **(Actor) + material process**.

Step 4: Identify any circumstance roles

There are two circumstances in this clause. The first is *to the Fishbowl*. This answers the question 'where?'. The type of meaning represented here is therefore a circumstance of **Location** in Space. The second is *for lunch*. This answers the question 'why?'. The type of meaning represented here is a circumstance of **Cause**.

Step 5: Identify the Finite type

The Finite is expressed by the main verb (*go*) and is a temporal Finite element (tense). This is shown by contrasting simple past tense with simple present tense: *(we) went to the Fishbowl for lunch / she went to the Fishbowl for lunch → we go to the Fishbowl for lunch / she goes to the Fishbowl for lunch.*

Step 6: Identify the Subject

Original clause: *(we) went to the Fishbowl for lunch.*

Add do-support: *we did go to the Fishbowl for lunch.*

Yes/no question: *did we go to the Fishbowl for lunch?*

The Finite has identified a boundary around the Subject, which is *we*; however in this clause the Subject is empty since it was ellipsed.

Step 7: Determine the mood of the clause

The Subject is followed by the Finite, which indicates declarative mood structure. This relationship holds even though the Subject is ellipsed.

Step 8: Identify any markers of modality and polarity

There is no modality or negative polarity expressed in this clause.

Step 9: Locate the experiential Theme

The experiential Theme is *we* (Actor/Subject/Theme) even though it is ellipsed.

Step 10: Check for any other thematic elements

There are no other thematic elements.

This completes the detailed presentation of the ten steps in analysing the clause. The grammatical analysis for each of the five remaining clauses is given below without a description of the steps taken in the analysis. These clauses are reproduced below.

[11] and then (we) did some shopping

[12] I got Robert the Thomas (train) with the case

[13] I was going to get him clothes

[14] as I saw some cute things

[15] but the Thomas thing is cute

Before looking at the complete analysis, you may wish to try to analyse these clauses on your own. The presentation of the guidelines, as was done above, is necessarily repetitive but it is by repeating the steps systematically that a thorough approach to grammatical analysis is developed. In my experience, when students are struggling with the analysis, it is often because they have skipped steps and consequently overlooked an important earlier step.

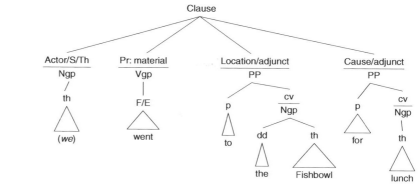

Experiential Meaning	(Actor)	Material process	Location: Space	Cause
Interpersonal Meaning	Subject	Finite/Predicator	Adjunct	Adjunct
	Declarative mood			
Textual Meaning	Experiential Theme	Rheme		

Figure 8.12 Tree and box diagram for *went to the Fishbowl for lunch*

Clause [11]

and then (we) did some shopping

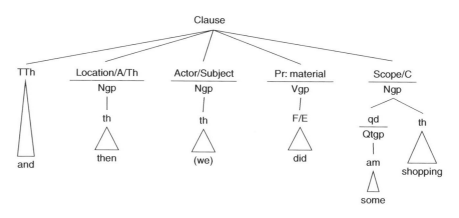

Figure 8.13 Tree and box diagram for *and then did some shopping*

Exp.		Location: Time	(Actor)	Material process	Scope
Int.		Adjunct	(Subject)	Finite/Predicator	Complement
			Declarative mood		
Tex.	Textual Theme	Marked Experiential Theme	Rheme		

Figure 8.13 (cont.)

Clause [12]

I got Robert the Thomas with the case

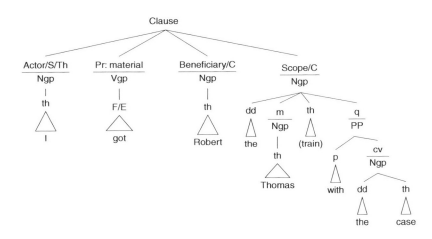

Experiential Meaning	Actor	Material process	Beneficiary	Goal	
Interpersonal Meaning	Subject	Finite/Predicator	Complement	Complement	
	Declarative mood				
Textual Meaning	Experiential Theme	Rheme			

Figure 8.14 Tree and box diagram for *I got Robert the Thomas with the case*

214

Clause [13]

I was going to get him clothes

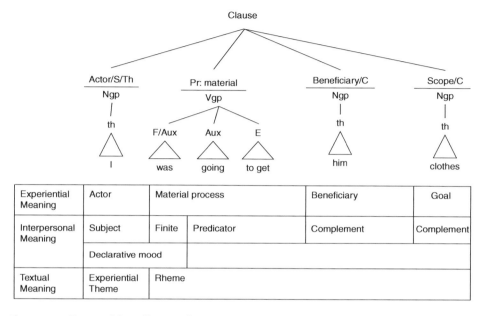

Figure 8.15 Tree and box diagram for *I was going to get him clothes*

Clause [14]

as I saw some cute things

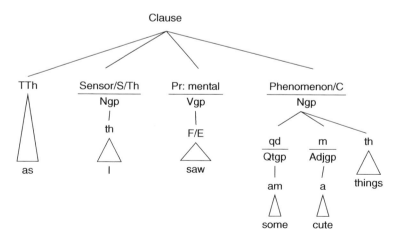

Figure 8.16 Tree and box diagram for *as I saw some cute things*

Experiential Meaning		Senser	Mental process	Phenomenon
Interpersonal Meaning		Subject	Finite/Predicator	Complement
		Declarative mood		
Textual Meaning	Textual Theme	Experiential Theme	Rheme	

Figure 8.16 (cont.)

Clause [15]

but the Thomas thing is cute

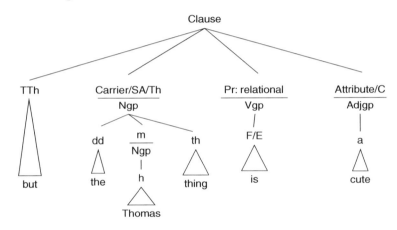

Experiential Meaning		Carrier	Relational process	Attribute
Interpersonal Meaning		Subject	Finite/Predicator	Complement
		Mood: Declarative		
Textual Meaning	Textual Theme	Experiential Theme		

Figure 8.17 Tree and box diagram for *but the Thomas thing is cute*

8.4 SUMMARY

It may seem that, despite the attempts to analyse grammar in a systematic way, the analysis itself is highly interpretive. This is true to some extent since, as Halliday (1994: xvi) points out, 'work of this kind ... is a work of interpretation'. In many cases the analysis is open to discussion and debate. There are no truly definitive answers since, when dealing with language, we have no way of verifying our claims. As Mel'čuk (1997: 2, my translation) explains:

> Linguistics is in the same situation as all other natural sciences. Language, which is a system of very complex rules, encoded in a speaker's brain in some unknown way, is inaccessible to the direct observation of 'pure' linguists: we cannot open up heads, neither can we penetrate them with electrodes in order to observe language as it is stored in the brain. The only solution we have is to develop models of language.

Therefore, our analysis is as good as our model and it can always be improved. In any case, language itself is not designed to conform to our models so there will always be instances that will perplex even the best one. Halliday (1994: xvi) explains that 'there are always indeterminacies, alternative interpretations, places where one has to balance one factor against another'. The ability to cope with this comes with experience and ideally, in return, it contributes to improving the model of language.

The grammatical analysis of an individual clause provides an in-depth account of the multiple meanings it expresses and the way it is structured in order to express these meanings. However, very clearly, the single clause tells us very little about the text we began with in the first stage of the analysis. There must be a transition from the analysis of the individual clauses of the fragmented text to the interpretation of the multifunctional nature of the text. Having now demonstrated the guidelines for analysing the clause, the next chapter in this book, Chapter 9, provides some direction in how to make this transition, returning the focus of the analysis to the text. This is not to say that there are never any good reasons for restricting analysis to the clause since many theoretical grammarians or syntacticians will focus almost exclusively on this. Similarly many language teachers, for example, may want to study language understanding or language production at the clause level. It always depends on the objectives of the study. For most students of English language, it is important to develop a firm understanding of the overall practice of grammatical analysis in a general sense so that they can apply it for whatever purpose is needed. Therefore, to round off the approach to analysing English grammar, Chapter 9 completes the picture with a focus on the interpretation of the grammatical analysis.

8.5 EXERCISES

Each exercise below includes the texts from the exercises in Chapter 7. Use the clause lists identified from those exercises to analyse each clause completely. You may wish to check your clause boundaries against the answers in Chapter 10 before doing the grammatical analysis.

Exercise 8.1

I always get to this computer later at night. John is out golfing and Jane is at a sleepover birthday party where they are sleeping outside in tents and Sue has three friends over for a sleep over. They are watching a movie now.

(Excerpt from a personal email written by an adult female to a female friend, June 2005)

Exercise 8.2

> When it first happened, there was a big thunderstorm that shook the house and the rain fell really fast. My brother was startled because he was outside. Now the water is knee-high but we're alright. We went canoeing to a nice park which is really fun! We saw some iguanas today, and we even had a black snake at our house and I saw a snake on a canoe too! Every time I go out we go out in a canoe or our dad carries us because me and my brother don't like going out in the water because of the snakes. We should be going back to school in three weeks. It's a long time off.

(BBC, CBBC Newsround. 2011. *Press Pack Reports: I'm stuck in the Australian floods.* http://news.bbc.co.uk/cbbcnews/hi/newsid_9340000/newsid_9341900/9341995.stm)

Exercise 8.3

> The future must see the broadening of human rights throughout the world. People who have glimpsed freedom will never be content until they have secured it for themselves. In a truest sense, human rights are a fundamental object of law and government in a just society. Human rights exist to the degree that they are respected by people in relations with each other and by governments in relations with their citizens. The world at large is aware of the tragic consequences for human beings ruled by totalitarian systems. If we examine Hitler's rise to power, we see how the chains are forged which keep the individual a slave and we can see many similarities in the way things are accomplished in other countries. Politically men must be free to discuss and to arrive at as many facts as possible and there must be at least a two-party system in a country because when there is only one political party, too many things can be subordinated to the interests of that one party and it becomes a tyrant and not an instrument of democratic government.

(Roosevelt, Eleanor. 1948. *The Struggle for Human Rights.* [speech] Paris, France, 28 September 1948. http://edchange.org/multicultural/speeches/eleanor_roosevelt_rights. html)

8.6 FURTHER READING

For approaches to analysing spoken language:
Eggins, S. and D. Slade. 1997. *Analysing Casual Conversation.* London: Cassell.
O'Grady, G. 2010. *A Grammar of Spoken English Discourse.* London: Continuum.

To supplement reading on analysing the clause:
Bloor, T. and M. Bloor. 2004. *The Functional Analysis of English: A Hallidayan Approach.* 2nd edn. London: Arnold.
Martin, J., C. Matthiessen and C. Painter. 1997. *Working with Functional Grammar.* London: Edward Arnold.
Thompson, G. 2004. *Introducing Functional Grammar.* 2nd edn. London: Arnold.

Chapter 9: There and back again: interpreting the analysis

9.1 INTRODUCTION

> Whatever the ultimate goal that is envisaged, the actual analysis of a text in grammatical terms is only the first step.
>
> (Halliday, 1994: xvi)

Throughout this book, the focus has been on understanding the clause both functionally and structurally. Chapters 1 to 7 have progressively constructed this understanding by focusing on specific individual aspects in turn. Chapter 8 summarized all of this by presenting a set of guidelines for a multifunctional analysis of the clause. In this final chapter, we have come full circle. As pointed out in Chapter 1, one of the main objectives of analysing language in a functional perspective is to consider language in context and gain an understanding of how language is used. It is the text not the clause that is socially relevant. This chapter completes the picture by exploring how the analysis of the clause informs the analysis of text.

It may be clear by now that analysing all the clauses in a text is a considerable amount of work, but it is only the first step. According to Halliday (2010), there are two main questions we might have when analysing text. The first is 'Why does the text mean what it does?' and the second is 'Why is the text valued as it is?' The answer to the first question is that 'it means what the linguist says it means' (Halliday, 2010), by relating to the system and exploring how the text comes to mean what it does. In order to achieve this, as Halliday (1994: xvi) states, 'there has to be a grammar at the base'. The answer to the second question is more difficult since 'it requires an interpretation not only of the text itself but also of its context (context of situation, context of culture), and of the systematic relationship between context and text' (Halliday 1994: xv). Halliday (2010) argues that there is not much point in trying to answer the second question without having already answered the first question. Therefore, irrespective of the goals one hopes to achieve in analysing text or discourse, a firm understanding of grammar is essential.

The meanings in the text are not immediately observable in most cases since they are expressed through the clause. This is why, before an understanding of the meanings in the text can be reached, it has to be segmented into its constitutive clauses so that these individual clauses can be analysed. The text is somewhat like a jigsaw puzzle in this sense; all the pieces must be taken apart and put back together before the full picture can be revealed.

9.1.1 Theory–description–use–theory cycle

Systemic functional linguistics presents both a theoretical model of language (a view of how language works) and a model of analysis (an analytical tool for describing language). There is a distinction to be made between considering the full potential of the grammar (language as system) and the perspective of 'analysis' when considering the actual instance of the grammar (language as text). The theory of SFL is based on the notion of choice and the modelling of the available choices in language as system networks.

Language, in this view, is seen as a resource for making meaning. In theory, semantics drives the production of language as speakers are considered to be selecting from semantic options which are related in a complex network. The output of the system is grammatical form. In analysing grammar, the analyst works backwards, in a sense, starting with the grammatical form (e.g. the clause as identified in text), and attempts to deduce the functions expressed by the speaker. There is a kind of necessarily symbiotic relationship between the theory and the application of the theory. The theory drives the approach to analysis and the results of any analysis will then, in turn, inform the theoretical model. These two very different strands have been referred to as 'theoretical-generative' and 'text-descriptive' respectively (Fawcett, 2000c: 78). Ideally, they work together in balance in what Halliday and Fawcett (1987, cited in Matthiessen and Bateman, 1991: xvi) refer to as the 'theory–description–use–theory cycle'. There should be open lines of communication between those who consider themselves architects of a theory and those who consider themselves appliers of a theory. Applied analysts need improvements to the model in order to better understand real-world concerns such as literacy, language disorders, media analysis, and so forth. Theorists need to test their model on real applications in order to adjust the theory, when necessary.

9.1.2 Goals of the chapter

The main goal of this chapter is to demonstrate how the analysis of the clause leads to an understanding of the text. This is often a difficult transition to make after focusing on individual clauses and it requires a different perspective from the micro-analysis that is done when working at the clause level. It is at this point, once the analysis of the clauses has been completed, that it is important to take a step back and look at the big picture.

A functional theory of language should be of interest and use to non-linguists and it should give 'insights into the way language works in social interaction' (Bloor and Bloor, 2004: 213). This chapter intends to move towards this goal and show how the results of the clause analysis can be compiled in order to both identify the patterns of meaning in the text and interpret them. As with many of the chapters in this book, the goal is to demonstrate an approach to grammatical analysis. In this chapter the focus is not on how to do the analysis (see Chapter 7 and 8) but on what to do with the results of this analysis. This is a difficult thing to model because interpreting grammatical analysis will be affected by the texts, the cultural and situational contexts involved, and the research aims of the analyst. Therefore, the presentation here should be seen as an example of one way to bridge the gap between grammatical analysis and discourse or text analysis. The discussion in this chapter is meant to be illustrative rather than exhaustive. For this reason, additional reading is suggested in section 9.5.

9.1.3 Organization of the chapter

This chapter will rely on two texts, as explained below, to illustrate one way of compiling, managing and interpreting the results of the grammatical analysis of text. The next section introduces the two texts and then presents the discussion of the results by considering each strand of meaning in turn. Examples will be given about how the results can be interpreted to show how the text means what it does. Once the meanings for each of the three meta-functions have been presented, a discussion of referent analysis is given which shows how a multifunctional view of specific referents can inform our understanding of the text. As this is the last main chapter in the book, section 9.3 offers some concluding remarks. Following this section 9.4 provides some exercises for readers to work through on their own with sample answers provided in Chapter 10. Finally, as with all other chapters, section 9.5 provides a list of suggested readings in text and discourse analysis.

9.2 PATTERNS OF MEANING IN TEXT

The analysis of the clause can be thought of as a kind of labelling exercise. The objective is to understand how meanings are expressed. This can provide a very detailed view of the clause. However, it does not really let us see the big picture, which is the text. The results from this analysis have to be collated so that the patterns of meaning in the text can be more easily seen and interpreted. This will be illustrated below using an example.

What is most relevant in the text is semantic rather than structural and while there is no direct correlation between grammatical realizations and semantic categories, there is a relationship between the two, albeit a complex one (Halliday, 1973: 75).

In this section, each strand of meaning will be considered in terms of patterns in text, leading to how results from analysis can be interpreted for a deeper understanding of the text. Sometimes, the meanings of the text are obvious and in fact so obvious that they can be difficult to notice (Thompson, 2004: 127). However, in other cases the meanings are perhaps obscured and only brought to consciousness by detailed analysis.

In order to begin to recognize patterns in the text, it can be very useful to organize the results. There are various ways in which this can be done. Generally, the results are grouped either manually or by using a software package. There are some very useful tools available for managing the analyses. One such tool is the UAM CorpusTool, developed by Mick O'Donnell (e.g. O'Donnell, 2008) and available for free on his website.[1] This software will assist the analyst in analysing single texts or collections of texts at multiple levels (for example, by text, clause or group) by keeping track of the analysis being done and managing the results. It also presents a very useful means of describing the results for the entire text or corpus and includes a statistical analysis package.

When working manually, it can be useful to compile the results of the analysis for each clause using tables for each strand of meaning. Tables can be created easily, and examples of this are given below for each metafunction. Some students have used spreadsheet software to enter clausal analysis in tabular form and others use the table function in word processor software. By doing so, an overview of the meanings in the text or in a section of the text can be seen at a glance.

As Thompson (2004: 127) points out, it is often easier to detect patterns by comparing two texts. To illustrate one way to compile the results of clause analysis in order to identify and interpret meaningful patterns in text, two texts will be presented and analysed by considering each metafunction individually. The two texts chosen are both what might be best called explanation texts since their purpose is to explain what an earthquake is. The first, Text 9.1,[2] was taken from the US Federal Emergency Management Agency (FEMA) website. It is intended for school-age children who are interested in learning about earthquakes. The second, Text 9.2,[3] was written for an adult audience and was taken from the British Geological Survey (BGS) website. The FEMA and BGS texts are quite similar in many respects, especially with regard to their shared immediate goal of explaining earthquakes. The BGS text is an excerpt rather than the entire text so that it would be comparable in word length and topic to the FEMA text. The BGS text is presented in an FAQ (frequently asked questions) format, and although the questions are included in the text presented here they have not been included in the analysis as only the text answering the questions is being considered.

Text 9.1 FEMA text: 'Earthquakes'

Earthquakes are the shaking, rolling or sudden shock of the earth's surface. Earthquakes happen along 'fault lines' in the earth's crust. Earthquakes can be felt over large areas although they usually last less than one minute. Earthquakes cannot be predicted – although scientists are working on it!

Most of the time, you will notice an earthquake by the gentle shaking of the ground. You may notice hanging plants swaying or objects wobbling on shelves. Sometimes you may hear a low rumbling noise or feel a sharp jolt. A survivor of the 1906 earthquake in San Francisco said the sensation was like riding a bicycle down a long flight of stairs.

The intensity of an earthquake can be measured. One measurement is called the Richter scale. Earthquakes below 4.0 on the Richter scale usually do not cause damage, and earthquakes below 2.0 usually can't be felt. Earthquakes over 5.0 on the scale can cause damage. A magnitude 6.0 earthquake is considered strong and a magnitude 7.0 is a major earthquake. The Northridge Earthquake, which hit Southern California in 1994, was magnitude 6.7.

Earthquakes are sometimes called temblors, quakes, shakers or seismic activity. The most important thing to remember during an earthquake is to DROP, COVER and HOLD ON. So remember to DROP to the floor and get under something for COVER and HOLD ON during the shaking.

Text 9.2 Excerpt from the BGS FAQ on earthquakes

What is an earthquake?

An earthquake is the sudden release of strain energy in the Earth's crust resulting in waves of shaking that radiate outwards from the earthquake source. When stresses in the crust exceed the strength of the rock, it breaks along lines of weakness, either a pre-existing or new fault plane. The point where an earthquake starts is termed the focus or hypocentre and may be many kilometres deep within the earth. The point at the surface directly above the focus is called the earthquake epicentre.

Where do earthquakes occur?

Anywhere! However, they are unevenly distributed over the earth, with the majority occurring at the boundaries of the major crustal plates. These plate boundaries are of three types: destructive, where the plates collide; constructive, where the plates move apart; and conservative plate boundaries, like the San Andreas Fault, where the plates slide past each other. Earthquakes also occur, less frequently, within the plates and far from the plate boundaries, as in eastern USA, Australia and the United Kingdom.

Which countries have the largest and most frequent earthquakes?

Around 75% of the world's seismic energy is released at the edge of the Pacific, where the thinner Pacific plate is forced beneath thicker continental crust along 'subduction zones'. This 40,000 km band of seismicity stretches up the west coasts of South and Central America and from the Northern USA to Alaska, the Aleutians, Japan, China, the Philippines, Indonesia and Australasia.

Around 15% of the total seismic energy is released where the Eurasian and African plates are colliding, forming a band of seismicity which stretches from Burma, westwards to the Himalayas to the Caucasus and the Mediterranean.

> **What is the biggest earthquake that has ever happened?**
> One of the largest earthquakes ever was the Chile event of 22 May 1960 with moment magnitude of 9.5 Mw. Other large earthquakes include Lisbon, 1 November 1755, magnitude 8.7 Ms; Assam, 12 June 1897, magnitude 8.7 Ms; Alaska, 28 March 1964, moment magnitude 9.2 Mw. Although the magnitude scale is open ended, the strength of the crustal rocks prior to fracturing limits the upper magnitude of earthquakes.

The details of the analysis are not discussed here in order to save space and to focus on how the results of the analysis can be interpreted. Segmenting the text into individual clauses was done following the guidelines given in Chapter 7 and the analysis of each clause was done following those given in Chapter 8. Before continuing in this chapter, it might be a useful exercise to work through the analysis of these two texts. It would help the understanding of the results presented in the tables that follow.

What follows is a discussion of the patterns found in each text. This discussion is organized by individual strand of meaning. The results of the analysis have been compiled in the form of tables. However, the tables given in each case are only intended as examples for illustrative purposes. They should be adapted to the needs of the analysis in each case, adding or removing detail as appropriate. If software such as the UAM CorpusTool is being used, then it will manage this organization. There is no fixed method for organizing results and it is up to each analyst to work out the best way to work with their text(s).

9.2.1 Experiential meaning

Experiential meaning, as explained in Chapter 4, involves the representation of the speaker's experience, including what they observe, what they think or perceive, and how they relate things. This experience is inherently subjective and consciously or unconsciously reflects how the speaker sees the world or, possibly, how they want others to see it.

Since experiential meaning is sub-categorized into six process types, it can be helpful to organize the results for each process type in separate tables so that the patterns in the text are easier to see. The results for both texts are presented below. The analysed clauses for Text 9.1 have been given in Tables 9.1 to Table 9.4 followed by Tables 9.5 and 9.6, which present the analysis of experiential meaning for Text 9.2. The tables for the interpersonal and textual analyses will be presented individually below.

These results will be discussed below in comparison with the results from the BGS text. However, some patterns may already be emerging, such as the type of experience being represented. The next set of tables (Tables 9.5 and 9.6) presents the results of the experiential analysis of the BGS text. There are only two tables since only two types of process were represented in this text.

It may seem immediately obvious from these tables that the two texts are not representing exactly the same experience. The FEMA text has a relatively high frequency of mental and relational processes as compared to a much higher frequency of material and relational processes in the BGS text (see Table 9.7 below). However, identifying other patterns related to experiential meaning requires a bit more digging. Thompson (2004: 127) provides a very useful overview of how transitivity can be interpreted by presenting a set of questions that help reveal the patterns. These questions, and any others that are relevant, can be used to guide the inquiry of the text:

Table 9.1: Material clauses in the FEMA text

Clause no.	Actor	Material process	Goal	Circumstance
[2]		happen	Earthquakes	Location: along 'fault lines' in the earth's crust
[6]	scientists	are working on	it	
[12]	the intensity of an earthquake	can be measured		
[14]	Earthquakes below 4.0 on the Richter scale	do not cause	damage	
[16]	Earthquakes over 5.0 on the scale	can cause	damage	

Table 9.2: Mental clauses in the FEMA text

Clause no.	Senser	Mental process	Phenomenon	Circumstance	Circumstance
[3]	(anyone)	can be felt	Earthquakes	Location: over large areas	
[5]	(anyone)	cannot be predicted	Earthquakes		
[7]	you	will notice	an earthquake	Extent: most of the time	Manner: by the gentle shaking of the ground
[8]	you	may notice	hanging plants swaying or objects wobbling on shelves		
[9]	you	may hear	a low rumbling noise	Extent: sometimes	
[10]	(you)	(may) feel	a sharp jolt		
[15]	(anyone) / (you)	can't be felt	earthquakes below 2.0		
[22]	(you)	remember	to DROP to the floor and get under something for COVER and HOLD ON during the shaking		

- What are the dominant process types? And why these?
- How do the process types match with other aspects (e.g. location in the text, appearing in commands vs. statements, etc.)?
- What (groupings of) participants are there?
- How do these compare with 'real-world' entities and events?
- What kinds of participants (e.g. concrete vs. abstract)?
- What transitivity role(s) do they have?

Table 9.3: Relational clauses in the FEMA text

Clause no.	Carrier or Identified	Relational process	Attribute or Identifier
[1]	Earthquakes	are (Identifying)	the shaking, rolling or sudden shock of the earth's surface
[4]	They	last (Attributive)	less than one minute
[13]	One measurement	is called (Identifying)	the Richter scale
[17]	A magnitude 6.0 earthquake	is considered (Attributive)	strong
[18]	a magnitude 7.0	is (Identifying)	a major earthquake
[19]	The Northridge Earthquake, which hit Southern California in 1994,	was (Attributive)	magnitude 6.7
[20]	Earthquakes	are called (Attributive)	temblors, quakes, shakers or seismic activity
[21]	The most important thing to remember during an earthquake	is (Identifying)	to DROP, COVER, and HOLD ON

Table 9.4: Verbal clauses in the FEMA text

Clause no.	Sayer	Verbal process	Verbiage
[11]	A survivor of the 1906 earthquake in San Francisco	said	the sensation was like riding a bicycle down a long flight of stairs

- How are any nominalizations used? Are they representing 'hidden' situations?
- What types of circumstances are included? Where are they in the text?
- What gets expressed as circumstance rather than in the 'nucleus' (process + participant)?

Although both texts rely on relational processes, the FEMA text has a broader range of experience represented. Relational processes, as discussed in Chapter 4, relate two participating entities in an abstract way. This is useful for explaining what an earthquake is (e.g. *An earthquake is the sudden release of strain energy in the Earth's crust resulting in waves of shaking that radiate outwards from the earthquake source*) or for describing an earthquake (e.g. *A magnitude 6.0 earthquake is considered strong*). The high frequency of mental processes in the FEMA text is interesting, and in order to understand how this works in the text it is necessary to consider the participants involved in these clauses.

The main participants in both texts are given in Table 9.8, where it is clear that, although both texts have earthquakes as a significant participant in terms of its representation in the texts, this is not done in the same way. The FEMA text has a much more concentrated representation of earthquakes and its main role in the text is as Phenomenon; in other words, it is represented as something that is to be experienced through the senses. The Senser in these mental processes always includes the addressee – that is, the reader of the text, who in this case is a school-age child. In contrast, the BGS text, while it does include

Table 9.5: Material clauses in the BGS text

Clause no.	Actor	Material process	Goal	Circumstance	Circumstance	Circumstance
[2]	(?)	breaks	it	Location (time): when stresses in the crust exceed the strength of the rock	Location (space): along lines of weakness, either a pre-existing or new fault plane	
[6]	(?)	are distributed	they	Manner: unevenly	Location: over the earth	Location: with the majority occurring at the boundaries of the major crustal plates
[8]		occur	Earthquakes	Extent: less frequently,	Location: within the plates and far from the plate boundaries, as in eastern USA, Australia and the United Kingdom.	
[9]	(earthquake)	is released	Around 75% of the world's seismic energy	Location: at the edge of the Pacific, where the thinner Pacific plate is forced beneath thicker continental crust along 'subduction zones'		
[11]	(earthquake)	is released	Around 15% of the total seismic energy	Location: where the Eurasian and African plates are colliding, forming a band of seismicity which stretches from Burma, westwards to the Himalayas to the Caucasus and the Mediterranean.		
[15]	the strength of the crustal rocks prior to fracturing	limits	the upper magnitude of earthquakes.			

Table 9.6: Relational clauses in the BGS text

Clause no.	Carrier or Identified	Relational process	Attribute or Identifier
[1]	An earthquake	is (Identifying)	the sudden release of strain energy in the Earth's crust resulting in waves of shaking that radiate outwards from the earthquake source
[3]	The point where an earthquake starts	is termed (identifying)	the focus or hypocentre
[4]	(it)	may be (Attributive)	many kilometres deep within the earth
[5]	The point at the surface [directly above the focus]	is called (Identifying)	the earthquake epicentre
[7]	these plate boundaries	are (Attributive)	of three types: destructive, where the plates collide; constructive, where the plates move apart; and conservative plate boundaries, like the San Andreas Fault, where the plates slide past each other.
[10]	This 40,000 km band of seismicity	stretches (Attributive)	up the west coasts of South and Central America and from the Northern USA to Alaska, the Aleutians, Japan, China, the Philippines, Indonesia and Australasia
[12]	One of the largest earthquakes ever	was (Identifying)	the Chile event of 22 May 1960 with moment magnitude of 9.5 Mw
[13]	Other large earthquakes	include (Identifying)	Lisbon, 1 November 1755, magnitude 8.7 Ms; Assam, 12 June 1897, magnitude 8.7 Ms; Alaska, 28 March 1964, moment magnitude 9.2 Mw.
[14]	the magnitude scale	is (Attributive)	open ended

Table 9.7: Comparison of process types in the FEMA and BGS texts

	FEMA text	BGS text
Material	5 (22.7%)	6 (40%)
Mental	8 (36.4%)	0
Relational	8 (36.4%)	9 (60%)
Verbal	1 (4.5%)	0
Total number of clauses	22	15

earthquakes as a participant, does so much less frequently and it is primarily represented as the Identified participant in a relational process, although it is represented implicitly as Actor in two passive material processes (clauses [9] and [11]). The addressee is never a participant in this text and there is a much greater variety of entities participating. One main participant in this text is *seismic energy*, which occurs most frequently as Goal in material processes.

Table 9.8: Comparison of the main participants in the FEMA and BGS texts

Referent	FEMA text	BGS text
\<earthquake\>	Phenomenon (4) Carrier (3) Identified (2) Goal (1)	Identified (3) Actor (2) Goal (2)
\<addressee\>	Senser (6)	–
\<seismic energy\>	–	Goal (2) Carrier (1)

Table 9.9: Comparison of circumstances in the FEMA and BGS texts

	FEMA text	BGS text
Manner	1	1
Location (space)	2	5
Extent	2	1
Total	5	7

The use of material processes in each text is considerably different. In the FEMA text, the role of Actor is explicitly stated (e.g. *the intensity of an earthquake, earthquakes below 4.0 on the Richter scale, earthquakes over 5.0 on the scale*). However, in the BGS text, the material processes are most frequently in the passive voice and the Actor is left covert (or unspecified). This suggests that a certain amount of geographical knowledge is expected of the reader. For example, it is never explicitly stated that the earthquake releases seismic energy.

A comparison of the use of circumstances is given in Table 9.9, which shows that the number of circumstantial elements is roughly equivalent in each text but that the BGS text has fewer clauses than the FEMA text. So, proportionally, the BGS text has far more circumstances per clause than the FEMA text. The use of manner circumstances differs in the texts since the FEMA text uses a manner circumstance in mental processes to describe how the phenomenon (*earthquake*) will be sensed (see clause [9]), whereas it occurs in material processes in the BGS text to show how something is done (see clause 6).

There is much more that could be said about the experience represented in these two texts (e.g. an analysis of the embedded clauses). The brief sample discussed above should provide an idea of how the results of the clause analysis combine to show what the text means experientially. Although the topic of each text is very similar, the analysis of the text shows that the goals are different. The FEMA text includes the addressee as a participating entity and focuses on earthquakes in terms of a phenomenon that the addressee can sense. The BGS text also represents the referent \<earthquake\> as a participating entity (i.e. as an entity participating in the situation), but it draws on other related entities (e.g. *seismic energy*, *rock* and *earth's surface*), primarily in relational processes, in order to define and describe earthquakes.

9.2.2 Interpersonal meaning

Interpersonal meaning was described in Chapter 5 as expressing the speaker's personal intrusion on the language situation and the speaker's use of language to interact with others. This involves the means by which the speaker's personal views are expressed through modalities of modalization (probability and usuality) and modulation (obligation and inclination). Speakers also express meanings that are related more directly to interaction through the use of mood choices to ask questions, give information or make requests.

Identifying patterns in the interpersonal meanings that are found in a text can be done following an approach which is similar to the one presented above. The results of the clause analysis can be grouped in a table which presents the relevant interpersonal meanings for the purpose of the study. The results of the interpersonal analysis for the FEMA text and the BGS text are given below in Tables 9.10 and 9.11. No column for mood has been included since all clauses in both texts (with one exception) are in the declarative mood. The use of the tables should be seen to help reveal relevant patterns easily. In this sense, they are simply a tool used in this stage of the analysis. Since the Subject and Finite elements have been stressed as being especially significant to interpersonal meaning in English, they should be seen as core elements to include. However, how they are included depends on the needs and interests of the analyst. In these tables, the Finite element has been included as a single column which can make it difficult to see at a glance the different forms of expression of the Finite (e.g. as expressed by the Auxiliary or Event element of the verb group). Also, in this example, modality is grouped in a single column which does not distinguish between modal auxiliary verbs and modal adjuncts. If this were an important distinction to consider, then it would be recommended to structure the tables differently so that this information is more readily available.

A set of guiding questions can also be used to help identify the patterns of interpersonal meaning in a text. A sample of such questions is listed below, which focuses on mood, modality and polarity. However it could also include, if appropriate, elements of the clause which express the roles of the speaker and addressee, indications of social status and relationships such as degrees of formality or familiarity:

- What is the dominant mood choice? How is mood being used in the interaction?
- What modality is expressed? How is it expressed?
- What polarity is expressed?
- What indicators of social status are present?
- What are the roles of the speaker and addressee?
- What indicators are there of the speaker's opinion or attitude?

The two texts do not differ significantly in their use of mood choice as all clauses are expressed in declarative mood except clause [22] in the FEMA text. The differences among the different types of mood choice (i.e. interrogative, declarative or imperative) relate to 'differences in the communication role adopted by the speaker in his interaction with a listener' (Halliday, 2002: 189). The use of the imperative mood expresses an obligation on the part of the addressee and reflects an unequal status between the speaker and addressee. The rest of the clauses in both texts are giving information about earthquakes and related topics.

There is considerable modality expressed in the FEMA text, which is in contrast to the BGS text, where there is only one instance of modalization (probability). The FEMA text uses a wider range of modality and includes it much more frequently, as shown in Table 9.12. The instances of modal probability express the degree of likelihood (or probability) of the experiences represented in the text, as illustrated in examples (1) to (3):

    (1) Most of the time, you <u>will</u> notice an earthquake by the gentle shaking of the ground (clause [7], FEMA)

Table 9.10: Interpersonal analysis of the FEMA text

Clause no.	Subject	Finite	Adjunct	Modality	Tense	Polarity
[1]	Earthquakes	are (Auxiliary)			simple present indicative	
[2]	Earthquakes	happen (Event)			simple present indicative	
[3]	Earthquakes	can (Auxiliary)		probability		
[4]	they	last (Event)	usually	usuality	simple present indicative	
[5]	Earthquakes	cannot (Auxiliary)		probability		negative
[6]	scientists	are (Auxiliary)			present progressive indicative	
[7]	you	will (Auxiliary)		probability		
[8]	you	may (Auxiliary)		probability		
[9]	you	may (Auxiliary)		probability		
[10]	(you)	(may) (Auxiliary)		probability		
[11]	A survivor of the 1906 earthquake in San Francisco	said (Event)			simple past indicative	
[12]	the intensity of an earthquake	can (Auxiliary)		probability		
[13]	one measurement	is (Auxiliary)			present passive indicative	
[14]	earthquakes below 4.0 on the Richter scale	do not (Auxiliary)	usually	usuality	simple present indicative	negative
[15]	earthquakes below 2.0	can't (Auxiliary)	usually	probability usuality	modalized	negative
[16]	earthquakes over 5.0 on the scale	can (Auxiliary)		probability	modalized	
[17]	a magnitude 6.0 earthquake	is (Auxiliary)			present passive indicative	
[18]	a magnitude 7.0	is (Event)			simple present indicative	
[19]	The Northridge Earthquake, which hit Southern California in 1994	was (Event)			present passive indicative	
[20]	Earthquakes	are (Auxiliary)	sometimes	usuality	present passive indicative	
[21]	The most important thing to remember during an earthquake	is (Event)			simple present indicative	
[22]	(you)	(Ø) (imperative)		obligation	imperative	

Table 9.11: Interpersonal analysis of the BGS text

Clause no.	Subject	Finite	Modality	Tense	Polarity
[1]	an earthquake	is (Event)		simple present indicative	
[2]	it	breaks (Event)		simple present indicative	
[3]	the point where an earthquake starts	is (Auxiliary)		present passive indicative	
[4]	(it)	may (Auxiliary)	probability	modalized	
[5]	the point at the surface directly above the focus	is (Auxiliary)		present passive indicative	
[6]	they	are (Auxiliary)		present passive indicative	
[7]	these plate boundaries	are (Event)		simple present indicative	
[8]	Earthquakes	occur (Event)		simple present indicative	
[9]	around 75% of the world's seismic energy	is (Auxiliary)		present passive indicative	
[10]	This 40,000 km band of seismicity	stretches (Event)		simple present indicative	
[11]	around 15% of the total seismic energy	is (Auxiliary)		present passive indicative	
[12]	one of the largest earthquakes ever	was (Auxiliary)		simple past indicative	
[13]	other large earthquakes	include (Event)		simple present indicative	
[14]	the magnitude scale	is (Event)		simple present indicative	
[15]	the strength of the crustal rocks prior to fracturing	limits (Event)		simple present indicative	

Table 9.12: Comparison of modality in the FEMA and BGS texts

Modality type	FEMA text	BGS text
Probability	9	1
Usuality	4	0
Obligation	1	0
Readiness	0	0

(2) You <u>may</u> notice hanging plants swaying or objects wobbling on shelves (clause [8], FEMA)

(3) Sometimes you <u>may</u> hear a low rumbling noise (clause [9], FEMA)

There is some evidence of the relationship between speaker and addressee in both texts. The FEMA text uses the personal pronoun *you* to refer to the addressee. This kind of interpersonal deixis allows the speaker to talk directly to the addressee by reference to the contextual situation even though the actual situation changes with every reader. Furthermore, as already stated, the use of the imperative pushes this relationship even further and raises the role of the speaker to one that has some power over the addressee. This means that the speaker is in a position of authority and can instruct the reader because of their knowledge and experience.

The speaker in both texts is in the role of expert who has specialist knowledge and therefore the status between speaker (writer) and addressee (reader) is necessarily asymmetrical. The BGS text maintains distance between the speaker and addressee due to the use of the declarative mood, the relative lack of modality and the absence of reference to speaker or addressee. These combine to contribute to a sense of detachment that is not found in the FEMA text. In the FEMA text, however, the detachment typically found in written texts is reduced by the use of addressee reference, modality and imperative mood.

9.2.3 Textual meaning

As was seen in Chapter 6, the textual metafunction has the function 'of creating text, of relating itself to the context – to the situation and the preceding text' (Halliday 1978: 48). The Theme element provides the link between the clause and text and, consequently, looking at the contents of Theme throughout the text will provide insight into the development of the text. Thompson (2004: 165) explains that one of the main functions of Theme is to signal 'the maintenance or progression of what the text is about'. In addition to this, other textual patterns can be identified by considering cohesion.

In terms of organizing the results of the textual analysis of the clause, the main organizing element will be Theme and the various types of Theme possible. The tables presenting these results may also include notes about cohesion, thematic progression or anything else related to the textual metafunction. The summary of the results for the FEMA and BGS texts are given in Tables 9.13 and 9.14. There were no interpersonal Themes in either text so this information has not been included.

Given that the texts are both about earthquakes, it would be reasonable to expect that most Themes would be expressed by nominal groups referring to earthquakes. Considering the content of Themes in a text is one way to identify the patterns in the text. There are other considerations. Here is a list of suggested questions for identifying patterns in textual meaning:

- What is the most frequent Theme?
- What is the use of any marked Themes (e.g. signalling a shift or transition in the development of the text)?
- How are any textual and/or interpersonal Themes being used?
- What is the text function of the use of any special thematic constructions?
- What are the patterns of thematic progression?
- What cohesive strategies are identifiable in the text?
- What are the main strategies for reference (e.g. endophoric/exophoric reference)?

In the FEMA text, Theme is expressed by an expression referring to earthquakes generally or to a specific earthquake in 11 of the 21 clauses (52.4 per cent). This is in contrast to only 4 such Themes in the BGS text (26.7 per cent), with Themes referring to seismic energy

Table 9.13: Summary of the textual analysis of the FEMA text

Clause no.	Textual Theme	Experiential Theme Unmarked	Marked	Notes
[1]		earthquakes		
[2]		earthquakes		
[3]		earthquakes		
[4]	although	they		anaphoric reference
[5]		earthquakes		
[6]	although	scientists		
[7]			most of the time	
[8]		you		exophoric reference
[9]			sometimes	
[10]	or	(you)		ellipsis
[11]		a survivor of the 1906 earthquake in San Francisco		
[12]		the intensity of an earthquake		
[13]		one measurement		
[14]		earthquakes below 4.0 on the Richter scale		
[15]	and	earthquakes below 2.0		
[16]		earthquakes over 5.0 on the scale		
[17]		a magnitude 6.0 earthquake		
[18]	and	a magnitude 7.0		
[19]		the Northridge Earthquake, which hit Southern California in 1994		
[20]		earthquakes		
[21]		the most important thing to remember during an earthquake		
[22]		remember		

forming 20.0 per cent of the Themes in the text. This suggests that the FEMA text maintains the topic of earthquakes much more than the BGS text does. It also points out that the BGS text uses Theme to progress the topic throughout the text. Both texts are quite similar in how they use multiple Themes. The use of textual Themes is very similar, and neither text includes any interpersonal Themes. Marked Themes were not common in either text.

It is interesting to note that the addressee (*you*) is only explicitly thematized in one clause (see clause [8] in Table 9.13), even though it expresses Subject in four clauses and Senser in six clauses in total. Therefore while the addressee is represented in the text in a significant way and he or she is addressed directly by the use of the imperative in clause [22], this reference is not an important thematic element. The text is not attempting to include the

Table 9.14: Summary of the textual analysis of the BGS text

Clause no.	Textual Theme	Experiential Theme		Notes
		Unmarked	Marked	
[1]		an earthquake		
[2]			when stresses in the crust exceed the strength of the rock	
[3]		the point where an earthquake starts		
[4]	and	(it)		ellipsis
[5]		the point at the surface directly above the focus		
[6]	however	they		anaphoric reference
[7]		these plate boundaries		
[8]		earthquakes		
[9]		around 75% of the world's seismic energy		
[10]		this 40,000 km band of seismicity		
[11]		around 15% of the total seismic energy		
[12]		one of the largest earthquakes ever		
[13]		other large earthquakes		
[14]	although	the magnitude scale		
[15]		the strength of the crustal rocks prior to fracturing		

addressee as a topic. The use of this kind of reference does contribute to the creation of text through exophoric reference to the context of situation by referring deictically to the addressee (reader).

9.2.4 Referent analysis

There are many ways to organize and interpret the results of a full multifunctional analysis of the clause. As shown above, one way to do so is to focus on individual strands of meaning. However, it can be revealing to concentrate on specific referents in the text by isolating them and considering the meanings they express throughout all strands of meaning. The approach presented here is adapted from Martin's (1992) reference chains and Halliday and Hasan's (1985) identity chains. Referent analysis combines all three metafunctions and considers the view the text has taken for a specific referent.

In this example, the referent <earthquake> is explored and this means that all expressions referring to an earthquake or earthquakes will be included. The results are presented in Tables 9.15 and 9.16, where any embedded reference to earthquakes is listed in italics.

Table 9.15: Referent analysis for <earthquake> in the FEMA text

Referring expression	Clause no.	Referring Strategy	Experiential Meaning	Interpersonal Meaning	Textual Meaning
earthquakes	[1]	indefinite lexical expression	Identified	Subject	Theme
earthquakes	[2]	lexical repetition (indefinite lexical expression)	Goal	Subject	Theme
earthquakes	[3]	lexical repetition (indefinite lexical expression)	Phenomenon	Subject	Theme
they	[4]	anaphoric reference	Carrier	Subject	Theme
earthquakes	[5]	lexical repetition (indefinite lexical expression)	Phenomenon	Subject	Theme
an earthquake	[7]	indefinite lexical expression	Phenomenon	Complement	Rheme
the 1906 earthquake in San Francisco	[11]	*definite expression*	*qualifier in Sayer*	*in Subject*	*in Theme*
an earthquake	[12]	*indefinite lexical expression*	*qualifier in Scope*	*in Subject*	*in Theme*
earthquakes below 4.0 on the Richter scale	[14]	indefinite lexical expression	Actor	Subject	Theme
earthquakes below 2.0	[15]	indefinite lexical expression	Phenomenon	Subject	Theme
earthquakes over 5.0 on the scale	[16]	indefinite lexical expression	Actor	Subject	Theme
a magnitude 6.0 earthquake	[17]	indefinite lexical expression	Carrier	Subject	Theme
a magnitude 7.0 (earthquake)	[18]	indefinite lexical expression with ellipsis	Identified	Subject	Theme
the Northridge Earthquake, which hit Southern California in 1994	[19]	definite lexical expression	Carrier	Subject	Theme
earthquakes	[20]	indefinite lexical expression	Identified	Subject	Theme
an earthquake	[21]	*indefinite lexical expression*	*circumstance in embedded clause as qualifier in Identified*	*in Subject*	*in Theme*

Table 9.16: Referent analysis for <earthquake> in the BGS text

Referring expression	Clause no.	Referring Strategy	Experiential Meaning	Interpersonal Meaning	Textual Meaning
an earthquake	[1]	indefinite lexical expression	Identified	Subject	Theme
an earthquake	*[3]*	*indefinite lexical expression*	*Actor in embedded clause as qualifier in Identified*	*in Subject*	*in Theme*
they	[6]	anaphoric reference	Goal	Subject	Theme
earthquakes	[8]	indefinite lexical expression	Goal	Subject	Theme
one of the largest earthquakes ever	[12]	indefinite lexical expression	Identified	Subject	Theme
other large earthquakes	[13]	indefinite lexical expression	Identified	Subject	Theme

These tables include the actual expression used, the clause number in the text, the referring strategy (e.g. definiteness of the expression and phoricity, such as anaphora), the experiential function of the expression, any interpersonal meaning, including modality and connotation, and textual meaning, which includes thematic role, cohesion and deictic functions.

A similar approach could be taken to comparing and contrasting different referents in a text or across texts. For example, it may be of interest to compare the references to political candidates in the media or in their own manifestos. In this example, these tables make it very clear that the main referent, <earthquakes>, is not used in the same way in each text. As the last two columns in each table show, <earthquakes> is primarily expressed as functioning as Subject/Theme. However, the main differences are found in the frequency of these referring expressions and in the experiential representation of the referent, as was already mentioned above.

There are also differences in the referring strategies used by the speaker in each text. The BSG text uses almost exclusively indefinite referring expressions. This is noted by the use of the indefinite article *an* and the use of the plural. This is directly related to the fact that no specific earthquake is being referred to. Other than through lexical repetition there is no overt cohesive tie amongst these clauses, with the exception of the contrastive use of *other* in clause [13], which ties it to the preceding clause. The expression in clause [12] is interesting because, although it is an indefinite expression, it is related in this clause to a specific earthquake. The FEMA text includes two definite referring expression, and these are used to refer to specific earthquakes rather than to earthquakes in a general sense. Both texts also include the use of cohesive reference (see the use of *they* in clause [4] in FEMA and clause [6] in BGS).

9.2.5 Summary

The objective of this section was to outline a method for identifying and interpreting the patterns of meaning in text. The discussion of these two texts has been necessarily brief but a detailed analysis would be able to reveal much more. A more detailed example of the interpretation of analysed text is provided in Chapter 10 in the sample answer to Exercise 9.1. As Halliday states, 'whatever the ultimate goal that is envisaged, the actual analysis of a text in grammatical terms is only the first step' (Halliday, 1994: xvi).

The interpretation of the results of text analysis as presented here has been done in abstract terms. In reality, this kind of text analysis, through grammar, would be done with a specific aim in mind. This might be, for example, to understand children's writing, the speech of a stroke victim or the meanings of political speeches. It may also be done with the aim of better understanding a particular theoretical area of the grammar such as the role of Theme in imperative clauses or the use of multi-word lexical items, such as phrasal verbs. The specific research aims will guide the explanation and interpretation of the grammatical analysis (see Chapter 10 and Exercise 9.2; see also Bloor and Bloor, 2004 and Coffin, Hewings and O'Halloran, 2004).

9.3 FINAL REMARKS

In writing this book, I set myself two challenges. The first was to write an introduction to analysing English grammar in a functional framework by focusing on the practical, 'how-to' aspects of analysis. There is an inherent paradox in grammatical analysis; to under-stand the clause (i.e. know and recognize it), you have to first understand the clause (i.e. know its components and configurations). This is why the presentation in this book compartmentalized the various aspects to analysis into manageable stages in order to construct a systematic approach to analysing grammar. The approach promoted here was built up incrementally so that the multiple functions of the clause could be clearly related to each other and directly associated to the structural units that serve to express them. For newcomers to functional analysis, this approach will be very useful as it will provide a practical set of guidelines for analysing English grammar. Those more experienced in systemic functional linguistics will have noted a hybrid approach which does not adhere strictly to one particular version of the theory but rather draws from various existing descriptions of the theory of systemic functional grammar, most notably from Halliday and Matthiessen (2004) and Fawcett (2000c).

The second challenge was to try to write it in such a way that grammatical analysis would seem less mysterious and more enjoyable. The funny thing is that speakers generally do not have any trouble understanding language but, as soon as analysing it involves terminology and theory, things quickly become more intimidating. It is import-ant to stress that fluent speakers of a language already know how language works since they use it successfully every day. However, developing skill at grammatical analysis offers a key to unlocking some of the mysteries. It is like becoming a professional language analyser with all the advantages that professional skill has over everyday general knowledge. It means you have a deeper and broader understanding of not only how language works but also how it can work. It means that you are in a specialist position for working on real problems related to language such as, for example, language learning, language disorders, applications such as translation and also the ways in which language is used to suppress, control or benefit people. There is very little we do in this world that does not involve language. As I said in the first chapter, if you end up enjoying grammar even just a bit more from having read this book then it will have been a great success.

9.4 EXERCISES

The exercises for this chapter focus on interpreting results. However, in obtaining an interpretation, all three stages of analysis are required: segmenting the text, analysing the clauses and interpreting the results. The text selected for these exercises comes from an assignment completed for my undergraduate course at Cardiff University. Only the text is given here; each exercise listed below asks you to complete one stage of the analysis for this text. A sample answer for each is given in Chapter 10. The analysis and discussion was completed by David Schönthal (2009), a former student, and it is reproduced here with permission.

Exercise 9.1

The text below is an extract from a text entitled 'Chief Seattle's Speech' and is generally accepted as being attributed to screenwriter Ted Perry in 1971. This version of the now famous text was taken from a web page that is no longer available, but a similar version can be found at www.ilhawaii.net/~stony/seattle2.html.

Segment the text below into a list of individual clauses (see Chapter 7) and analyse it fully using the guidelines presented in Chapter 8. In Chapter 10, the full clause list is given for this text and a sample three-strand analysis is provided in the form of box diagrams. Only a selection of clauses will be analysed for illustrative purposes due to the length of the text.

Chief Seattle's Speech

How can you buy or sell the sky, the warmth of the land? The idea is strange to us. If we do not own the freshness of the air and the sparkle of the water, how can you buy them?

Every part of this earth is sacred to my people. Every shining pine needle, every sandy shore, every mist in the dark woods, every clearing and humming insect is holy in the memory and experience of my people. The sap which courses through the trees carries the memories of the red man.

The white man's dead forget the country of their birth when they go to walk among the stars. Our dead never forget this beautiful earth, for it is the mother of the red man. We are part of the earth, and it is part of us. The perfumed flowers are our sisters; the deer, the horse, the great eagle, these are our brothers. The rocky crests, the juices in the meadows, the body heat of the pony, and man – all belong to the same family.

. . .

The rivers are our brothers, they quench our thirst. The rivers carry our canoes and feed our children. If we sell you our land, you must remember, and teach your children, that the rivers are our brothers, and yours, and you must henceforth give the rivers the kindness you would give any brother. We know that the white man does not understand our ways. One portion of the land is the same to him as the next, for he is a stranger who comes in the night and takes from the land whatever he needs. The earth is not his brother but his enemy, and when he has conquered it he moves on. He leaves his father's graves, and his children's birthright is forgotten. He treats his mother, the earth, and his brother, the sky, as things to be bought, plundered, sold like sheep or bright beads. His appetite will devour the earth and leave behind only a desert.

. . .

There is no quiet place in the white man's cities. No place to hear the unfurling of leaves in the spring, or the rustle of an insect's wings. But perhaps it is because I am a savage and do not understand. The clatter only seems to insult my ears. And what is there to life if a man cannot hear the lonely cry of the whippoorwill or the arguments of the frogs around a pond at night? I am a red man and do not understand. The Indian prefers the soft sound of the wind darting over the face of a pond, and the smell of the wind itself, cleansed by rain or scented with the pine cone.

The air is precious to the red man, for all things share the same breath: the beast, the tree, the man, they all share the same breath. The white man, they all share the same breath. The white man does not seem to notice the air he breathes. Like a man dying for many days, he is numb to the stench. But if we sell you our land, you must remember that the air is precious to us, that the air shares its spirit with all the life it supports. The wind that gave our grandfather his first breath received also his last sigh. And if we sell you our land, you must keep it apart and sacred, as a place where even the white man can go to taste the wind that is sweetened by the meadow's flowers.

Exercise 9.2

Based on the analysis done in the previous exercise, use the approach developed in this chapter to organize and interpret the results of the functional analysis. A sample presentation of the tables of results is given in Chapter 10 along with Schönthal's (2009) discussion as a sample of a possible interpretation of the grammatical analysis.

9.5 FURTHER READING

Bartlett, T. forthcoming. *Analysing Powers in Text*. London and New York: Routledge.

Butt, D., R. Fahey, S. Feez, S. Spinks and C. Yallop. 2001. *Using Functional Grammar: An Explorer's Guide*. 2nd edn. Sydney: NCELTR.

Coffin, C., A. Hewings and K. O'Halloran, eds. 2004. *Applying English Grammar: Corpus and Functional Approaches*. London: Hodder Arnold.

Halliday, M. A. K. and R. Hasan. 1985. *Language, Context, and Text: Aspects of Language in a Social-Semiotic Perspective*. Oxford University Press.

Hasan, R. 1985. *Linguistics, Language and Verbal Art*. Deakin University Press.

Martin, J. 1992. *English Text: System and Structure*. Amsterdam: John Benjamins.

Thompson, G. 2004. *Introducing Functional Grammar*. 2nd edn. London: Arnold.

Threadgold, T., E. Grosz, G. Kress and M. A. K. Halliday, eds. 1986. *Semiotics, Ideology, Language*. Sydney Association for Studies in Society and Culture.

Chapter 10: Answers to exercises

10.1 CHAPTER 1

Exercise 1.1
Clause recognition exercise

Text 1.1
Hello there. How are you? How are you managing with work, school and the boys? Are you finding time for yourself at all? Again, sorry I have been so long in getting back to you. Work has been crazy too. I always feel like I am rushing. So now, when I feel that, I try and slow myself down. I also have the girls getting more prepared for the next morning the night before and that has seemed to help the mornings go more smoothly. I will be glad when we don't have to bother with boots, hats and mitts. The days are getting longer so hopefully it will be an early spring.

Text 1.2
This module aims to offer an introduction to a functionally oriented approach to the description of the English language and to provide students with an understanding of the relationship between the meanings and functions that are served by the grammatical structures through which they are realized. The major grammatical systems will be explored through a functional framework. At all stages the description and analysis will be applied to a range of text types. By so doing, we will be able to explore both the meaning potential that speakers have and how particular choices in meaning are associated with different texts.

Exercise 1.2

There are many ways to answer this question. There is considerable similarity in what each person is saying about themselves and in relation to the political party of which they are a member. However, Tony Blair is expressing an act of choosing and he is representing himself as the one doing the choosing and the Labour party as having been chosen by him. Nick Clegg is saying something similar but he expresses it very differently. He is describing himself as a liberal. There does not seem to be the same active agency in what Clegg says as compared to Blair.

10.2 CHAPTER 2

Exercise 2.1 Word class recognition

Lexical categories	Examples from the text
nouns	work, school, boys, time, back, work, girls, morning, night, mornings, boots, hats, mitts, days, spring
verbs	are, managing, finding, have, been, getting, has, feel, am, rushing, try, slow, prepared, seemed, to help, go, will, be, don't, to bother
pronouns	how, you, yourself, all, I, now, when, that, myself, when, it
prepositions	with, for, at, in, to, down, before
adjectives	long, crazy, sorry, next, glad, longer, early
adverbs	so, smoothly, hopefully
articles and numerals	the, more, more, an
conjunctions	and, so, like
other (but these might be grouped with adverbs)	again, too, always, also

Exercise 2.2

The process in each clause has been underlined and the outcome of the process test is given in the right-hand column.

Jack Sprat could <u>eat</u> no fat	In a process of eating, we expect someone to be eating something. Two-participant process.
His wife could <u>eat</u> no lean	In a process of eating, we expect someone to be eating something. Two-participant process.
And so between the two of them, they <u>licked</u> the platter clean	In a process of licking, we expect someone to be licking something. Two-participant process.
Jack <u>ate</u> all the lean	In a process of eating, we expect someone to be eating something. Two-participant process.
Joan <u>ate</u> all the fat	In a process of eating, we expect someone to be eating something. Two-participant process.
The bone they <u>picked</u> it clean	In a process of picking, we expect someone to be picking something. Two-participant process.
Then they <u>gave</u> it to the cat	In a process of giving, we expect someone to be giving something to someone. Three-participant process.

Exercise 2.3 Ambiguity

The ambiguity for each sentences is explained below each example.

1. ***He gave her dog treats*** There are three participants in this situation but we can't tell whether dog treats were given to her or whether treats were given to her dog. The ambiguity is based on whether *her dog* is one group and *treats* is another group, or whether *her* is one group and *dog treats* is a separate group.

2. ***She saw the man from the store*** The ambiguity in this sentence is just like the Groucho Marx example. This is a process of seeing but we can't tell if the second participant is one group, *the man*, which is a separate group from *from the store* or whether the second participant (i.e. who was seen) is expressed by a single group, *the man from the store*.

3. ***He painted the canvas in the bedroom*** The ambiguity here is the same as in the previous sentence. There are two readings. In one, *the canvas in the bedroom* is a single group which means that there is more than one canvas and the one that was painted was in the bedroom. Alternatively, if what was painted was *the canvas*, expressed as a separate group from *in the bedroom*, then the *in the bedroom* is expressing where the canvas was painted.

4. ***The girl teased the cat with the ribbon*** The ambiguity is the same here as well. The thing that was teased by the girl is either the single group, *the cat*, or *the cat with the ribbon*, where in this case *with the ribbon* is part of the group and is describing which cat was teased.

10.3 CHAPTER 3

Exercise 3.1

The nominal groups have been indicated in boxes.

> ⟨I⟩ do have ⟨asthma⟩. ⟨I⟩'m not getting ⟨enough oxygen⟩ into ⟨my⟩ ⟨blood stream⟩. ⟨I⟩ must find ⟨a doctor⟩.
> ⟨I⟩ hope that ⟨things⟩ are on ⟨the mend⟩ ⟨now⟩ for ⟨Rowan⟩. ⟨It⟩'s good that ⟨he⟩ is being checked out so well. Hopefully ⟨the chamber thing⟩ will deliver ⟨the meds⟩ better and get to ⟨the problem⟩. ⟨Breathing problems⟩ are so weird. ⟨One of the most important things that I've learned⟩ is staying calm. ⟨There⟩ is ⟨an automatic response to get excited⟩ when unable to breathe, and ⟨the added stress⟩ makes ⟨it⟩ more difficult to breathe.

Exercise 3.2

The tree diagrams for the nominal groups are given in Figures 10.1 to 10.3.

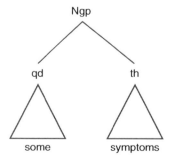

Figure 10.1 Tree diagram for the nominal group *some symptoms*

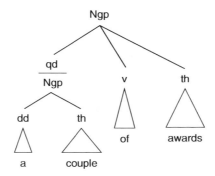

Figure 10.2 Tree diagram for the nominal group *a couple of awards*

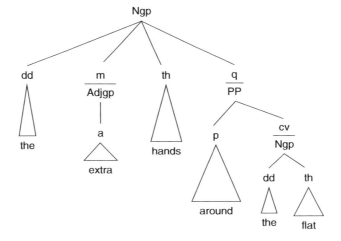

Figure 10.3 Tree diagram for the nominal group *the extra hands around the flat*

10.4 CHAPTER 4

Exercise 4.1

The tree diagrams for each clause are given in Figures 10.4 to 10.19.

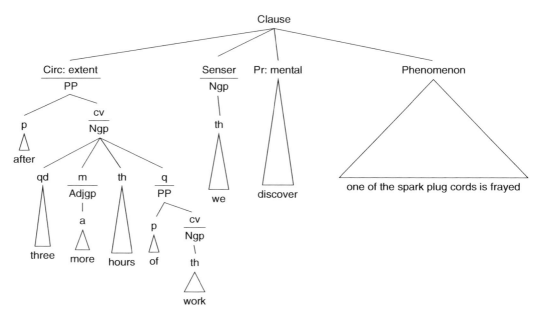

Figure 10.4 Tree diagram for *After three more hours of work we discover one of the spark plug cords is frayed*

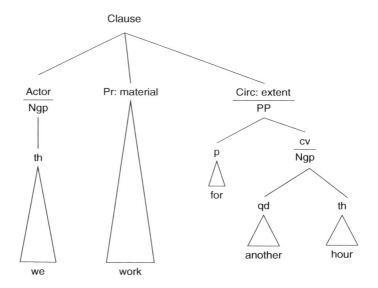

Figure 10.5 Tree diagram for *We work for another hour*

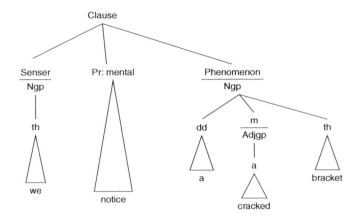

Figure 10.6 Tree diagram for *We notice a cracked bracket*

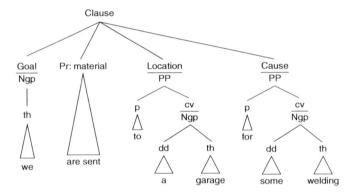

Figure 10.7 Tree diagram for *We are sent to a garage for some welding*

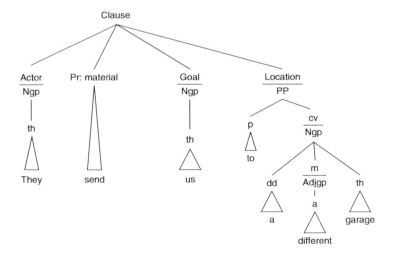

Figure 10.8 Tree diagram for *They send us to a different garage*

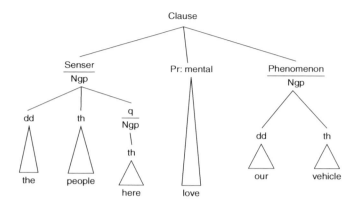

Figure 10.9 Tree diagram for *The people here love our vehicle*

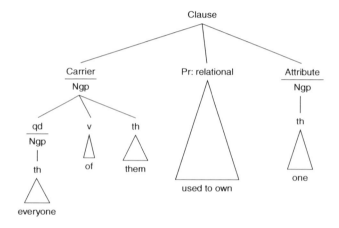

Figure 10.10 Tree diagram for *Everyone of them used to own one*

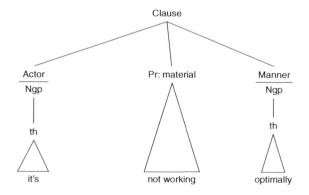

Figure 10.11 Tree diagram for *It's not working optimally*

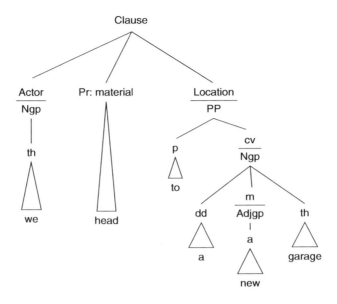

Figure 10.12 Tree diagram for *We head to a new garage*

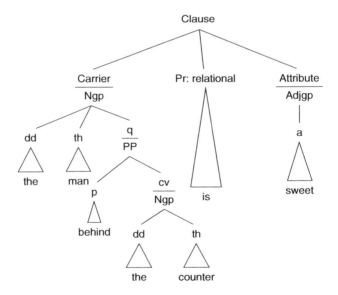

Figure 10.13 Tree diagram for *The man behind the counter is sweet*

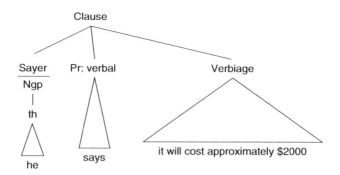

Figure 10.14 Tree diagram for *He says it will cost approximately $2000*

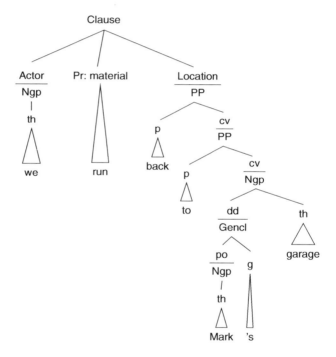

Figure 10.15 Tree diagram for *We run back to Mark's garage*

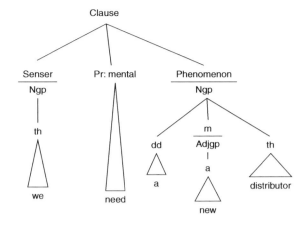

Figure 10.16 Tree diagram for *We need a new distributor*

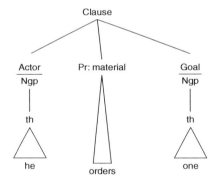

Figure 10.17 Tree diagram for *He orders one*

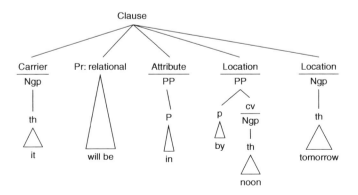

Figure 10.18 Tree diagram for *It will be in by noon tomorrow*

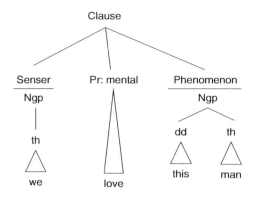

Figure 10.19 Tree diagram for *We love this man*

10.5 CHAPTER 5

Exercise 5.1

The analysis of the interpersonal strand of meaning is given below. The Subject is enclosed and the Finite is underlined. Modality and polarity are indicated in italics. Embedded clauses are indicated by square brackets.

1. In the event of an emergency over water, [you] *must* put on your life jacket
2. [The life jacket] is located in a bag under your seat
3. [You] *will* find a belt at your side
4. On the chest, [there] are two pull-tabs
5. [These lights] *will* guide you to the exits during an emergency
6. [The location of the nearest emergency exit] *should* be known
7. Do [you] know the location of the nearest emergency exit?

Exercise 5.2

The analysis of the interpersonal function for these clauses is given below. The Subject is enclosed and the Finite is underlined. Modality and polarity are indicated in italics. Mood is given in curly brackets. Any ellipsed elements are given in parentheses. Embedded clauses are indicated by square brackets.

1. [The President] says [my proposed reduction of tax rates would be inflationary] {declarative}
2. Well, ([you]) (___) let me [ask him a simple question in economics] {imperative}
3. Why is [it] inflationary {interrogative}
4. if [you] keep more of your earnings {declarative}
5. and ([you]) spend them [the way you want to] {declarative}
6. but [it] isn't inflationary {declarative}
7. if [he] takes them {declarative}
8. and ([he]) spends them [the way he wants to] {declarative}
9. The fact is [this program] *will* give us a balanced budget by 1983, and possibly by 1982 {declarative}
10. [We] also *need* faster, less complex depreciation schedules for business {declarative}

11. Outdated depreciation schedules now prevent many industries from [moderniz-ing their plants] {declarative}
12. Faster depreciation *would* allow these companies [to generate more capital internally, permitting them to make the investment necessary to create new jobs, to help workers become more productive, and to become more competitive in world markets] {declarative}
13. Another vital part of this strategy concerns government regulations [which work against rather than for the interests of the people] {declarative}
14. No one argues with the intent of regulations [dealing with health, safety, and clean air and water] {declarative}
15. But we *must* carefully re-examine our regulatory structure [to assess to what degree regulations have cost jobs and economic growth] {declarative}
16. There *should and will* be a thorough and systematic review of the thousands of federal regulations [that affect the economy] {declarative}

10.6 CHAPTER 6

Exercise 6.1

The three-strand analysis for each clause is given in Figure 10.20 in the form of box diagrams.

1	There	's		a divinity that shapes our ends
	Ngp	Vgp		Ngp
Exp		Pr: existential		Existent
Int	Subject	Finite/Predicator		Complement
	declarative mood			
Text	Theme	Rheme		

2	(you)		Consider	the case of Henry Pifield Rice, detective
			Vgp	Ngp
Exp	(Senser)	–	Pr: mental	Phenomenon
Int	Subject	Finite	Predicator	Complement
	imperative mood			
Text	Theme			Rheme

Figure 10.20 Three-strand analysis for the clauses from Exercise 6.1

3

3	I	must	explain	Henry	early,	to avoid disappointment
	Ngp	Vgp		Ngp	Advgp	clause
Exp	Senser	Pr: mental		Phenomenon	Location	Cause
Int	Subject	Finite	Predicator	Complement	Adjunct	Adjunct
	declarative mood					
Text	Theme	Rheme				

4

4	if	I	simply	said	he was a detective
		Ngp	Advgp	Vgp	Ngp
Exp		Senser		Pr: mental	Phenomenon
Int		Subject	Adjunct (modal)	Finite/Predicator	Complement
		declarative mood			
Text	Textual Theme	Experiential Theme	Rheme		

5

5	and	(I)	let	it go	at that
			Vgp (semi-fixed expression)		PP
Exp		Actor	Pr: material		Extent
Int		Subject	Finite	Predicator	Adjunct
		declarative mood			
Text	Textual Theme	Experiential Theme	Rheme		

6

6	I	should	be obtaining	the reader's interest	under false pretences
	Ngp	Vgp		Ngp	PP
Exp	Actor	Pr: material		Goal	Manner
Int	Subject	Finite (modal)	Predicator	Complement	Adjunct
	declarative mood				
Text	Theme	Rheme			

Figure 10.20 (cont.)

7	he	was	really	only	a sort of detective, a species of sleuth
	Ngp	Vgp	Advgp	Advgp	Ngp
Exp	Carrier	Pr: relational			Attribute
Int	Subject	Finite/Predicator	Adjunct (modal)	Adjunct (modal)	Complement
	declarative mood				
Text	Theme	Rheme			

8	at Stafford's International Investigation Bureau in the Strand where he was employed	they	did not	require	him to solve mysteries which had baffled the police
	PP	Ngp	Vgp		clause
Exp	Location	Senser	Pr: mental		Phenomenon
Int	Adjunct	Subject	Finite/negator	Predicator	Complement
		declarative mood			
Text	Marked Experiential Theme	Rheme			

9	he	had	never	measured	a footprint	in his life
	Ngp	Vgp…	Advgp	…Vgp	Ngp	PP
Exp	Actor	Pr: material			Goal	Location
Int	Subject	Finite	Adjunct (modal)	Predicator	Complement	Adjunct
	declarative mood					
Text	Theme	Rheme				

10	and	what he did not know about bloodstains	would	have filled	a library
		clause	Vgp		Ngp
Exp		Actor	Pr: material		Goal
Int		Subject	Finite (modal)	Predicator	Complement
		declarative mood			
Text	Textual Theme	Experiential Theme	Rheme		

Figure 10.20 (cont.)

11	the sort of job they gave Henry	was	to stand outside a restaurant in the rain and note what time someone inside left it
	Ngp	Vgp	Clause
Exp	Identified	Pr: relational	Identifier
Int	Subject	Finite/Predicator	Complement
	declarative mood		
Text	Theme	Rheme	

Figure 10.20 (cont.)

10.7 CHAPTER 7

Exercise 7.1

Clause list:

1. I always get to this computer later at night
2. John is out golfing
3. and Jane is at a sleepover birthday party
4. where they are sleeping outside in tents
5. and Sue has three friends over for a sleep over
6. They are watching a movie now

Exercise 7.2

Clause list:

1. When it first happened, there was a big thunderstorm that shook the house
2. and the rain fell really fast
3. My brother was startled
4. because he was outside
5. Now the water is knee-high
6. but we're alright
7. We went canoeing to a nice park which is really fun
8. We saw some iguanas today
9. and we even had a black snake at our house
10. and I saw a snake on a canoe too
11. Every time I go out we go out in a canoe
12. or our dad carries us
13. because me and my brother don't like going out in the water because of the snakes
14. We should be going back to school in three weeks
15. It's a long time off

Exercise 7.3

Clause list:
1. The future must see the broadening of human rights throughout the world
2. People who have glimpsed freedom will never be content until they have secured it for themselves
3. In a truest sense, human rights are a fundamental object of law and government in a just society
4. Human rights exist to the degree that they are respected by people in relations with each other and by governments in relations with their citizens
5. The world at large is aware of the tragic consequences for human beings ruled by totalitarian systems
6. If we examine Hitler's rise to power
7. we see how the chains are forged which keep the individual a slave
8. and we can see many similarities in the way things are accomplished in other countries
9. Politically men must be free to discuss and to arrive at as many facts as possible
10. and there must be at least a two-party system in a country
11. because when there is only one political party
12. too many things can be subordinated to the interests of that one party
13. and it becomes a tyrant and not an instrument of democratic government

10.8 CHAPTER 8

Exercise 8.1

The analysis is given here in the form of tree diagrams, in Figures 10.21 to 10.26.

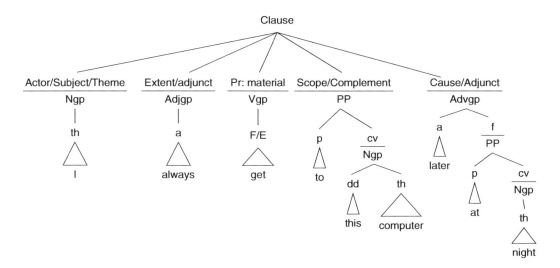

Figure 10.21 Tree diagram for *I always get to this computer later at night*

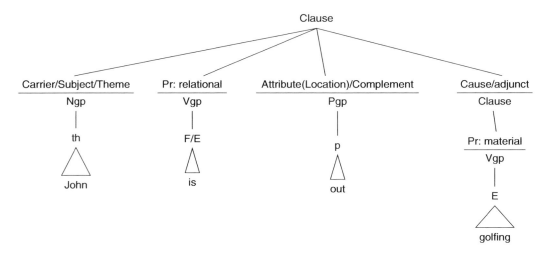

Figure 10.22 Tree diagram for *John is out golfing*

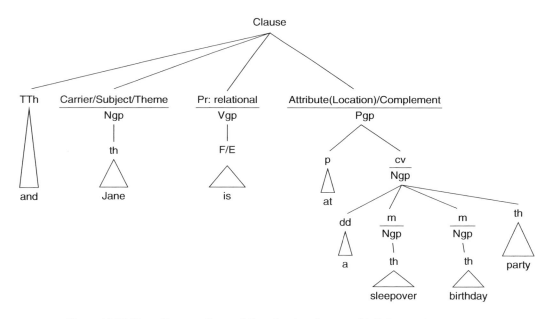

Figure 10.23 Tree diagram for *and Jane is at a sleepover birthday party*

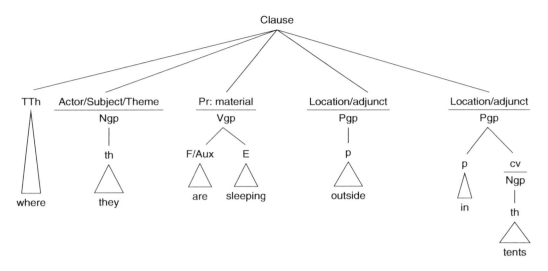

Figure 10.24 Tree diagram for *where they are sleeping outside in tents*

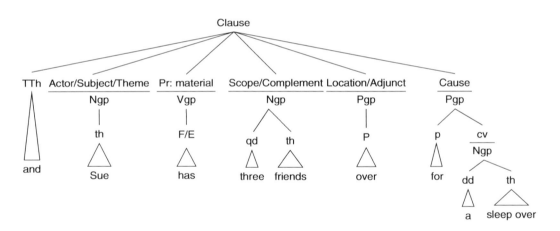

Figure 10.25 Tree diagram for *and Sue has three friends over for a sleep over*

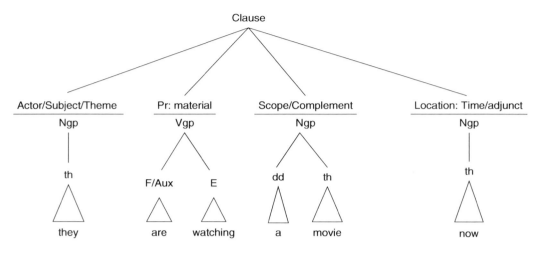

Figure 10.26 Tree diagram for *they are watching a movie now*

Exercise 8.2

The three-strand analysis for each clause is given in Figure 10.27 in the form of box diagrams.

1	when	it	first	happened
		Ngp	Adjgp	Vgp
Exp		Goal	Location	Pr: material
Int		Subject	Adjunct	Finite/Predicator
		declarative mood		
Text	Textual Theme	Experiential Theme	Rheme	

2	there	was	a big thunderstorm that shook the house
	Ngp	Vgp	Ngp
Exp		Pr: existential	Existent
Int	Subject	Finite/Predicator	Complement
	declarative mood		
Text	Experiential Theme	Rheme	

Figure 10.27 Three-strand analysis for the clauses from Exercise 8.2

3	and	the rain	fell	really fast
		Ngp	Vgp	Adjgp
Exp		Goal	Pr: material	Manner
Int		Subject	Finite/Predicator	Adjunct
		declarative mood		
Text	Textual Theme	Experiential Theme	Rheme	

4	my brother	was	startled
	Ngp	Vgp	
Exp	Goal	Pr: material	
Int	Subject	Finite	Predicator
	declarative mood		
Text	Experiential Theme	Rheme	

5	because	he	was	outside
		Ngp	Vgp	PP
Exp		Carrier	Pr: relational	Attribute (Location)
Int		Subject	Finite/Predicator	Complement
		declarative mood		
Text	Textual Theme	Experiential Theme	Rheme	

6	now	the water	is	knee-high
	Ngp	Ngp	Vgp	Adjgp
Exp	Location	Carrier	Pr: relational	Attribute
Int	Adjunct	Subject	Finite/Predicator	Complement
	declarative mood			
Text	Marked Experiential Theme	Rheme		

Figure 10.27 (cont.)

7	but	we	're	alright
		Ngp	Vgp	Adjgp
Exp		Carrier	Pr: relational	Attribute
Int		Subject	Finite/Predicator	Complement
		declarative mood		
Text	Textual Theme	Experiential Theme	Rheme	

8	we	went	canoeing	to a nice park which is really fun
	Ngp	Vgp		PP
Exp	Actor	Pr: material		Location
Int	Subject	Finite	Predicator	Adjunct
	declarative mood			
Text	Experiential Theme	Rheme		

9	we	saw	some iguanas	today
	Ngp	Vgp	Ngp	Ngp
Exp	Senser	Pr: mental	Phenomenon	Location
Int	Subject	Finite/Predicator	Complement	Adjunct
	declarative mood			
Text	Experiential Theme	Rheme		

10	and	we	even	had	a black snake	at our house
		Ngp		Vgp	Ngp	PP
Exp		Carrier		Pr: relational	Attribute	Location
Int		Subject	Adjunct (modal)	Finite/Predicator	Complement	Adjunct
		declarative mood				
Text	Textual Theme	Experiential Theme	Rheme			

Figure 10.27 (cont.)

11	and	I		saw	a snake	on a canoe	too
		Ngp		Vgp	Ngp	PP	
Exp		Senser		Pr: mental	Phenomenon	Location	
Int		Subject		Finite/Predicator	Complement	Adjunct	Adjunct
		declarative mood					
Text	Textual Theme	Experiential Theme		Rheme			

12	every time	I	go	out
	Ngp	Ngp	Vgp	PP
Exp		Actor	Pr: material	Location
Int		Subject	Finite/Predicator	Adjunct
		declarative mood		
Text	Textual Theme	Experiential Theme	Rheme	

13	we	go	out	in a canoe
	Ngp	Vgp	PP	PP
Exp	Actor	Pr: material	Location	Manner
Int	Subject	Finite/Predicator	Adjunct	Adjunct
	declarative mood			
Text	Experiential Theme	Rheme		

14	or	our dad	carries	us
		Ngp	Vgp	Ngp
Exp		Actor	Pr: material	Goal
Int		Subject	Finite/Predicator	Complement
		declarative mood		
Text	Textual Theme	Experiential Theme	Rheme	

Figure 10.27 (cont.)

15	because	me and my brother	don't	like	going out in the water	because of the snakes
		Ngp	Vgp		clause	PP
Exp		Senser	Pr: mental		Phenomenon	Cause
Int		Subject	Finite/negator	Predicator	Adjunct	Adjunct
		declarative mood				
Text	Textual Theme	Experiential Theme	Rheme			

16	we	should	be going	back to school	in three weeks
	Ngp	Vgp		PP	PP
Exp	Actor	Pr: material		Location (Space)	Location (Time)
Int	Subject	Finite (modal)	Predicator	Adjunct	Adjunct
	declarative mood				
Text	Experiential Theme	Rheme			

17	it	's	a long time off
	Ngp	Vgp	Ngp
Exp	Carrier	Pr: relational	Attribute
Int	Subject	Finite/Predicator	Complement
	declarative mood		
Text	Experiential Theme	Rheme	

Figure 10.27 (cont.)

Exercise 8.3

The three-strand analysis for each clause is given in Figure 10.28 in the form of box diagrams.

1	the future	must	see	the broadening of human rights	throughout the world
	Ngp	Vgp		Ngp	PP
Exp	Senser	Pr: mental		Phenomenon	Location
Int	Subject	Finite (modal)	Predicator	Complement	Adjunct
	declarative mood				
Text	Experiential Theme	Rheme			

2	People who have glimpsed freedom	will	never	be	content	until they have secured it for themselves
	Ngp	Vgp…		…Vgp	Adjgp	PP
Exp	Carrier	Pr:relational			Attribute	Extent
Int	Subject	Finite	Adjunct (modal)	Predicator	Complement	Adjunct
	declarative mood					
Text	Experiential Theme	Rheme				

Figure 10.28 Three-strand analysis for the clauses from Exercise 8.3

3	in a truest sense	human rights	are	a fundamental object of law and government	in a just society
	PP	Ngp	Vgp	Ngp	PP
Exp		Carrier	Pr: relational	Attribute	Location
Int	Adjunct (modal)	Subject	Finite/Predicator	Complement	Adjunct
		declarative mood			
Text	Interpersonal Theme	Experiential Theme	Rheme		

4	human rights	exist	to the degree that they are respected by people in relations with each other and by governments in relations with their citizens
	Ngp	Vgp	PP
Exp	Carrier	Pr: relational	Attribute (Contingency)
Int	Subject	Finite/Predicator	Complement
	declarative mood		
Text	Experiential Theme	Rheme	

5	the world at large	is	aware of the tragic consequences for human beings ruled by totalitarian systems
	Ngp	Vgp	Adjgp
Exp	Carrier	Pr: relational	Attribute
Int	Subject	Finite/Predicator	Complement
	declarative mood		
Text	Experiential Theme	Rheme	

Figure 10.28 (cont.)

6	if	we	examine	Hitler's rise to power
		Ngp	Vgp	Ngp
Exp		Actor	Pr: material	Goal
Int		Subject	Finite/Predicator	Complement
		declarative mood		
Text	Textual Theme	Experiential Theme	Rheme	

7	we	see	how the chains are forged which keep the individual a slave
	Ngp	Vgp	Clause
Exp	Senser	Pr: mental	Phenomenon
Int	Subject	Finite/Predicator	Complement
	declarative mood		
Text	Experiential Theme	Rheme	

8	and	we	can	see	many similarities	in the way things are accomplished in other countries
		Ngp	Vgp		Ngp	PP
Exp		Senser	Pr: mental		Phenomenon	Location
Int		Subject	Finite (modal)	Predicator	Complement	Adjunct
		declarative mood				
Text	Textual Theme	Experiential Theme	Rheme			

Figure 10.28 (cont.)

9	Politically	men	must	be	free to discuss and to arrive at as many facts as possible	
	Advgp	Ngp	Vgp		Adjgp	
Exp	Manner	Carrier	Pr: relational		Attribute	
Int	Adjunct	Subject	Finite (modal)	Predicator	Complement	
		declarative mood				
Text	Marked Experiential Theme	Rheme				

10	and	there	must	be	at least	a two-party system in a country
		Ngp	Vgp		PP	Ngp
Exp			Pr: existential			Existent
Int		Subject	Finite (modal)	Predicator	Adjunct (modal)	Complement
		declarative mood				
Text	Textual Theme	Experiential Theme	Rheme			

11	because	when there is only one political party	too many things	can	be subordinated	to the interests of that one party
		Clause	Ngp	Vgp		PP
Exp		Contingency	Goal	Pr: material		Manner
Int		Adjunct	Subject	Finite (modal)	Predicator	Adjunct
		declarative mood				
Text	Textual Theme	Marked Experiential Theme	Rheme			

Figure 10.28 (cont.)

12	and	it	becomes	a tyrant and not an instrument of democratic government
		Ngp	Vgp	Ngp
Exp		Carrier	Pr: relational	Attribute
Int		Subject	Finite/Predicator	Complement
		declarative mood		
Text	Textual Theme	Marked Experiential Theme	Rheme	

Figure 10.28 (cont.)

10.9 CHAPTER 9

Exercise 9.1

Clause list:

1. How can you buy or sell the sky, the warmth of the land?
2. The idea is strange to us
3. If we do not own the freshness of the air and the sparkle of the water
4. how can you buy them?
5. Every part of this earth is sacred to my people
6. Every shining pine needle, every sandy shore, every mist in the dark woods, every clearing and humming insect is holy in the memory and experience of my people
7. The sap which courses through the trees carries the memories of the red man
8. The white man's dead forget the country of their birth when they go to walk among the stars
9. Our dead never forget this beautiful earth
10. for it is the mother of the red man
11. We are part of the earth
12. and it is part of us
13. The perfumed flowers are our sisters
14. the deer, the horse, the great eagle, these are our brothers
15. The rocky crests, the juices in the meadows, the body heat of the pony, and man – all belong to the same family
16. The rivers are our brothers
17. they quench our thirst
18. The rivers carry our canoes
19. and feed our children.
20. If we sell you our land

21. you must remember and teach your children, that the rivers are our brothers, and yours

22. and you must henceforth give the rivers the kindness you would give any brother

23. We know that the white man does not understand our ways

24. One portion of the land is the same to him as the next

25. for he is a stranger who comes in the night and takes from the land whatever he needs

26. The earth is not his brother

27. but (the earth is) his enemy

28. and when he has conquered it he moves on

29. He leaves his father's graves

30. and his children's birthright is forgotten

31. He treats his mother, the earth, and his brother, the sky, as things to be bought, plundered, sold like sheep or bright beads

32. His appetite will devour the earth

33. and (it will) leave behind only a desert

34. There is no quiet place in the white man's cities

35. (There is) No place to hear the unfurling of leaves in the spring, or the rustle of an insect's wings

36. But perhaps it is because I am a savage and do not understand

37. The clatter only seems to insult my ears

38. And what is there to life

39. if a man cannot hear the lonely cry of the whippoorwill or the arguments of the frogs around a pond at night?

40. I am a red man

41. and (I) do not understand

42. The Indian prefers the soft sound of the wind darting over the face of a pond, and the smell of the wind itself, cleansed by rain or scented with the pine cone

43. The air is precious to the red man

44. for all things share the same breath

45. the beast, the tree, the man, they all share the same breath

46. The white man, they all share the same breath

47. The white man does not seem to notice the air he breathes

48. Like a man dying for many days, he is numb to the stench

49. But if we sell you our land

50. you must remember that the air is precious to us, that the air shares its spirit with all the life it supports

51. The wind that gave our grandfather his first breath received also his last sigh

52. And if we sell you our land

53. you must keep it apart and sacred, as a place where even the white man can go to taste the wind that is sweetened by the meadow's flowers

Sample clause analysis

Clauses [36] to [53] have been analysed for the three main metafunctions and are presented in Figure 10.29 in the form of box diagrams.

36	But	perhaps	it	is	because I am a savage and do not understand.		
Exp			Carrier	Pr: relational		Attribute	
Intp		Adjunct (modal)	Subject	Finite	Predicator	Complement	
			declarative mood				
Text	Textual Theme	Interpersonal Theme	Experiential Theme	Rheme			

37	The clatter	only	seems	to insult	my ears
Exp	Sayer		Pr: verbal		Receiver
Intp	Subject	Adjunct (modal)	Finite (modal)	Predicator	Complement
	declarative mood				
Text	Theme		Rheme		

38	And	what	is	there	to life
Exp		Existent	Pr: existential		Angle
Intp		Complement	Finite/Predicator	Subject	Adjunct
			interrogative mood		
Text	Textual Theme	Experiential Theme	Rheme		

Figure 10.29 Three-strand analysis for clauses [36] to [53] from Exercise 9.1

39	if	a man	can	not hear	the lonely cry of the whippoorwill or the arguments of the frogs around a pond at night
Exp		Senser	Pr: mental		Phenomenon
Intp		Subject	Finite (modal)	Predicator	Complement
		declarative mood			
Text	Textual Theme	Experiential Theme	Rheme		

40	I	am	a red man
Exp	Carrier	Pr: relational	Attribute
Intp	Subject	Finite/Predicator	Complement
	declarative mood		
Text	Theme	Rheme	

41	and	(I)	do	not	understand
Exp		Senser	Pr: mental		
Intp		Subject	Finite	Negator	Predicator
		declarative mood			
Text	Textual Theme	Experiential Theme	Rheme		

Figure 10.29 (cont.)

270

42	The Indian	prefers	the soft sound of the wind darting over the face of a pond, and the smell of the wind itself, cleansed by rain or scented with the pine cone
Exp	Senser	Pr: mental	Phenomenon
Intp	Subject	Finite/Predicator	Complement
	declarative mood		
Text	Theme	Rheme	

43	The air	is	precious	to the red man
Exp	Carrier	Pr: relational	Attribute	Angle
Intp	Subject	Finite/Predicator	Complement	Adjunct
	declarative mood			
Text	Theme	Rheme		

44	for	all things	share	the same breath
Exp		Actor	Pr: material	Scope
Intp		Subject	Finite/Predicator	Complement
		declarative mood		
Text	Textual Theme	Experiential Theme	Rheme	

45	the beast, the tree, the man,	they all	share	the same breath
Exp		Actor	Pr: material	Scope
Intp		Subject	Finite/Predicator	Complement
		declarative mood		
Text	Preposed experiential Theme (marked)	Rheme		

Figure 10.29 (cont.)

46	The white man,	they all	share	the same breath
Exp		Actor	Pr: material	Scope
Intp		Subject	Finite/Predicator	Complement
		declarative mood		
Text	Experiential Theme	Rheme		

47	The white man	does	not seem to notice	the air he breathes
Exp	Senser		Pr: mental	Phenomenon
Intp	Subject	Finite	Predicator	Complement
	declarative mood			
Text	Experiential Theme	Rheme		

48	like a man dying for many days,	he	is	numb to the stench
Exp	Manner	Carrier	Pr: relational	Attribute
Intp	Adjunct	Subject	Finite/Predicator	Complement
		declarative mood		
Text	Marked Experiential Theme	Rheme		

49	But	if	we	sell	you	our land
Exp			Actor	Pr: material	Beneficiary	Goal
Intp			Subject	Finite/Predicator	Complement	Complement
			declarative mood			
Text	Textual Theme	Textual Theme	Experiential Theme	Rheme		

Figure 10.29 (cont.)

50	you	must	remember	that the air is precious to us, that the air shares its spirit with all the life it supports.
Exp	Senser	Pr: mental		Phenomenon
Intp	Subject	Finite (modal)	Predicator	Complement
	declarative mood			
Text	Theme	Rheme		

51	The wind that gave our grandfather his first breath	received	also	his last sigh
Exp	Beneficiary	Pr: material		Goal
Intp	Subject	Finite/Predicator	Adjunct	Complement
	declarative mood			
Text	Theme	Rheme		

52	And	if	we	sell	you	our land
Exp			Actor	Pr: material	Beneficiary	Goal
Intp			Subject	Finite/Predicator	Complement	Complement
			declarative mood			
Text	Textual Theme	Textual Theme	Experiential Theme	Rheme		

Figure 10.29 (cont.)

273

53	you	must	keep	it	apart and sacred, as a place where even the white man can go to taste the wind that is sweetened by the meadow's flowers
Exp	Actor	Pr: material		Goal	Manner
Intp	Subject	Finite (modal)	Predicator	Complement	Adjunct
	declarative mood				
Text	Experiential Theme	Rheme			

Figure 10.29 (cont.)

Exercise 9.2

The following is a sample discussion of the text, taken from Schönthal (2009).

The nature of red and white: the influence of the experiential and interpersonal metafunction of language on the portrayal of two opposing viewpoints

1. Introduction In 1854, Chief Seattle, a leader among the Puget Sound Indians of America, gave a memorable speech, which is still remembered today. Much controversy has taken place around this speech, mostly because there are several written versions of it and because it has never been proven that any of them follow the exact wording of the actual speech of 1854. One of the most famous versions is now generally believed to have been written by screenwriter Ted Perry in 1971. It is a short extract from this version that will be discussed in this report.

Ted Perry wrote the speech in Chief Seattle's voice talking about the possibility of selling the red man's land to the American government and depicting his people's beliefs and relationship with nature. In this paper the contrast between representations of the red man and the white man in this speech will be analysed in terms of the experiential and interpersonal strands of meaning in order to reach a deeper understanding of the representation of the two opposing viewpoints.

Halliday (Halliday and Matthiessen, 2004: 60) claims that 'the clause is constituted not of one dimension of structure but of three, and that each of the three construes a distinctive meaning'. The different meanings portrayed function simultaneously within the clause (Thompson, 2004: 86). From the experiential perspective, language comprises a set of resources for referring to entities in the world and the ways in which those entities act on or relate to each other (Thompson, 2004: 86).

Hence, the experiential metafunction looks at how experience is represented in the clause. This is done by dissecting the clause into its constituents – process, participants and circumstances (Thompson, 2004: 87) – and identifying the process 'with respect to . . . the number and kind of participants involved' (Martin et al. 1997: 102). The interpersonal metafunction, on the other hand, is the part of meaning where speakers establish what

Table 10.1 Circumstances of Angle

Clause no.	Occurrence	Type of circumstance
3	to us	Angle
6	to my people	Angle
7	in the memory and experience of my people	Angle
26	to him	Angle
45	to the red man	Angle
52.1	to us	Angle

Table 10.2 The use of 'mood' and 'role in exchange'

No.	Clause	Mood	Role in exchange	Perspective
12	We are part of the earth	declarative	statement	red man stating his viewpoint
1	How can you buy (the sky, the warmth of the land)?	interrogative	question	red man tries to understand white man's viewpoint
22	you must remember that the rivers are our brothers, and yours	declarative	command	red man imposes his viewpoint onto white man

they want to achieve with their message: Whether they are 'giving' or 'demanding' 'information' or 'goods and services' (Eggins, 2004: 144–5). Furthermore, it contains the function of whether the given information in the clause is 'affirmed or denied, ... including a number of choices of degree of certainty, or of usuality' (Eggins, 2004: 172). It is these elements and features of the clause that will be used to discuss the representation of the red and the white man in Chief Seattle's speech.

2. **Two opposing viewpoints** In Chief Seattle's speech, two opposing viewpoints of how to treat nature are being presented. This becomes apparent when looking at a specific kind of circumstance, which is used throughout the text. Within the short extract chosen for this analysis, the speaker makes use of a circumstance expressing an angle or a point of view, six times. These six occurrences are presented in Table 10.1.

Furthermore, the use of mood and the clauses' role in exchange illustrate the presence of two different viewpoints as well. In seventy-three out of eighty-two finite clauses the mood structure is a declarative forming a statement, presenting the two different perspectives, which creates a sense of factuality. In the nine remaining clauses, however, there is a shift in perspective when the red man, namely Chief Seattle, tries either to understand the white man's position or to impose his own position onto the white man. This is done four times by using an interrogative mood structure asking for information and five times by using a declarative mood structure issuing a command with the help of the modal verb *must*. An example for each of these three uses of the interpersonal metafunction is given in Table 10.2.

Table 10.3 Material processes with the white man as Actor

No.	Process	No.	Process
1	buying	30.1	conquering
2	selling	33	treating
27.2	taking	33.2	plundering
55	keeping	34	devouring

3. **The depiction of the white man** Let us now consider how these two opposing standpoints are represented individually by the experiential and interpersonal metafunction, focusing on the different participant roles in which the two parties may be found. Throughout the extract, the white man occupies the role of Actor nineteen times out of thirty-two occurrences as participant. In Hasan's 'scale of dynamism' (1985: 46) Actor is placed at the very top of the continuum, identifying it as an active participant. In most of these cases the material process is realized by a verb with negative connotation in relation to nature, which is shown in Table 10.3.

In all but one of these nineteen clauses, aspects of nature occupy the participant role of either Goal or Scope. Hence, considering the different material processes, illustrated in Table 10.3, the white man is represented as an Actor in processes that either anticipate possession – the land is something that can be acquired (buying, taking, conquering), owned (keeping) and given away (selling) – or maltreatment (plundering, devouring, treating) of nature.

In addition to material processes, the white man is also represented as Senser in six further clauses with parts of nature. In Hasan's scale of dynamism, Senser is placed in the middle of the continuum, hence it is less active and more passive than Actor. This would diminish the white man's 'activeness' attributed to him by the material processes. However, in three of these cases, the polarity of the process is negative. Therefore, it follows that he is not a Senser. In the other three instances it is twice the red man who insists that if he sold the land to the white man he *must* honour it in return (see clauses 22 and 52) and once Chief Seattle makes use of a negatively connotated process, namely *forgetting* (see clause 9). Thus, in all the clauses where the white man is represented as a Senser, experiencing nature, it is done so negatively.

4. **The depiction of the red man** In contrast to the depiction of the white man's relationship with nature, the red man's connection to his land is attributed with positive features. First, the red man carries the function of Actor only three times, in all of which Chief Seattle talks about the hypothetical case of him selling the land to the white man, hence shifting his perspective towards the white man's point of view of how nature can be treated. In all the other cases where the red man is a participant within a material process he occupies the position of Goal which, having a strong sense of passivity, features near the lower end of Hasan's scale of dynamism. In these instances it is nature itself which is the Actor of the material process. In any further clauses with nature as Actor, it simultaneously occupies the function of Goal too. Thus, nature either acts upon itself or the red man, which places them on an equal position. Moreover, on all these occasions the process is represented by a verb implying either support or care, as shown in Table 10.4.

In almost all other clauses where the red man is occupying an '-er role' (Hasan 1985: 45) which refers to the participant that is the source (i.e. the active part) of the process, the red

Table 10.4 Material processes with nature as Actor

No.	Process	No.	Process
18	quenching	44.3	scenting
19	carrying	52.3	supporting
20	feeding	55.3	sweetening

Table 10.5 Kinship terms in relational attributive processes

No.	Carrier	Process	Attribute
11	it (the earth)	is	the mother of the red man
14	The perfumed flowers	are	our sisters
17	The rivers	are	our brothers

man is either a Senser or a Carrier, both of which are placed versus the lower end of the scale of dynamism. In fact, the most frequent process type in which the red man appears within a participant role is relational attributive. Most often he is incorporated indirectly within the Attribute as possessive determiner of kinship terms, such as brother, sister or mother. The Carrier of these clauses is always an aspect of nature. Three instances of such an occurrence are given in Table 10.5.

These clauses support the fact that the red man and nature are on equal hierarchical levels, which is emphasized by the following statement: 'We are part of the earth, and it is part of us.'

5. **Conclusion** In this report, the opposing viewpoints of the white man and the red man have been discussed in terms of their grammatical representation in relation to nature in an excerpt from Ted Perry's version of Chief Seattle's speech. Circumstances of Angle and the varying use of mood and the role of the clause in exchange have been identified as setting up the two opposing positions. Furthermore, the different participant roles of the white man and the red man have been shown to contribute to their contrasting depiction. The white man is depicted negatively as dominating nature, whereas the red man is shown to share the same level with nature, being part of the same family.

Notes

Chapter 2: The units of language analysis

1 "situation n." *The Oxford American Dictionary of Current English*. Oxford University Press, 1999. Oxford Reference Online (accessed on 7 August 2010), www.oxfordreference.com/views/ENTRY.html?subview=Main&entry=t21.e28706.

Chapter 3: The grammar of things: the nominal group

1 Rothman, D. 2008. 'Pirate leader Falkvinge: "Our enemy has no intellectual capital to bring to the battle."' *TeleRead*. www.teleread.com/copy-right/pirate-leader-falkvinge-our-enemy-has-no-intellectual-capital-to-bring-to-the-battle.

Chapter 6: Organizing language

1 "text *noun*." *Oxford Dictionary of English*. Edited by Angus Stevenson. Oxford University Press, 2010. Oxford Reference Online (accessed on 1 April 2011): www.oxfordreference.com/views/ENTRY.html?subview=Main&entry=t140.e0855780.

2 Baum, L. Frank. 1900. *The Wonderful Wizard of Oz*. Project Gutenberg, 2008. www.gutenberg.org/files/55/55-h/55-h.htm.

3 http://eo.ucar.edu/webweather/blizzard2.html.

4 Baum, L. Frank. 1900. *The Wonderful Wizard of Oz*. Project Gutenberg, 2008. www.gutenberg.org/files/55/55-h/55-h.htm.

5 Wodehouse, P. G. (1917) *The Man with Two Left Feet and Other Stories*. Project Gutenberg, 2003. www.gutenberg.org/ebooks/7471.

Chapter 9: There and back again: interpreting the analysis

1 www.wagsoft.com/CorpusTool.

2 www.fema.gov/kids/quake.htm (URL accessed on 5 May 2011).

3 www.earthquakes.bgs.ac.uk/education/faqs/faq_index.html.

References

Bache, C. 1995. *The Study of Aspect, Tense and Action: Toward a Theory of the Semantics of Grammatical Categories*. New York: Peter Lang.

Barkow, B. and U. Rutenberg. 2002. *Improving the Effectiveness of Aircraft Cabin Safety Briefings*, www.bteam.com/reports/Aircraft_safety_briefings_TP%2013973E.pdf.

Bartlett, T. forthcoming. *Analysing Powers in Text*. London and New York: Routledge.

Berry, M. 1996. 'What is Theme? – A(nother) personal view', in M. Berry, C. Butler, R. Fawcett and G. Huang, eds., *Meaning and Form: Systemic Functional Interpretations. Meaning and Choice in Language: Studies for Michael Halliday*. Norwood, NJ: Ablex: 1–64.

Bloor, T. and M. Bloor. 2004. *The Functional Analysis of English: A Hallidayan Approach*. 2nd edn. London: Arnold.

Butt, D., R. Fahey, S. Feez, S. Spinks and C. Yallop. 2001. *Using Functional Grammar: An Explorer's Guide*. 2nd edn. Sydney: NCELTR.

Coffin, C., J. Donohue and S. North. 2009. *Exploring English Grammar: From Formal to Functional*. London: Routledge.

Coffin, C., A. Hewings and K. O'Halloran, eds. 2004. *Applying English Grammar: Corpus and Functional Approaches*. London: Hodder Arnold.

Daneš, F. 1974. 'Functional sentence perspective and the organization of the text', in F. Daneš, ed., *Papers on Functional Sentence Perspective*. Prague: Academia: 106–28.

Davies, M. 1994. '"I'm sorry, I'll read that again": information structure in writing', in S. Čmejrková and F. Sticha, eds., *The Syntax of Sentence and Text*. Amsterdam: John Benjamins: 75–88.

Eggins, S. 2004. *An Introduction to Systemic Functional Linguistics*. 2nd edn. London: Continuum.

Eggins, S. and D. Slade. 1997. *Analysing Casual Conversation*. London: Cassell.

Fawcett, R. 2000a. 'In place of Halliday's "verbal group", part 1: evidence from the problems of Halliday's representations and the relative simplicity of the proposed alternative', *Word*, 51.2: 157–203.

Fawcett, R. 2000b. 'In place of Halliday's "verbal group", part 2: evidence from generation, semantics and interruptability', *Word*, 51.3: 327–75.

Fawcett, R. 2000c. *A Theory of Syntax for Systemic Functional Linguistics*. Amsterdam: John Benjamins.

Fawcett, R. 2007a. 'Modelling "selection" between referents in the English nominal group: an essay in scientific inquiry in linguistics', in C. Butler, R. Hidalgo Downing and J. Lavid, eds., *Functional Perspectives on Grammar and Discourse: Papers in Honour of Professor Angela Downing*. Amsterdam: John Benjamins: 165–204.

Fawcett, R. 2007b. *The Many Types of 'Theme' in English: Their Semantic Systems and their Functional Syntax*, Research Papers in the Humanities www.cardiff.ac.uk/chri/researchpapers/humanities/papers1-10/4Fawcett.pdf.

Fawcett, R. 2008. *Invitation to Systemic Functional Linguistics through the Cardiff Grammar: An Extension and Simplification of Halliday's Systemic Functional Grammar*. 3rd edn. London: Equinox.

Fawcett, R. and A. Neale. 2005. 'Transitivity analysis for the 21st century' [workshop]. *European Systemic Functional Linguistics Conference and Workshop (ESFLCW)*. London: Kings College.

Fries, P. 1995. 'Themes, methods of development, and texts', in R. Hasan and P. Fries, eds., *Subject and Theme: A Discourse Functional Perspective*. Amsterdam: John Benjamins: 317–59.

Halliday, M. A. K. 1973. *Explorations in the Functions of Language*. London: Edward Arnold.

Halliday, M. A. K. 1976. 'Functions and universals', in G. Kress, ed., *Halliday: System and Function in Language*. London: Oxford University Press: 26–35.

Halliday, M. A. K. 1978. *Language as Social Semiotic: The Social Interpretation of Language and Meaning*. London: Edward Arnold

Halliday, M. A. K. 1994. *An Introduction to Functional Grammar*. 2nd edn. London: Arnold

Halliday, M. A. K. 2002. 'Language structure and language function', in J. Webster, ed., *On Grammar*. London: Continuum: 173–95.

Halliday, M. A. K. 2005. 'Grammar, society and the noun', in J. Webster, ed., *On Language and Linguistics*. New York: Continuum: 50–76.

Halliday, M. A. K. 2010. 'Lexicogrammatical features and functional explanations' [workshop]. *LinC Summer School in Systemic Functional Linguistics*. Cardiff University, Room 031, 14 September.

Halliday, M. A. K. and R. Fawcett, eds. 1987. *New Developments in Systemic Linguistics. Volume 1: Theory and Description*. London: Pinter.

Halliday, M. A. K. and R. Hasan. 1976. *Cohesion in English*. London: Longman.

Halliday, M. A. K. and R. Hasan. 1985. *Language, Context, and Text: Aspects of Language in a Social-Semiotic Perspective*. Oxford University Press.

Halliday, M. A. K. and C. Matthiessen. 1999. *Construing Experience through Meaning: A Language-Based Approach to Cognition*. London: Cassell.

Halliday, M. A. K. and C. Matthiessen. 2004. *An Introduction to Functional Grammar*. 3rd edn. London: Hodder Arnold.

Hasan, R. 1985. *Linguistics, Language and Verbal Art*. Deakin University Press.

Hunston, S. and G. Thompson, eds. 1999. *Evaluation in Text: Authorial Stance and the Construction of Discourse*. Oxford University Press.

Jackson, H. and E. Zé Amvela. 2007. *Words, Meaning and Vocabulary: An Introduction to Modern English Lexicology*. 2nd edn. London: Cassell.

McCabe, A. 2011. *An Introduction to Linguistics and Language Studies*. London: Equinox.

Martin, J. 1992. *English Text: System and Structure*. Amsterdam: John Benjamins.

Martin, J., C. Matthiessen and C. Painter. 1997. *Working with Functional Grammar*. London: Edward Arnold.

Matthiessen, C. and J. Bateman. 1991. *Text Generation and Systemic-Functional Linguistics: Experiences from English and Japanese*. London: Pinter.

Mel'čuk, I. 1997. *Vers une linguistique Sens-Texte. Leçon inaugurale* [speech], Collège de France, Chaire internationale. 10 January, http://olst.ling.umontreal.ca/pdf/melcuk-ColldeFr.pdf.

Morley, D. G. 2000. *Syntax in Functional Grammar*. London: Continuum.

Morley, D. G. 2004. *Explorations in Functional Syntax: A New Framework for Lexicogrammatical Analysis*. London: Equinox.

O'Donnell, M. 2008. 'The UAM CorpusTool: software for corpus annotation and exploration', in C. Bretones Callejas, J. F. Fernández Sánchez, J. R. Ibáñez Ibáñez, E. García Sánchez, E. Cortés de los Ríos, S. Salaberri, S. Cruz, N. Perdú and B. Cantizano, eds., *Applied Linguistics Now: Understanding Language and Mind*. Almería: Universidad de Almería; 1433–47.

O'Grady, G. 2010. *A Grammar of Spoken English Discourse*. London: Continuum.

Quirk, R., S. Greenbaum, G. Leech and J. Svartvik. 1985. *A Comprehensive Grammar of the English Language*. London: Longman.

Schönthal, D. 2009. *The Nature of Red and White: The Influence of the Experiential and Interpersonal Metafunction of Language on the Portrayal of Two Opposing Viewpoints*. [coursework assignment] SE1375 Describing Language, Cardiff University, unpublished.

Simon-Vandenbergen, A.-M., M. Taverniers and L. Ravelli, eds. 2003. *Grammatical Metaphor: Views from Systemic Functional Linguistics*. Amsterdam: John Benjamins.

Tench, P. 1996. *The Intonation Systems of English*. London: Cassell Academic.

Thompson, G. 2004. *Introducing Functional Grammar*. 2nd edn. London: Arnold.

Thompson, G. 2007. 'Unfolding theme: the development of clausal and textual perspectives on Theme', in R. Hasan, C. Matthiessen and J. Webster, eds., *Continuing Discourse on Language: A Functional Perspective*, Vol. 2. London: Equinox: 669–94.

Threadgold, T., E. Grosz, G. Kress and M. A. K. Halliday, eds. 1986. *Semiotics, Ideology, Language*. Sydney Association for Studies in Society and Culture

Tucker, G. 1998. *The Lexicogrammar of Adjectives: A Systemic Functional Approach to Lexis*. London and New York: Cassell.

Index

36746293R00162

Printed in Great Britain
by Amazon